# African International Relations

**Dr Olatunde J. C. B. Ojo**
**Dr D. K. Orwa**
**Dr C. M. B. Utete**

Longman

London, New York, Lagos

Longman Group Limited,
Longman House, Burnt Mill,
Harlow, Essex CM20 2JE, England
and Associated Companies throughout the World

Longman Nigeria Limited
Ikeja, Ibadan, Owerri,
Zaria and representatives throughout Nigeria

Published in the United States of America
by Longman Inc., New York

First published 1985

**British Library Cataloguing in Publication Data**

Ojo, Olatunde, J. C. B.
African international relations.
1. Africa – Foreign relations – 1960 –
I. Title   II. Orwa, D. K.   III. Utete, C. M. B.
327'.096   DT3.0.5
ISBN 0 582 64394 5
ISBN 0 582 64393 7 Pbk

**Library of Congress Cataloguing in Publication
Data**

Ojo, Olatunde J. C. B.
African international relations.
Bibliography: p.
Includes index.
1. Africa – Foreign relations – 1960 –
Addresses, essays, lectures.   I. Orwa, D. K.
II.   Utete, C. Munhamu Botsio.   III. Title.
DT30.5.036   1984   327'.096   85 – 794
ISBN 0 582 64394 5
ISBN 0 582 64393 7 Pbk

Produced by Longman Group (FE) Ltd
Printed in Hong Kong

# Contents

# List of tables

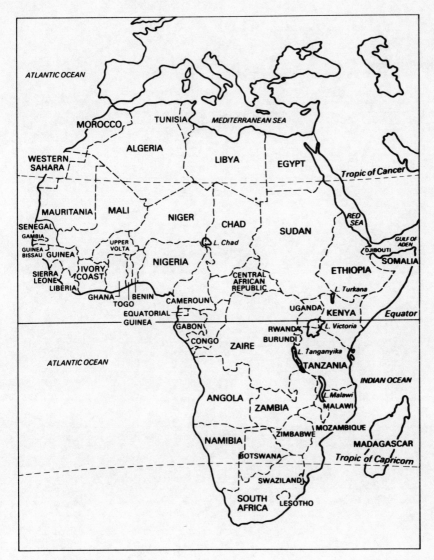

*Political map of Africa*

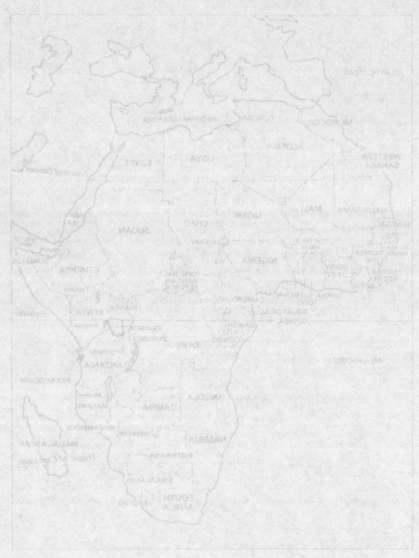

Political map of Africa

# 1   Theories of international relations

## The nature of international relations

Our world is the only known planet in which humans live. It is one world divided into five main geographical land masses called continents. Each continent is composed of sovereign and independent nation-states, though one still finds in some of the continents dependent territories. Each independent nation-state grants citizenship to its people, has its own political system and government, pursues its own economic goals and propagates its own brand of ideology. Nature also determined that this one world be inhabited by racial types. All these make our one world 'many worlds'.

The continents of the world do not exist in complete isolation from each other. Nor do the nation-states. The nation-states, which are the main units of a continent, have to carry on some of their activities in the world environment. Thus they not only come into contact with each other on their own continent, but they also interact with nation-states in other continents. This world-wide interaction takes place in what we call the 'international system'.

A system is 'an autonomous unit capable of adaptive behaviour' (Goldsmith, 1970: 16). It is 'a set of complexes standing in interaction' (Bertalanffy, 1965: 20–4). Each set of elements in the system is living and dynamic and has an environment. The dynamic of the system is created by interactions among the system's elements and between the system itself and its environment among others. These promote the system's adaptive behaviour and its goal seeking functions. Thus a system is an organized whole in dynamic interaction.

An international system is an organized whole in dynamic interaction. It is 'The totality of all boundary-crossing interactions of whatever kind among whatever units' (Reynolds, 1971: 193). It is 'a decentralized political system dominated by competing, relatively autonomous, territorially based political organizations' (Coplin, 1971: 331). The main units of the international system are the sovereign and independent nation-states and the international and regional organizations.

Quincy Wright defines nation in a Western European context. It is 'a considerable group united by common culture, values, standards, and political aspirations, occupying a definite territory and usually enjoying legal sovereignty' (Wright, 1955: 3–8). The limitation of this definition is, however, corrected by Fred A. Sondermann and William C. Olson who define nation as an ethnic group which has a common heritage, language, culture and a sense of common identity (Olson and Sondermann, 1966: 25). This view is inclusive because it recognizes that several nations may occupy a definite territory and enjoy legal sovereignty. Thus the state is defined as a body of people politically organized under one government with sovereign rights and recognized by other sovereign states as having legal status. The main elements of the state are, therefore, geography, people, government and sovereignty. These, when taken together, form the basic units and bases of power in an international system.

Sovereignty refers to the exclusive legal jurisdiction that a state possesses within its territory and its freedom to act in international affairs without being subjected to any legal control by another sovereign state. It is sovereignty that confers upon each state total jurisdiction on the utilization of the strength of its people and resources in whatever manner it wishes, without regard to any political authority inside or outside the national territory. When the state is able to display this quality, it is said to be sovereign and independent. Government refers to the organization within a state which makes and enforces the laws of the state, decides and carries out the state's policies, both domestic and international, and conducts its official relations with other states operating in the international system.

The nature of the relations of states reflects the nature of the international system. The main feature of the international system is *anarchy*. Unlike the nation-state system, the international system lacks a central authority to regulate activities and arbitrate between the conflicting interests of nation-states which constitute the main units operating within it. Thus the relations which nation-states have with each other are characterized by *conflict and co-operation*. Therefore, in the international system power considerations are of immense importance. The ability of each state to use its power in self-defence will determine its sovereignty and effective participation in the international system. A state has to rely on its own power in conducting its relations with other sovereign states. Where its own power is inadequate it might find it necessary to enter into an alliance with any one or more states with which co-operation would be more beneficial. But co-operation in the international system today does not preclude conflict tomorrow, and vice versa. Hence the relations of states must be seen as 'a complex of conflicts and co-operations embracing hundreds of different kinds of situations in some of which power is virtually at stake and others of which mutual convenience is the real issue' (Hartmann, 1967: 4).

All the participants in the international system have diverse historical, cultural and social backgrounds. Their values and goals have been, are and will continue to be, dissimilar. This situation reflects the absence of 'easily achievable consensus among the various groups which participate in international relations'. Therefore, no state can expect only 'gains for its own position on all values, at all times and in all places' (Olson and Sondermann, 1966: 2, 4). All states recognize that in the international system there are gains and losses to be made, compromises to be reached, and conflicts and threats to be faced. In efforts to realize certain gains it might be necessary to deploy force involving extensive destruction.

## The growth of international relations

International relations deals with human behaviour. Therefore, the study attempts to include almost the totality of human knowledge (Reynolds, 1971: 4). States, which are the main units in the interactions occurring in the international system, are static, occupying immovable geographical regions. The safety of the state depends on the behaviour of its people, particularly those holding political office as well as those involved in major international transactions such as international trade.

This is especially important because, as already noted, the international system lacks institutions that can give some order to the interactions that occur within it. At times these interactions have resulted in costly conflicts. Thus writings on international relations have been the result of human desire 'to structure and explain the political interaction(s) of nations' in the hope of developing 'a device for imposing order and meaning on the complexities of international affairs' (Spanier, 1972: 4).

The Chinese philosopher Mancius (4th Century B.C.) and Chief Minister Kautilya of India (326–298 B.C.) wrote about the international relations of their time. Machiavelli, writing in the early sixteenth century, advised that:

A Prince should therefore have no other aim or thought, nor take up any other thing for his study, but war and its organization and discipline, for that is the only art that is necessary, to one who commands, and it is of such virtue that it not only maintains those who are born princes but often enables men of private fortune to attain to that rank. And one sees, on the other hand, that when princes think more of luxury than arms, they lose their state. The chief cause of the loss of states is the contempt of this art, and the way to acquire them is to be well versed in the same (Machiavelli, 1952: 81).

Mancius, Kautilya and Machiavelli all wrote to counsel their emperors on how best they could manage state affairs so as to promote national interest. Their concern was with the preservation of their respective states but their writings were devoid of generalized analysis of international relations of states.

The growth of nation-states, particularly in Europe, led to increasing interest in international relations during the eighteenth and nineteenth centuries. However, writings on the subject concentrated on military thought and strategies, although international law and diplomacy also received considerable attention. Similarly, the idea of a world organization, early supporters of which included Pierre Dubois in 1306, George Podebrad in 1460 and Emeric Cruce in 1623, appealed to the intellectual imagination of many peace lovers. The movement for some form of international order culminated in the founding of the League of Nations in 1919 and the United Nations in 1945 (Kuehl, 1969; Divine, 1967).

The 'internationalists' proposed to end wars through the establishment of international bodies to which all nation-states would turn for peaceful resolution of disputes. They appealed to the rational and moral man. Hence they ignored analysis of why states behaved the way they did. They took for granted the actors in the international system. No writer seemed interested in questioning and identifying who the actors on the international stage were, or the manner in which they made policy. Was it the process of policy-making that conditioned the behaviour of the state? Or was it the behaviour of the state which determined the policy process? The 'internationalists' were, however, able to recognize the principle of 'balance of power' in the relations between states. Nevertheless, they made little attempt to analyze the processes associated with balance of power behaviour. As a result they left many questions unanswered.

## Emergence of international relations as an autonomous discipline

International relations as a field of study developed because of the realization of man's capacity for mass destruction. This raised the need for preventive measures. The First World War convinced many that man must study the causes of war if future wars were to be prevented. The concern with future peace led to the introduction in the United States' universities of a field of study called 'international relations'. Students of international affairs now saw the need to seek a greater understanding of the causes of conflicts among nation-states and to create institutions and norms that could ensure international peace.

The effects of the war sharpened the perceptions of writers on international relations. Systematic analysis of international relations began. But post-First World War studies were dominated by Utopian thought engrossed in rationalist theory. Shying away from the realism of Aristotle and Machiavelli, many students of international relations attempted to revive the Platonic concept of philosopher-king. Man was naturally good and peaceful. He had only been corrupted by his environment. All he needed was education so that he would be enlightened, because governments headed by enlightened leaders would seek peace and not war.

President Woodrow Wilson believed that war would be permanently eliminated if the civilized nations of the world undertook to do a number of things. First, all absolute governments must go and be replaced by democratic governments. Second, self-determination ought to be extended to all people because wars were caused by oppressive regimes. The advocates of self-determination thus found consolation in the growth of nationalism, which they assumed would enhance prospects for world peace. Finally, the world needed an organization which could police it and maintain law and order. The League of Nations was created to meet this need and when it collapsed it was replaced by the United Nations.

The rationalist approach to international relations demonstrated a number of weaknesses. First, scholars and commentators on the subject concentrated on the analysis of the causes of war and of international treaties, international law and international organizations. Second, most of the studies were descriptive, legalistic and moralistic. They had what K. J. Holsti has referred to as 'normative orientation' (Holsti, 1967: 6). Third, they did not sufficiently identify variables that influence the behaviour of states in the international system. Finally, international relations as a discipline in the social sciences remained undefined and its boundaries unstated.

Events in the 1930s that culminated in the Second World War raised doubts about the appropriateness of the rationalist theory of international relations. The rise of Hitler in Germany, with his outward looking German nationalism, cast a shadow on the assumption that nationalism would be a potent force against war. Scepticism arose among many scholars. They questioned the nature of international relations, the motives behind a state's expansionist and security policies, the mechanisms of diplomacy, the factors that influence international trade and how the trade influences international relations. These questions pointed towards the emergence of international relations as a science.

A new brand of international relationists devoted to 'systematic and comparative studies of objectives, processes and means, as well as the "basic forces" assumed to affect a state's foreign policy behaviour' took charge (Holsti, 1967: 6). They became convinced that such determinants of foreign policy as nationalism, geography and power needed to be conceptually analyzed. They further concluded that the field of international relations must be defined and scientific theories of international relations formulated. (Rosenau, 1961: 5–6). The recognition that international relations was too broad and too encompassing – international political relations, international law, international organization, trade, diplomacy, foreign aid, espionage, cultural exchange, olympic games, international piracy, all fall within the field of international relations – reinforced the need for precise definitions of the field itself and concepts used in the study of international relations.

By the 1950s it came to be generally accepted that the discipline that dedicates itself to the study of the relations between states was 'international relations'. It was further recognized that the subject was 'something more than contemporary history' that had 'to evolve as a legitimate academic specialty', including within it international politics and foreign policy (Fox, 1969: ix; Rosenau, 1961: 6). In 1955 Quincy Wright provided a more inclusive definition of international relations. He observed that international relations refers both to a condition and the study of that condition (the international system and the interactions that occur within it). It is concerned with relations which take place beyond the national boundaries, and between the groups of major importance in the life of the world at any period in history, in particular those of territorially organized nation-states, and the dynamics of these relationships (Wright, 1955: 9). Charles A. McClelland added in 1958 that international relations is 'a study of all exchanges, transactions, contacts, flows of information and meaning, and the attending and resulting behavioural responses between and among separately organized societies (including their components) in both the immediate and more remote past' (McClelland, 1961: 24).

A student of international relations works in a science which 'is concerned with observation and analysis, and theorising in order to explain (processes) and predict (outcome) (Burton, 1967: 5). He observes 'the nature, conduct of, and influence upon, relations among individuals of groups operating in [the international system] within the framework of anarchy, and . . . the nature of, and the change factors affecting, the interactions among them'. (Reynolds, 1971: 10).

Accordingly, international relations includes not only the study of the processes of interactions, but also the interactions themselves – the politics of these interactions, their likely consequences, the effects on the international system, and vice versa. Therefore external policies and powers of the basic units in the international system fall within the study of international relations, as do the politics of these interactions (Hoffman, 1960: 6; Pfaltzgraff, 1967: 1–2).

Politics is 'the art of influencing, manipulating, or controlling [other groups] so as to advance the purpose of some against opposition of others' (Wright, 1955: 130). It is the process by which issues are 'agitated' through negotiations, arguments, discussions, persuasion and the application of force (Meyerson, 1955: 304). International politics is the area of international relations in which power, coercion and bargaining are used to determine how world resources will be allocated among various states. Hans Morgenthau has argued that 'international politics, like all politics, is a struggle for power'. It is power which is dominant in the interactions of states (Morgenthau, 1973: 28). In the international system, the questions of 'war and peace, stability and change, freedom and tyranny' fall within the area of international politics and foreign policy (Rosenau, 1961: 1).

Foreign policy is the process by which states identify goals in the international system. It refers to actions designed to achieve a set of goals. Thus foreign policy can be viewed as the range of actions taken by various sections of government of a state in its relations with other bodies or states similarly acting on the international stage in the hope of advancing their own interests. While international relations is general and all encompassing, foreign policy is specific.

International relations will therefore have to involve agreement and disagreement over objectives (policy goals), persuasion and coercion, including occasional blatant use of force. Power in international relations is the process by which one group may gain control over another group in the struggle for group goals.

# Theories of international relations

What emerges from the preceeding discussion is that international relations is broad and complex. It involves the use of many variables and the treatment of numerous interactions. This has always made it hard to comprehend fully the dynamics of the international system and all the interactions within the system. In an effort to deal with this situation, scholars in the field of international relations have formulated theories and made attempts to develop tools of analysis that facilitate a better understanding of the behaviour of states in the international system. The need for 'a unifying conceptual framework comprising a manageably small number of conceptual elements and therefore for a high degree of abstraction' (Nitze, 1959: 1) expressed itself more forcefully during the first two decades of the second half of this century. Students of international relations came to believe that if they constructed a model which could 'structure and explain the political interaction(s) of nations' they might be able to develop 'a device for imposing order and meaning on the complexities of international relations' (Spanier, 1972: 4). Hence the call for a theoretical formulation.

Theory is a set or sets of propositions and/or hypotheses that are logically related to each other (Coplin, 1971: 9). Theory brings organization and the capacity to accumulate knowledge to a field and it enables scholars to tie together the propositions they have developed at different levels. In the words of Stanley Hoffman, 'Theory is understood as a set of inter-related questions capable of guiding research both of the empirical and of the normative variety' (Hoffmann, 1960: 80).

The movement for a general theory of international relations during the 1950s and 1960s stemmed from disaffection with (a) the rationalist theory that had dominated the post-First World War studies of international relations, (b) the failure of the League of Nations to prevent a second war, (c) the failure of the United Nations to prevent the Cold War, and (d) the development of nuclear weapons. This situation produced two major rival theories – realism or power theory and systems theory, the latter being the offshoot of the behavioural approach.

## Power theory

Power theory is based on realism. It began with the publication of E. H. Carr's *The Twenty Years' Crisis, 1919–1939* in 1946, but received a more authoritative restatement in Hans Morgenthau's 1948 *Politics Among Nations*. Realism sees the state as the main actor in the international system. It starts from the premise that universal conformity is not possible. Hence international conflicts must arise and must persist, as few nation-states want to surrender their sovereignty to international institutions, and international institutions are bound to fail since they lack power to sustain them. Furthermore, the responsibility of each state is to promote the interests of its people against the opposition of other groups in the international system.

To the realists, the behaviour of states in the international system can best be understood in terms of international politics, defined as 'a struggle for power'. In relations between states the power factor is dominant and is 'inescapable in the history of international relations of states'. The struggle for power is therefore 'universal in time and space'. It is a 'fact of experience' that cannot be denied and, in the ultimate goals of states, power 'is always the immediate aim'. The struggle for power overrides all other factors (Burton, 1967: 17; Morgenthau, 1973: 27–9). Every government is preoccupied with this struggle, and every government must adjust its actions to its power requirements.

Furthermore, power position and the overall power distribution in the international system allows a nation-state only a limited number of policy choices. Hence a state can either choose the status quo (maintenance of the balance of power) or expansion (imperialism and increase of power), or prestige (demonstration of power held by a state).

Power, being the dominant factor in the international relations of states, must also be seen as a psychological relationship in which one actor (the state) is able to control the behaviour of another actor. Power politics dictates that a rational political actor be concerned mainly with the promotion of his vital interest. That is that he acts to seek power and to develop capability and willingness to control others, for this is the 'law' of nature. To overlook this law is to endanger one's own survival. Therefore the law of nature does not expect a rational political actor to be bound by morals or ideology. He is to be pragmatic and use morals and ideology only as a means to an end – the promotion of personal interest. He must recognize the central role of power and must pursue it, while being able to adapt his pursuit according to the power position of other power seekers. Hence he must always be guided by pragmatism. In the final analysis power theory is a theory of power relationships.

Without question, power is a major factor in the relations between states. Each state is the sole guardian of its security and independence in the international system. All states seek power equilibrium, which they perceive as 'balanced power'. Balanced power is 'neutralized power', the only guarantee of achieving state security (Spykman, 1942: 21). John Spanier, a non-realist, has noted that 'a balance of power is the prerequisite of each nation's security . . . as well as for the preservation of the system itself. Any attempt by any nation to expand its power and attain dominance . . . which would allow it to impose its will upon the other states, will be resisted. When the balance is disturbed, the tendency will be for it to return to a position of equilibrium'. Thus the international system has assigned to the states the role of maintaining this equilibrium (Spanier, 1971: 10).

The lessons of history convinced the realists that the key to international relations lay in the history of power politics. Herein one finds the flaw of the power theory. Power theory, with its faith in the balance of power system, is one directional. Power is presented solely as an end in itself which states must pursue all the time, a fact that E.H. Carr, a leading realist, lamented, noting that the theory is static and deals with 'what is' and ignores 'what ought to be' and 'what is becoming'. Moreover, the power theory sees power as an independent variable when power can also be a dependent variable. Furthermore, the theory contains a near dogmatic belief in its presentation of power as the vital national interest that states pursue and defend above all else.

## The scientific school

The scientific school of international relations arose as a reaction to the limitations inherent in the power theory. This school rejected realists' claims that power theory was scientific. Its advocates feel that power theory, like the rationalist theory, lacks the precision and the explicitness of a real science. The power theory is too vague and too inclusive to provide adequate explanations of international political behaviour and of the nature of the international system. The theory is impressionistic, broad and too flexible to withstand the test of rigorous scientific verification. A theory of international relations must, therefore, overcome the imprecision of the power theory.

The quest for conceptual theories of international relations found its initial advocacy in the movement for a rigorous behavioural approach to the study of human activities, a movement that has been called a 'behavioural revolution' (Haas and Becker, 1970: 479–510). Behaviouralists rejected institutions as forming basic units of social and political analysis. They shifted emphasis from institutions to human actors. Thus they called for the application of the most precise techniques for observing, classifying and measuring data, the development of quantitative formulations, a greater use of statistical methods, and an orderly separation of empirical statements from normative ones so that a systematic theory of political science capable of giving scientific explanations to political interactions and the accompanying consequences could be discovered (Kirkpatrick, 1977: 23, 64). The scientific school of international relations seeks this noble objective.

The scientists argue that the field of international relations belongs to the experimental social sciences, and can even draw from natural sciences. Its theories therefore ought to be based on empirical method, combining inductive reasoning with comprehensive testing of deductive hypotheses. Detailed rules for definition and coding of observations must be adhered to. A study of international relations qualifies as scientific if it meets the following basic minimum requirements:

(a) involves the formulation of generalizations (universal and statistical) which must be confirmed by their 'positive instances'

(b) involves the construction of general theories, understood to be logically homeomorphic to theories in physics

(c) involves precise measurement and analysis in an articulated data-language (Spegele, 1980: 195–6).

All formulations, definitions and analysis must be derived from systematic and comprehensive observation of human behaviour. Only generalizations found in empirical evidence should be formulated, following testing and retesting according to scientific methods. Quantification is, therefore, essential to the scientific method of international relations. Scholars and students should always aim at conceptual theories and models of international relations rather than resort to descriptive analysis of international events.

## General systems theory

Systems theory is based on the assumption that 'political activity is a life process' that can best be approached from the perspective of systems analysis (Joynt and Corbett, 1978: 66–7). It treats the political system as a living system capable of adjusting to changes in its environment while retaining those basic characteristics that identify it as the same system. Systems theory is, therefore, an attempt to develop a unified theory of politics which is applicable to all political systems. As a theory, systems analysis is applicable to the state systems as well as to the international system (Aron, 1967: 94; Lerche, 1963: 95).

Systems theory comprises two types of theories – medium-range and long-range theories. Medium-range theories concentrate on one aspect of international relations; for example, behaviour of individuals or groups or organizations which are viewed as major actors in the international system. Long-range theories, on the other hand, look at the totality of the system. Thus international relations are treated 'as sets of interactions of many different kinds and which concern themselves with the nature of interactions and relationships, and how and why and in what senses they change or remain stable' (Reynolds, 1971: 17). Systems analysis will therefore embody all the components of sovereign states and will focus on relationships among the units and on their interdependence (Spanier, 1972: 9). The study of such complex relationships, the scientist argues, is best approached from the perspective of a general system theory.

General systems theory of international relations owes much to Morton Kaplan (1957, 1965, 1968). It is the scientist's answer to the need for 'the most general conceptual framework in which scientific theory or a technological problem can be placed without losing the essential features of the theory or the problem' (Joynt and Corbett, 1978: 65). The theory is characterized by the provision of related definitions, assumptions and postulates about all levels of the system (state and international). It concentrates on the building of conceptual models which make definitions operational through the application of systematic empirical analysis. The aim is to discover laws, recurrent patterns and regularities in a system's activities. Once these discoveries are made, it is possible to predict more accurately the behaviour of states in the international system.

Therefore, a scholar or a student of international relations should concentrate on building mathematical models and equations. He must carefully observe, code and quantify observable phenomena. He should be able to discern patterns of similarity in the phenomena being studied acting in much the same way as a natural or physical scientist.

Systems theory has noble objectives. It has moved the study of international relations a step further by asking broader and more direct questions about the international system and the nature of interactions that occur within that system. It permits the examination of international relations in a multi-dimensional context, something that the power theory fails to do. Indeed, there is much that takes place in the international system, trends in international economics and military armament, for example, that can effectively be analyzed through observation, coding and quantification.

However, in the final analysis, international relations are concerned with human behaviour. Behaviour is highly flexible and is changing faster than the advocates of general systems theory are willing to admit. The flexibility and complexity that are characteristic of human behaviour cannot easily be reduced to a mathematical equation. Human behaviour cannot be understood by separating the actor from his action. Otherwise, governments would find it totally unnecessary to charge an individual with murder, for murder abstracted from the individual ceases to be an act committed by the actor.

By the same token, it would be unnecessary for a student of international relations to worry about the actions of statesmen when studying the causes of war. His interest would be centred on quantifiable data such as the number of guns, bullets, aircraft, tanks, bombs and with this knowledge alone he would hope to explain past wars and predict the prospect for future ones. But this approach is clearly not sufficient. To dismiss what the principle actors in the international system say is tantamount to claiming that international actions occur beyond the realm of human beings. Such a dehumanized science of international relations can never be a science at all. As Roger D. Spegele has rightly noted, 'A spurious correlation coefficient does not transform itself into a causal law by defining conditions of causality . . . [In international politics] the truth will be shown to lie in power after all, the power of the dominant forces within a society' (Spegele, 1980: 194).

It is with this point in mind that Hedley Bull, a leading advocate of power theory, has observed that:

> By confining themselves to what can be logically or mathmatically proved or verified according to strict procedure, the practitioners of the scientific approach are denying themselves the only instruments (history and philosophy) that are at present available for coming to grips with the substance of the subject. By abstaining from what Morton Kaplan calls 'intuitive guesses' or what William Riker calls 'wisdom literature' they are committing themselves to a course of intellectual puritanism that keeps them as remote from the substance of international politics as the inmates of a Victorian nunnery were from the study of sex (Bull, 1969: 52).

## Dependency analysis

Europe and North America have provided the most influential theories of social science. These theories evolved out of the political and social experience in these geographical areas and until the 1950s were applied with little modification to Third World countries. It was seldom suspected that the application of some of these theories to the Third World inhibited a fuller understanding of developments in this region. The impact of colonialism and imperialism on underdeveloped countries was taken as a mere historical stage which give way to the forces of development upon the attainment of political independence. However, by the 1950s experience in Latin America had demonstrated conclusively that political independence was not in itself sufficient to achieve development.

The emergence of dependency analysis as a tool for the study of international politics has its roots in the Latin American historical experience. Latin America had the longest contact with European colonialism. Having been colonized in the fifteenth century, the region did not regain political independence until the first two decades of the nineteenth century. In Africa colonialism lasted less than one century. Latin America has also had the longest struggle with the situation of underdevelopment. No region has seen so frequent direct and indirect military, political and economic interventions by a dominant power than has Latin America. The post-Second World War imperialist behaviour of the United States throughout the world hit Latin America hardest. In the 1960s some social scientists began to construct theories to explain the inability of Latin American countries to escape from the limits imposed upon them by their former colonial powers and by the regional dominance − both political and economic − of the United States. These theories came to be known under the general heading of 'dependency' theory (Stein and Stein, 1970; Frank, 1969; Cockroft, Frank and Johnson, 1972; Chilcote, 1974; Bath and James, 1976).

Dependency means 'a situation in which the economies of certain countries are conditioned by the development and expansion of another economy to which the former is subjected' (Dos Santos, 1970: 231−6). In this situation the dominant economies, usually those of industrialized capitalist states, expand and maintain self-sustaining growth while the dependent economies of the non-industrial countries can only expand and grow as a reflection of the expansion of the former. This relationship produces 'the condition of underdevelopment' (Bath and James, 1976: 5).

Dependency analysis initially emphasized economic factors as being decisive in shaping the kind of relationship an underdeveloped country might have with a powerful industrially developed state. Colonialism incorporated Latin America's 'undeveloped' economies into European worldwide mercantilist and capitalist systems causing Latin America to become a satellite of metropolitan Europe and later of the United States. Thus began Latin America's historical role as a supplier of raw materials for the expansion of metropolitan industries and as a consumer of metropolitan manufactured goods. The prices of raw materials were determined in the metropolis, far away from the control of the exporter. At the same time the prices of manufactured goods were also fixed in the metropolis. Therefore, there existed an unequal relationship in which Latin America was exploited for the development of Europe. Income derived from the export of raw material, which in most countries comprized one or two agricultural or mineral products, was usually small and was not enough to finance the establishment of industries in Latin America. This deformed the process of Latin America's economic expansion and intensified the situation of dependence upon the metropolis. After independence Latin America failed to break with colonial dependence. The role of a metropolitan power passed over to the United States. Thus Latin American economies could only expand as a reflection of the expansion of North American economies, with the consequence that underdevelopment has remained a characteristic of Latin American societies.

By the 1970s dependency analysis became widely used as a tool for studying the relations between other Third World countries and the industrialized countries of Europe and North America. In 1974, using dependency analysis, Walter Rodney published *How Europe Underdeveloped Africa*. The 1970s also saw a growing sophistication in the use of dependency analysis. Emphasis on foreign economic and political factors was retained but internal structures and domestic factors which contribute to dependency and underdevelopment were also included (Leys, 1975; Smith 1979; Ake, 1978; Bath and James, 1976: 33–4). Dependency could now be analyzed by examining the process of economic, political and cultural intercourse between the underdeveloped countries and the developed capitalist and socialist worlds. Dependency became a comprehensive theory of international politics.

Nzongola-Ntalaja who, like Colin Leys, prefers the use of 'neo-colonialism' to dependency, wrote with particular reference to United States relations with Zaire and Angola that 'the preservation of the anti-communist ideas once championed by the ideological apparatus of the colonial state is one of the major tasks that imperialism has assigned to the neo-colonial state'. In order to maintain a neo-colonial state, or what the dependency approach calls a dependent state, the metropolitan powers set up training programmes for trade union leaders and journalists, and created scholarships for university students – all these being 'part of the American and Western ideological stake' (Nzongola, 1978: 153).

Both the economic and cultural/ideological versions of dependency take the colonial era as their starting points for analysis. Like the power theory of international relations it is a theory which draws on historical experience. Clearly, dependency theory is of great relevance to the study of African international relations.

# Theory and the study of African international relations

The study of African international relations is only just beginning to attract the interest of scholars and students. This fact is underscored by the lack of relevant texts on the subject and by the absence of debate on the theoretical framework for the study of African international relations. The systems theory of international relations is not particularly well suited to Africa. This is partly because it was developed to explain international relations in the industrialized world, partly because much of the data that is needed to make it applicable to Africa simply is not available and partly because of the uniqueness and complexity of the African case.

Power theory, resting on certain universal assumptions about the nature of man, is easier to apply to Africa. Its emphasis on the importance of the struggle for survival (achieved through the acquisition of power) finds many sympathetic listeners in Africa. Ali Mazrui, for example, who approaches African international relations from the perspective of political philosophy and political sociology, sees African international relations as a struggle against dependency, a situation imposed upon the continent by its historical experience (Mazrui, 1977).

African states are concerned with the preservation of their sovereignty and independence, which they see threatened from both within and outside the continent. The international politics of African states are, therefore, characterized by a struggle for power – power seen as both an end in itself and as a means to an end. Economic power, for example, is pursued both as a goal worthwhile in itself and as a means of purchasing greater military power and of increasing a state's prestige and influence.

A critical look at African international relations reveals the dominance of power politics. In Africa alliances are short-lived and tend to be entered into in order to balance out the power of either a potential aggressor or a domineering state and for the purposes of preserving sovereignty and independence.

The emergence of the Casablanca, Brazzaville and Monrovia–Lagos blocs of states in the early 1960s served the needs of the respective member states. The conservative Morocco belonged to the Casablanca Group because it supported Morocco's claim on Mauritania against the opposition of the Brazzaville group. Egypt, on the other hand, found co-operation with the Casablanca states necessary because it needed Africa's support in its struggle against Israel. The Brazzaville–Lagos–Monrovia axis was created by a shared fear that the Casablanca states, dominated by the declared Marxists Nkrumah and Nasser, would dominate Africa and introduce communism.

Power politics can also be seen in the Nile Valley and in the Horn of Africa. For years Sudan has viewed Egypt as a threat to its security and has always feared Egyptian domination. However, the feeling in Sudan today that it is Libya which threatens its security has led to a military and economic alliance with Egypt. Egyptian military support is seen as balancing out Libyan military superiority. In the Horn of Africa Somalia's challenge to both Kenyan and Ethiopian sovereignty has produced a military alliance between Kenya and Ethiopia. This alliance continues regardless of ideological differences between Kenya and Ethiopia. In both the Nile Valley and the Horn the struggle for power appears to be generating an arms race as states in the regions strive to maintain a balance of power.

Economic dependence has been another feature of African international relations. The declared goal of all African states is economic independence. An observer of East African state relations will discover that the conflict between Kenya and Tanzania lies in the struggle for economic independence. Tanzania, which for years has served as a periphery to Kenya's capital, is determined to break its dependence on Kenya. Tanzania argues that it is through Kenya that external capital gains economic domination in the region. Therefore, in its effort to break from a dependency situation, Tanzania has restricted its economic relations with Kenya and has taken steps to isolate Kenya through the creation of Tanzania-led economic communities. Examples of this policy include the Kagera Basin Development Organization, consisting of Tanzania, Burundi, Rwanda and Uganda, and the Southern Africa Development Co-ordination Conference (SADCC), grouping together the Front Line states.

Kenya recognizes the threat presented by Tanzania. Thus Kenya supports the 'Preferential Trade Area' (PTA) for Eastern and Southern Africa. Kenyan policy-makers believe that the PTA will be able to undermine Tanzania's growing influence in both East and Southern Africa, thus permitting Kenya's economy to continue its domination of the East African market.

In conclusion, it seems that African international relations are best approached from the perspectives of power and dependency theory. Power theory is valuable for any descriptive analysis of power politics within the continent. Dependency theory draws our attention to variables outside Africa, for in dependency theory the 'centre-periphery' relation is of great importance and can be seen to operate at both a global and a continental level.

# References

AKE, CLAUDE (1978) *Revolutionary pressures in Africa,* Zed Press, London.

AMIN, SAMIR (1972) Underdevelopment and dependence in black Africa: origin and contemporary forms. *Journal of Modern African Studies,* **X** (4).

ARON, RAYMOND (1967) *Peace and war,* New York, Praeger.

BATH, RICHARD C and JAMES, DILMUS D (1976) Dependency analysis of Latin America: some criticisms, some suggestions. *Latin America Research Review,* **XI** (3),

BERTALANFFY, LADWIG (1965) General system theory. In J David Singer (ed) *Human Behaviour and International Politics,* Rand McNally, Chicago.

BULL, HEDLEY (1969) International theory: the case of classical approach. In Robert L. Pfaltzgraff Jr. (ed) *Politics and the International System,* J. B. Lippincott, Philadelphia.

BURTON, J W (1967) *International relations: a general theory* Cambridge University Press, Cambridge.

CHILCOTE, RONALD H (1974) Dependency theory: a reassessment. *Latin American Perspective,* **I** (1).

COCKROFT, J D, FRANK, A GUNDER and JOHNSON D L (1972) *Dependence and underdevelopment: Latin America's political economy* Doubleday, N.Y.

COPLIN, D WILLIAM (1971) *Introduction to international politics: A theoretical overview*, Markham Publishing Co., Chicago.

DIVINE, ROBERT A (1967) *Second chance: the triumph of internationalism in America during World War II*, New York, Aitheneum.

DOS SANTOS, THEOTONIO (1970) The structure of dependence. *The American Economic Review*, **LX**.

FOX, T R WILLIAM (ed) (1959) *Theoretical Aspects of International Relations*, Notre Dame, University of Notre Dame Press.

FRANK, ANDRÉ GUNDER (1969) *Latin America, underdevelopment or revolution: essays on the development of underdevelopment and the immediate enemy*, Monthly Review Press, New York.

GOLDSMITH, C (1970) Societies and ecosystems, *Ecologist*. **I** (16).

HARTMANN, H F (ed) (1967) *World in crisis: readings in international relations*, 3rd edn., Macmillan, London.

HOFFMAN, STANLEY (1960) *Contemporary theory in international relations,* Prentice-Hall, N.J.

HOLSTI J K (1967) *International politics*, Prentice-Hall, N.J..

JOYNT, B CARREY and PEVENT CORBETT (1978) *Theory and reality in world politics*, Macmillan, London.

KIRKPATRICK, E M (1977) From past to present. In Donald M Freeman (ed) *Foundations of Political Science*, The Free Press, New York.

KUEHL, F WARREN (1969) *Seeking world order*, Vanderbilt University Press, Nashville.

LEGUM, C (ed) (1979) *Africa contemporary record, 1977–1978,* Africana Publishing Co., London.

LERCHE, CHARLES O Jr. (1963) *Concepts of international politics*, Prentice-Hall, N.J..

LEYS, C (1975) *Underdevelopment in Kenya: the political economy of neo-colonialism, 1964–1971,* University of California Press, Berkeley, Calif.

MACHIAVELLI, NICCOLO (1952) *The Prince*. Introduction by Christian Gauss, translated by Luigi Ricci and revised E R P Vincent. New American Library, New York.

McCLELLAND, A CHARLES (1961) The social sciences, history and the international relations, in J R Rosenau (ed) *International Politics and Foreign Policy*, The Free Press, New York.

MAZRUI, A A (1977) *African international relations: the diplomacy of dependency and change*, Heinemann, London.

MARTIN, MEYERSON (1955) *Politics, planning and public interest*, Free Press, New York.

MORGENTHAU, HANS (1973) *Politics among nations: the struggle for power and peace*, 5th edn., Scientific book agency, Calcutta.

NITZE, H PAUL Necessary and sufficient elements of a general theory of international relations. In T R W Fox (ed) *Theoretical aspects of international relations*, Notre Dame Press, Notre Dame.

NZONGOLA-NTALAJA (1978) US, Zaire and Angola, in René Lemarchand (ed) *American policy in Southern Africa: stakes and stance,* University Press of America, Washington, D. C.

PFALTZGRAFF, L ROBERT Jr. (ed) (1967) *Politics and the international system.* J. B. Lippmeott Co., Philadelphia.

REYNOLDS, P A (1971) *Introduction to international relations,* Schenkman Publishing Co., Cambridge, Mass..

ROSENAU, N J (1961) *International politics and foreign policy,* The Free Press, New York.

SMITH, TONY (1979) The underdevelopment of development literature: the case of dependency theory. *World Politics,* **XXXI** (2).

SONDERMAN, A FRED and OLSON, WILLIAM C (eds) (1966) *The theory and practice of international relations.* 2nd ed, Prentice-Hall, N.J.

SPANIER, JOHN (1972) *Games nations play: analyzing international politics,* Praeger, New York.

SPEGELE, D ROGER (1980) The neoclassical empiricist research programme for international relations, a reconsideration, *Il Politico,* XLV (2).

SPYKMAN, J NICHALAS (1972) *America's strategy in world politics: the United States and the balance of power,* Harcourts Brace, New York.

STEIN, S J and STEIN, B H (1970) *The colonial heritage of Latin America: essays on economic dependence in perspective,* Oxford University Press, New York.

WRIGHT, QUINCY (1955) *The study of international relations,* Appleton-Century Crift, New York.

ZARTMAN, WILLIAM (1966) *International relations of the new African states,* Prentice-Hall, New Jersey.

ZARTMAN, WILLIAM (1967) Africa as a subordinate state system in international relations, *International Organization,* **XXI**.

# 2   The international actors

## Who is an international actor?

In Chapter 1 states were identified as actors both in the international system as a whole and in the African subordinate system. An international actor has been defined as 'a relatively *autonomous* unit that exercises influence on the behaviour of other autonomous actors'. The key word is *autonomy,* 'the ability to behave in ways that have consequences in international politics and cannot be predicted entirely by reference to other actors or authorities' (Hopkins and Mansbach, 1973: 4). Until recently states alone were thought to have this quality because they possess sovereignty – that is, legal independence without accountability to any higher authority. They were therefore regarded as the fundamental actors in international politics. Accordingly international politics was largely analyzed in terms of relations among states (or nation-states as they are sometimes called). Indeed, the very notion of *international* politics assumes that the state is the fundamental actor. Hans Morgenthau, for example, called his monumental work *Politics among Nations.*

## The mixed actor view

Since the First World War, and particularly after the Second, many theorists have challenged this state-centric view of international politics. The complex arguments against the state-centric view can be reduced to four.

First, the concept of state has become too ambiguous to serve as a useful frame on which to base the analysis of international politics. It has been argued that the traditional attributes of states are meaningless in the contemporary world because many entities that call themselves states and are recognized as such do not possess the attributes of states. Many so-called states, especially the 'new states' in Africa are said to have a fluid rather than a clearly defined territorial (geographical) basis, to have a shifting rather than a stable, permanent population, to lack a viable and effective central government and to be so dependent on powerful foreign states as to compromise their sovereignty (Young, 1972; Cooper 1968; Emerson, 1960).

The second argument against the state-centric view of international politics is that states are not hard-shelled, impermeable units within which political and economic activities are confined and human security and welfare assured. Rather, in our nuclear age with its revolutionary developments in communication, transportation, technology, commerce and industry, the territorial state is increasingly 'penetrated' by other states. In addition it has declined and become obsolescent and ineffective in terms of achieving human security and welfare. In consequence there has been a dramatic increase in the number of human activities promoting welfare and security which cut across state lines. Thus there has been an expansion of the role of non-state entities which cannot be thought of as wholly dependent on, or subsidiary to, state initiatives. Even such organizations as the United Nations (UN) and the Organization of African Unity (OAU) which are composed of states, sometimes operate as semi-autonomous entities in international relations. All these developments have in turn resulted in the fractionalization of human loyalty. Nationalism is currently at a low ebb, as it is competing with internationalism and supranationalism which can be seen in the various moves for political unification and in the growth of transnational non-governmental entities such as the multinational corporations. It is unrealistic, therefore, to base analysis of international policy solely on an entity – the state – which appears to be in such decline (Herz, 1959; Etzioni 1968; Falk 1966; Young 1972).

The third line of argument against the state-centric view is that by focusing on states we lose sight of the human beings for whom and through whom the state plays the game of international politics. The state is reified and assumed to be capable, like human beings, of thinking and acting, of having desires and preferences and of choosing goals and means. State 'interests' become elevated above those of its citizens who are often asked to make sacrifices in the 'interests' of the state. If we attribute human qualities to the state, and regard it as an actor in its own right we run the risk of making the state into a monster which accords its own interests primacy over those of human individuals. As a result international politics becomes 'dehumanized' (Wolfers, 1962; 4–5).

The fourth and final argument is that historically non-state entities such as banks, trading companies, religious movements and institutions all played an important role in world politics before the modern nation-state came into existence. And today similar entities are more important than many states. For example, it could be said that the American Telephone and Telegraph Company (ATT) whose profit of $5 000 million in 1980 was larger than the GNP of many African states, plays a more prominent and effective economic role in international politics than the poorer African states. Indeed, a study in 1968 showed that nearly ninety multinational corporations had sales volumes that exceeded the GNP of 57 states and that surpassed the expenditures of 86 of the 126 central governments then existing in the world. This awesome power, combined with their mode of operation, enables the corporations to restrict the effective choices of those who act in the name of the state (Modelski, 1968. For an account of the organizational growth of multinationals and their effects, see Vernon, 1971; Rolfe and Damm, 1970).

In the light of these arguments against the state-centric or state-as-actor view of international politics, it has been suggested that we should regard as actors all individuals (whether private or official), groups, and other non-state entities which independently enter into transactions and relationships that are political in quality or have political consequences but at the same time are international in scope. Thus international organizations and institutions, multinational corporations and hundreds of private individuals may be regarded as international actors, provided their activities are both international and to some degree political in character. Some proponents of this 'mixed actor' view have identified and classified actors by the scope of their constituencies (i.e. what constitutes the entity) and by the type of tasks they perform in the political system. Five types of actors have been identified: (1) inter-state governmental organizations, e.g. the UN and the OAU; (2) inter-state non-governmental organisations, e.g. the West African Chambers of Commerce, Industry, Agriculture and Mines; (3) intra-state governmental institutions, e.g. the Kenya Government or Tanzania's State Trading Corporation; (4) intra-state non-governmental organizations, e.g. the Ghana Chamber of Commerce, the Trade Union Congress or the Popular Front Party and simialr interest groups; (5) certain powerful individuals acting as individuals rather than as representatives or spokesmen of larger social unit, e.g. Count Carl Gustaf Von Rosen, the Swedish nobleman who provided and helped to fly seventeen light airplanes and two old converted fighter-bombers in support of Biafra during the Nigerian Civil War (Hopkins and Mansbach, 1973: 5–9). Each type of actor can also be classified

**TABLE 2.1 Types of actors by constituency and task in the mixed-actor scheme**

| Constituency | Security | Political | Economic | Socio-Technical Public Interest | Group Identity |
|---|---|---|---|---|---|
| Intra-State Governmental | Ministry of Defence | Ministry of External Affairs | 1. State Trading Corporation<br>2. Ministry of Finance | Ministry of Education | Kano State |
| Intra-State Non-Governmental | Baganda<br>Fanti<br>UNITA | Political Parties<br>Owegbe cult | Nairobi Chambers of Commerce<br>Trade Unions<br>Utuks Motors (Nigeria) Ltd. | Nigerian Bar Association<br>The Anti-Corruption League | 1. Egbe Omo Oduduwa<br>2. Ibo State Union |

| Constituency | Security | Political | Economic | Socio-Technical Public Interest | Group Identity |
|---|---|---|---|---|---|
| Inter State Governmental | 1. African High Command<br>2. Royal West African Frontier Force | Union of Central African States<br>OCAMM<br>The Front line Five | ECOWAS<br>UDEAC<br>Conseil de l'Entente | 1. Trans-Sahara Highway Committee<br>2. West African Examinations Council | The Non-Aligned Group<br>The African Bloc |
| Inter State Non-Governmental | 1. The Polisario Front<br>2. African Youth Command | AAPSO<br>African National Congress | Shell (BP)<br>Unilever Brothers<br>CFAO<br>Club of Dakar<br>West African Chambers of Commerce | 1. African Adult Education Association<br>2. Association of African Universities<br>3. Amnesty International | All Africa Conference of Churches |
| Individual | Savimbi | Nelson Mandela<br>Alan Paton<br>Funmilayo Ransome-Kuti | M.K. Abiola | Mary Slessor<br>Albert Schweitzer | 1. Maitatsine<br>2. Usman Dan Fodio<br>3. Emir of Borno |

Adapted from Raymond Hopkins and Richard Mansback (1973) *Structure and process in international politics,* Harper and Row, New York, p. 7

according to one or more of the following tasks which it performs in the polity: physical protection, economic development and regulation, social welfare and provision of group status. Table 2:1 shows African examples of 'actors' by constituency and the task performed.

This 'mixed actor' system is said to be more reflective of the real world of international politics where 'several qualitatively different types of actor interact in the absence of any settled pattern of dominance – submission (or hierarchial) relationships' (Young, 1972: 136). Relationships can at one level, involve two or more representatives of the same type of actor between themselves producing as many different patterns of political relationships as there are types of actors. At another level two or more different types of actors may be involved and this would result in an even greater number of patterns of political relationships.

## The case for state-as-actor

The arguments against the state-as-actor are, however, not entirely convincing and the alternative mixed actor concept is in many ways misleading and irrelevant to the student of international relations.

The argument that the 'new states' are in some sense incomplete states does not stand up to critical examination. It is an example of Western ethnocentrism (and racism) which disparages or dismisses as unreal anything that does not conform totally to Western ideas and conceptions. Thus if African states do not exhibit to the same degree the attributes of Western states, then these new states must be seen as a 'perversion' of the Western ideal. More importantly, this line of argument is vulnerable empirically. Many states, especially those in Africa, may be 'inchoate, economically absurd, administratively ramshackle and impotent', to borrow Stanley Hoffman's phrase. But they are nevertheless 'dangerous in international politics' as the bloody wars in the Horn of Africa, Vietnam and elsewhere in the Third World remind us. They 'remain the basic units in spite of all remonstrations and exhortations . . . They go on *faute de mieux* despite their alleged obsolescence; indeed their very existence is a formidable obstacle to their replacement' (Hoffman, 1966: 897). Oran Young, a proponent of the mixed actor view, himself admits that 'states and nation-states are still remarkably resilient:

> As experience even with such relatively successful ventures as the European communities makes clear, the modern state cannot be superceded with ease even under comparatively favourable circumstances. And in many other parts of the world (particularly in Africa, one might add), there is every evidence that the state is only now coming to its own as the dominant form of political organization. Even nationalism, with its thrust toward the idea of nation-states, is still a potent and rising political force in many areas of the world . . . perhaps because of . . . imperial activities of various great powers (Young, 1972: 135).

The argument about the demise or obsolescence of the state is a dangerous one which could be employed to endanger the 'new states' in Africa. For if we accept this argument we inevitably undermine the basis of such time-honoured principles as state sovereignty and non-intervention in internal affairs. Such a development could lead to an unrestrained use of force by the powerful against the weak.

The possibility of the state-as-actor view being a dehumanizing influence in international politics is a very remote one. For to talk of states-as-actors is not to attribute human quality of thought and action to an abstract entity. Of course only human beings think, choose between alternatives and act on behalf of the state. States-as-actors, then, is no more than a way of referring to those human beings who authoritatively speak and act in the name of the state concerned. The particular predispositions of these decision-makers will be essential variables in their dealings with similar authorities in other states. Their personal value preferences, temperament and rationality will be important in deciding the 'state interests', the priorities among those interests and the level of energy and available resources to be devoted to the pursuit of these interests. Thus state-as-actor does not preclude human actors and human interests from the analysis. Rather it calls for an understanding of international politics both in terms of 'the behavior of states as organized bodies of men, [and] of human beings upon whose psychological reactions the behavior credited to states ultimately rests'. For in the final analysis 'State interests are indeed human interests' as percieved by the decision-makers and 'a sufficient number of men [still] identify themseleves with their state or nation to justify and render possible governmental action in the name of state interests' (Wolfers, 1962: 6).

There are, of course, serious phenomenological (and therefore methodological) issues that arise once we accept authoritative decision-makers as surrogates for the state. Is the behaviour of decision-makers on behalf of the state motivated by objective factors or by the decision-makers' perception of the objective factors, or both? Can the individual's perception of objective factors be measured in an accurate and systematic fashion? For a group of decision-makers it is possible to identify some sort of corporate perception? But these issues will arise equally in the mixed actor model, since that model also deals with integral social units even if of a different character and with different attributes to those of states.

Finally, it is true that historically states are late-comers into international politics. But their rise has transformed the nature of international politics and has eclipsed the dominant role which non-state actors previously played. And while it is possible that the state may be replaced by some other entity as the principal actor in international politics that possibility belongs to the future and, therefore, to the realm of speculation. As yet the state has not been superceded anywhere in the world, and supernational developments (e.g. the European Economic Community (EEC)) have counterparts in micro-national movements everywhere, including the United Kingdom (cf. the Irish struggle for self-determination).

The arguments advanced in favour of the alternative mixed actor view of international relations have serious weaknesses. Firstly, while the mixed actor view may reflect the complexity of the real world of international politics by distinguishing patterns of relations involving the *same* type of actors and those involving *different* types of actors, the mixed actor model is itself too complicated to serve as a useful tool of analysis. If, for example, we take the five types of actors which have been identified in terms of scope of constituency and the four categories of tasks which each type performs in a political system, we would have twenty functional specific *types* of actors (see Table 2.1). The possible combinations of relations for these twenty types of actor is statistically in the thousands. Thus the types of actors and the possible combination of relationships among them become too unwieldy to be encompassed by any one theory of international politics. And the relative importance of these relationaships becomes impossible to systematize and analyze except on an *ad hoc* basis.

Secondly, the attempt to be comprehensive disguises the fact that the state is still 'the significant unit of political action' and is going to remain so for many years to come and that 'strategies of action and commitment of resources . . . continue to be decided at the national level' (Synder, Bruck and Sapin, 1962: 62–3). Only states and inter-state governmental agencies are endowed with an international legal status which enables them to participate in high politics and to resolve issues of war and peace. Intra-state and inter-state non-governmental organizations and groups are not members of, and do not participate in, such international fora as the UN, the OAU and the Non-Aligned Movement except as observers. They cannot appeal to international tribunals except through the instrumentalities of states and only after local legal procedures have been exhausted. Thus, for instance, a British company operating in Nigeria cannot sue the Nigerian government in an international court until it has gone through the hierarchy of the Nigerian courts up to the Supreme Court without obtaining satisfaction. But even then the case could go to an international tribunal only if the British government takes it up as its own.

On account of these shortcomings it is hardly surprising that most texts which claim that there are actors other than states nevertheless proceed to analyse international politics exclusively in terms of *nation* and *state*. The other so-called actors are either ignored in the analysis or are treated separately and without reference to the larger system.

## A state-as-actor model

Because of the shortcomings of the mixed actor conception of international politics we adopt the view in this study of the state-as-actor. We view states (or rather those individuals and agencies acting authoritatively in the name of the state) as the only actors. This is mainly because only states have autonomy expressed in terms of the capacity to exercise exclusive jurisdiction within a geographical space. All the other units which the mixed actor proponents regard as actors are in this context regarded as part of the milieu in which states operate. They are, therefore, influencers rather than actors in their own right (Coplin, 1971: 62–92).

The Sprouts have suggested that inter-governmental organizations should be treated as *structures* of the international system. Thus the UN could be viewed as the structure of the global system and the OAU could be seen as a structure of the African subordinate system. These inter-governmental organizations (and indeed other non-governmental ones) are 'elements of the milieu within which unfold the interactions and interrelationships of the legally sovereign communities called states.' As elements of the milieu these structures, and other elements such as the multinational corporations exercise a 'more or less constraining influence on even the most powerful legally sovereign governments'. (Sprout and Sprout, 1971: 85). But this quality or ability does not make them international actors in the strictest sense.

There are two main considerations for sticking to the state–as–actor view. One is the advantage of its conceptual simplicity, the other is its conformity with the legal (and practical) reality. Conceptually, by treating states as the actors while regarding non-state entities as influencers, international politics can be reduced to a simple model represented by figure 2.1.

Figure 2:1 shows patterns of inter-state relations. State A represents any state interacting with another State B. Each state comprises its decision-makers and its influencers – both indigenous and non-indigenous – operating within its boundaries. The various channels of interaction are:

a)    government to government
b)    government to other state's influencers (and vice versa)
c)    influencers to influencers
d)    government to its own influencers (and vice versa)

Channels *a* and *b,* which involve governments, represent international politics and together with channel *c* they comprise the totality of international relations. Channel *d* represents domestic politics.

Channel *a* is the normal channel of diplomacy as well as of military operations. Channel *b* is the indirect channel of diplomacy whereby one

*Figure 2:1    A model of states-as-actors*

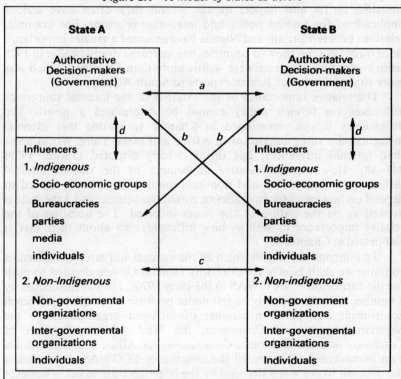

Adapted from Duchacek (1970: 43), Sprout and Sprout (1971: 63, 140–1).

government attempts to influence another by influencing the other government's indigenous influencers or manipulating the non-indigenous groups. For instance Nigeria attempted to influence British government policy over Zimbabwe's independence by nationalizing British Shell and British Petroleum in Nigeria. The threat of further nationalizations of British companies presumably led these companies to put pressure on the British government and thus contributed to a change in British policy in favour of measures that hastened Zimbabwe's independence. Conversely, the United States, Britain and other Western countries, exercise pressure on multinational corporations to adopt measures that will force other states to change or adopt certain policies. This was done to Nkrumah's and to Busia's government in Ghana (Thompson, 1969; Libby, 1976: 67–89). Channel *b* then is clearly the main channel of propaganda, subversion, sabotage and other convert operations. Between them channels *a* and *b* exhibit all the techniques of international statecraft, that is the techniques of the art of conducting international public affairs.

Channel *c* is the channel of trade, finance, technical and cultural exchanges, tourism, private correspondence and telecommunication. Although private, these activities are normally regulated by governments – by means of, for example, immigration controls, foreign exchange controls, tariffs and import quotas – and they often have serious implications for foreign policy and inter-state relations. For example, relations between Britain and Nigeria have assumed a greater importance since trade between the two countries has increased dramatically: in 1978 British exports to Nigeria were worth more than $1 billion which was more than the value of British exports to South Africa.

The relative importance of the external or the internal sources of influences on foreign policy cannot be determined a priori. The dependency school, mentioned in Chapter 1, assume that external influences are more important in Africa and other Third World areas than internal influences, but this is widely disputed (Smith, 1979: 247–88). However, the relative importance of the various internal influencers – indigenous and non-indigenous – is generally agreed to depend on how open (democratic) or closed (non-democratic) the state is as well as on the nature of the issues involved. The question of the relative importance as well as how influencers go about their task is elaborated in Chapter 3.

To illustrate the way in which all the internal and external influences combine we shall briefly consider why General Gowon decided to push for the formation of ECOWAS in the early 1970s. He was influenced by a number of factors: partly he felt under pressure from a hostile French government and partly a number of different organizations – the Nigerian Chamber of Commerce, the West African Chamber of Commerce and the Economic Commission for Africa – along with his own bureaucracy all favoured the creation of ECOWAS. Nevertheless the decision to act was a decision by the Nigerian *state* to act – however much individuals, external powers, intra- and inter-state organizations may have contributed to the decision to act.

In sum, by treating international organizations, both governmental and non-governmental as well as intra-state non-governmental units and private individuals as influencers and as a part of the milieu in which states transact international political business, we conceptually simplify international politics allowing us to focus analytically on state behaviour. We can then show (1) how and why the activities of these other non-state entities (which constitute a part of what states have to deal with) affect the behaviour of different kinds of states (developed or underdeveloped, open or closed, for instance); (2) the relative roles and importance of these non-state entities under varying conditions in the formulation and implementation and, therefore, outcome of the foreign policies of different kinds of states; and (3) the implications of all of these for the international system as a whole. Thus we avoid the problem of the alternative view where other actors besides states are identified only then to be largely ignored in the analysis of the actual workings of the international system.

In other words, it is the state-centric view alone which permits both a comprehensive understanding of the international system as a whole and a comprehension of its parts. For in both the systemic and subsytemic level of analysis the empirical referents remain the same – the state. Such phenomena as the creation and dissolution of coalitions, the frequency and stability of specific power configurations and the impact of these on the various parts, which are all objects of system analysis, cannot be discussed meaningfully without reference to the state. The subsystem analysis focuses on the nature and processes of interaction of the parts (the states) between themselves and with the formal and informal organizations that influence and regulate these processes (Singer, 1961: 77–92).

A second consideration for adopting the state-as-actor model is that to a considerable degree it conforms to the legal and, therefore, practical reality. International actors other than states remain subject to state authority and jurisdiction or, in the case of international governmental organizations, operate according to the will of the states which are its sole members. Thus intra-state organizations – political parties, the media interest groups, for example – are regulated by, and operate within, the confines of state laws. So are international non-governmental organizations. Even multinational corporations which appear to be independent of any one state authority are at least nominally regulated by the state in which they are formally incorporated – the state where their headquarters are situated.

Similarly in such international governmental organizations as the UN and the OAU the identity and policy-making capacity of individual states remain unscathed and are, in fact, preserved by their respective charters. Certainly no collective action of these organizations can be easily explained without reference to actions in the various member states.

Except for the special case of individuals and international organizations which have been accorded an international personality, it is essential that states are internationally recognized. Recognition is an act whereby actors in the international system confer membership and legal status to a new member. The act could be some appropriate declaration or a mere entering of diplomatic relations, but it always means that the recognizing state regards the new state as legitimate. For example, Tanzania, Ivory Coast, Gabon and Zambia recognized Biafra during the Nigerian Civil War and by that act indicated their intention to treat Biafra as a legitimate autonomous actor to be treated on an equal footing as any other state. It gave Biafra a moral boost. Recognition of a state, once accorded, cannot be withdrawn unless of course the recognized state disappears, as was the case with Biafra.

New governments are also normally recognized as a signal that the new regime will be regarded as a qualified spokesman of the state. Recognition can be *de facto,* when the regime is the effective spokesman or *de jure,* when the regime is the rightful spokesman, but in either case it can be withdrawn or denied. Denial of recognition to a state and denial or withdrawal of recognition to a government 'represents an attempt either to exclude the political community in question from the international political system or brand [the ] government as an outlaw, unqualified to speak for its community in dealings with other members of the society of nations' (Sprout and Sprout, 1971: 70–1).

Recognition, then, is the acid test of legitimacy and the formal mode of acquiring status in the international system. It is a practical test to decide who the actors are. The practical reality is that only those units so recognized participate in high politics and function in such global and regional international fora as the UN and the OAU.

In summary, states constitute the 'populations' or the 'legal citizens' of the international system. Other units whose activities and transactions have implications for international politics are, therefore, no more than powerful elements of the environment which influence the state actors. This position is consistent with our definition of the international system in Chapter 1 as 'a decentralized political system dominated by competing, relatively autonomous, territorially based political organizations' (Coplin, 1971: 331).

## The bases of power and capabilities of state actors

The attributes of statehood – territory, population, government, economy and political culture (the way of life and those shared values, beliefs and customs that give a sense of belonging to one group rather than to another) – constitute the base of power and capabilities of the state. As such they significantly affect the determination of state international attitudes and policies.

### Territory

When we talk of territory in the context of a territorial state we mean more than the mere expanse of land: we include both the expanse (geographical size and shape) as well as the location, climatic conditions and natural resources such as minerals. This geographical dimension has long been recognized as critical to the power capabilities of a state and, thus, to its foreign policy. 'The geographical position of a nation', the famous French diplomat, Jules Cambon, once wrote, 'is the principal factor conditioning its foreign policy' (Cambon, 1930: 173). Sir Austen Chamberlain (1931) and Sir Eyre Crowe (1950) of the British Foreign Office as well as the German diplomatist Richard Kühlmann (1931) not only fully concur with Cambon, but have also been instrumental in making the influence of geography on political history a commonplace of modern thought.

Indeed the whole field of geopolitics – the study of the relation of geography to politics – is concerned with theories and hypotheses that explain or predict international political patterns and relationships in terms of the configuration of the seas, oceans and lands, the topography of places, the climatic variations in time and space and the distribution of mineral and other natural resources. The assumption is that these geographical factors are decisive in the development of military/naval power, which in turn determines the global patterns of domination. Sir Halford Mackinder (1919), for example, sees Africa, Europe and Asia as one land mass and as an island surrounded by the Atlantic, Indian, Pacific and Arctic Oceans. This 'world island', as he calls it, has two critically important parts for world power and domination: Eastern Europe and the 'heartland', the latter comprising approximately what is today the Soviet Union.

Mackinder theorizes that:

Who rules East Europe commands the Heartland;
Who rules the Heartland commands the World Island;
Who rules the World Island commands the World (Cited in Morgenthau, 1962: 158).

Centuries earlier, Kaultiya, the fourth century Indian philosopher, had delved in geopolitics and stated as a general principle that geographical neighbours are always political enemies while neighbours' neighbours are friends (Coplin, 1971: 140–1). Relatively more recent writers such as Ellsworth Huntington (1915) and C. A. Mills (1949) have argued that climate is the key variable which sets a limit to human achievement and thus determines the global pattern of power distribution (see Sprout and Sprout, 1971: 268–97 for detailed discussion).

Whatever the approach and theories relating geography to international politics, one thing is clear: the size, shape and location of a territorial state, its climatic conditions and natural endowments can be great assets to that state. But they can also be a liability. A geographically large state, completely landlocked, with a hot, dry climate and few mineral resources (e.g. Mali or Upper Volta) is, other things being equal, more handicapped in terms of the cost and rate of economic development and, therefore, in terms of what it can do internationally than an equally large state, with ready access to the sea, a warm and wet climate and abundant natural resources (e.g. Zaire or Nigeria). But then Upper Volta may be relatively safe from attack by covetous states –

because there is little to covet — than the larger, better endowed Zaire. It is no accident that since its independence in 1960 Zaire has been subjected to Euro-American interventions such as Shaba I and II.

## Population

It is commonly supposed that the larger the population the larger the manpower available to the state for economic and military mobilization. Thus population is equated with manpower which then is equated with political power conceived in terms of economic and military power.

A more sophisticated view is that technological advancement is today the decisive factor in power relationships among states. Technological advancement of a state, however, is brought about by its men and women of genius, especially in the fields of science and technology. The incidence of such men and women is not racially or geographically determined: they appear at random in the population of the world. It follows that the number of such geniuses to be found in any state will, all things being equal, be directly proportional to the size of the population. In other words the larger the population, the larger the number of geniuses likely to be found, and, as a result, the better for technological advancement and international power the state will be (Sprout and Sprout 1971: 298–372 for detailed discussion).

This view, best articulated by the British scientist, B. K. Blount (1957a; 1957b), seems to have been embraced by many Third World countries. This in part explains their opposition to birth-control measures aimed at stemming what is now generally regarded as a population explosion. These countries feel that population control is the West's sinister method of preventing Blount's prediction from coming true. Blount had concluded from his analysis that the great centres of population in Afro-Asia, countries like China and India and, in the case of Africa, Nigeria, will become the leading nations of the world, eclipsing the less populated countries of Western Europe.

A large population is not always an advantage, however. For it can be argued that the quality is more important than the size of the population. A state with a large but poor quality manpower through being ill-fed, ill-clad, ill-housed, diseased and uneducated, is always at a disadvantage in political-military terms to a state with a small but high quality, and, therefore, more efficient population. The case of Israel and the Arab States in the 1967 and 1973 wars is illustrative of the importance of quality as opposed to quantity. Furthermore, the larger the population the heavier the demands on food supply and other raw materials. Given the fact that in most parts of the world the population growth (average of 2.5 per cent annually in the Third World) outpaces the growth of the economy, these demands cannot be met, resulting in a further deterioration of the quality rather than in its improvement. A larger population in Afro-Asia, Dr Frank Notestein has argued 'spells poverty and not power — except power to absorb suffering and punishment' (Notestein, 1951: 25).

High quality manpower depends on a high level of economic

development. But the latter is much more difficult without the former. However, high quality manpower is difficult to achieve where there is a large population and a high rate of population growth. The level of economic development sets a limit on the capital resources that can be allocated to education and training which is essential to high quality manpower. The lower the level of development the less the resources available and the fewer the children that are educated and trained. The talents of the unlucky children are thus wasted, and in their adulthood become social liabilities rather than assets.

## Economy

From what has been said above, it is clear that geography and population have a direct bearing on a state's potential for economic development. Economic development can be defined as higher growth in the production of goods and services and in the efficiency and equity with which these goods are allocated within a state. It is a result of effective integration and utilization of its human and non-human resources. To be effectively integrated the economy must allocate goods and services and other resources between consumption and investment in the best possible way. Investment may be in the form of capital investment or investment in education and research. This is the task of government. The task is not an easy one and often entails the need to acquire extra foreign exchange through increased exports and external aid which is then used to finance capital imports and technology transfer. The foreign exchange needs are so great that most developing states are reduced to greater dependence through trade, aid and investments on the more developed states.

Obviously the requirements and the performance of each economy differ. This differential need and performance in turn affects the power capabilities and thus the foreign policies of the state actors. Indeed, theories abound which depict the foreign policy of a state as a function of its level of economic development. Apart from Lenin's theory that imperialism represented the highest stage in capitalist development, there are more specific theories linking stages of economic growth to the foreign policy behaviour of states. W. W. Rostow (1963) identifies five stages of economic growth: the traditional, the pre-take-off, take-off, maturity and high mass-consumption. A. F. K. Organski (1968) and G. Lovell Field (1968) have merged Rostow's traditional and pre-take-off into one stage, the pre-industrial stage. The succeeding stages are the industrial, the post-industrial and overabundance which correspond to Rostow's last four stages.

The pre-industrial stage is characterized by foreign policy of national consolidation − consolidation of national territory, population and resources. As such the state is cautious, conservative, non-aligned and avoids hostility. The industrial stage is characterized by what might be called adolescent exuberance, with the state acting without balancing expenditure and resources. It pursues prestige policies involving regional aggression and local imperialism as a way of generating domestic support in the face of the social disequilibrium occasioned by economic progress. The post-industrial stage for its part is concerned with national security since its industrial achievements might be coveted by others. However, this stage is characterized by a sense of measure, by calculation and balancing of expenditure and resources. In practice this means playing the balance of power game in order to preserve the status quo. However, if a state has a massive industrial base this often entails further expansion – anti-imperialist imperialism – in order to pre-empt a rival, ideological posturing in order to win satellites and buffers and arms transfers to smaller states to fight proxy wars. The final stage, that of overabundance, is characterized by a foreign policy best described as 'extravagance and international goodwill'. Self-abnegation becomes the order of the day. This involves the pursuit of altruistic goals which may even run counter to the national interest – but no state has yet reached this stage in its foreign policy.

The discussions of various theories have taken us far afield, but they do indicate the degree of importance which scholars and practitioners attach to state attributes as a base of power capabilities and, therefore, as a limiting factor in foreign policy and international politics.

## Government and political culture

Government, the legitimate authority for the exercise of power of the state within a country, has the task of regulating and controlling the economy. This task is performed through fiscal (tax) and monetary (banking and currency control) measures, through development planning and through other legislative and indirect measures that independently and collectively change population trends, savings and investment habits, attitude to work, and the kinds of tools employed for production.

A government's ability to perform these functions obviously depends on many factors. One of these is the congruence of governmental forms and structures with the political culture. Any lack of congruence between political structures and political culture results in instability and disorder. For example, democratic forms and structures in authoritarian society will create disjunctions, instability and disorder. To restore order and stability either the democratic forms and structures must be transformed to suit the authoritarian culture, or the culture must change to accommodate the democratic norms. This explains, in part, why in post-colonial Africa the democratic forms adopted at independence have had to be adjusted to suit the authoritarian culture inherited from both the traditional and the colonial past. The changes to one-party states and from Parliamentary to Presidential systems are examples of this adjustment.

Obviously the form and actual mode of operation of government (democratic or dictatorial, open or closed) will affect its ability to develop, mobilize and harness its resources. It will, therefore, also affect its estimate of its own capabilities and as a result has a bearing on its foreign policy. It was once thought that monarchies based on an aristocracy were peace-loving while democratic Republics caused international disorder. The modern variant, developed initially by the early nineteenth–century French political philosopher, Alexis de Tocqueville, is that liberal democracies are peace-loving but inefficient in international statecraft while Socialist democracies (Communist states) cause international disorder but are efficient in statecraft (Lippmann, 1955).

A more sophisticated theory has been advanced by Henry Kissinger (1969). The structure of government, Kissinger contends, along with the values of society and the experiences of leaders during their rise to prominence are the three factors that determine the nature of leadership which in turn largely determines the nature of foreign policy. Kissinger identifies three contemporary leadership types – ideological, bureaucratic-pragmatic and revolutionary charismatic. These types, when added to the differences in structures and values which produce them, cause a gulf between reasonable aims and methods of international statecraft as well as producing conflicting criteria for resolving differences. Indeed, often differences arising from conflicting domestic sets of values are one of the principal issues of international politics, as states feel that their own set of values are being threatened by those of another state.

It is clear, in sum, that the power capabilities of state actors derive from the attributes of states. It should come as no surprise then that these attributes constitute the core interest or nation-entity value (which may be defined as the value attached to the survival of the nation as an entity) which the state upholds and defends at all times. Core interests include (1) the defence of the territorial integrity against both external aggression and internal secessionist movements; (2) the protection and preservation of the political independence; (3) the protection of the integrity of government, which makes sedition and treason the most heinous crimes; and (4) the quest for economic development and self-reliance. Other values that states value and uphold are either private but assimilated to state interests or they are transient. Examples of the former are foreign exchange controls and import restrictions which are primarily for the benefits of entrepreneurial individuals, groups or organizations whose activities are regarded as ultimately beneficial to the state. Examples of transient values are the international fight against apartheid, support for liberation movements and the projection of an 'African personality'.

It is clear that there are qualitative and quantitative differences in the extent to which states are endowed with the attributes of statehood, and that changes occur in these over time. Thus populations change in number and quality, the economy develops, and even territory may be lost to or gained from neighbours. States, though sovereign equals (i.e. equal in the legal sense) are unequal in power capabilities. This inequality results in unequal influence and, therefore, creates a hierarchy of states based on power and influence. It is for this reason that A. F. K. Organski (1958) sees world politics as a pecking order system, with states struggling for high places in the hierarchy.

# Actors in Africa: the unequal equals

In Africa, there are fifty independent states, the primary actors on the continent. Namibia is expected to join the ranks soon. The states vary enormously in size and population. At one extreme is Nigeria with over 72 million people, nearly twice the population of the next largest, Egypt (40 million). At the other extreme are Seychelles with a population of about 70 000, Sao Tome and Principe (100 000), Equatorial Guinea (200 000) and Cape Verde (300 000). There are differences in the composition (age, sex, occupational groups), the density and the quality (level of education, teachers and doctors per thousand people) of the population.

The African states also differ widely in geographic size and, to a degree, climate. Sudan (967 491 sq miles), Algeria (919 590 sq miles) and Zaire (905 559 sq miles) are much larger than any other state. At the opposite end of the territorial scale are Seychelles (107 sq miles) Reunion (970 sq miles), Cape Verde (1 557 sq miles), Gambia (4 361 sq miles) and Swaziland (6 704 sq miles).

The size and performance of the economy is as varied. In 1978 Nigeria and the Republic of South Africa with GNPs of $44.5 billion and $41.2 billion respectively topped the list, followed by Algeria ($21.9 billion), Libya ($19.5 billion) and Egypt ($16.0 billion). Among those at

**TABLE 2.2 Basic data on African states**

| State | Area in[1] sq. miles | Population[2] in millions (1975) | GNP in[2] millions (1978) | GNP per capita[2] |
|---|---|---|---|---|
| Algeria | 919,590 | 17.6 | 21,877 | 1,157 |
| Angola | 481,400 | 6.5 | 3,049 | 436 |
| Benin | 43,483 | 3.3 | 679 | 191 |
| Botswana | 220,000 | 0.7 | 459 | 611 |
| Burundi | 10,759 | 4.1 | 613 | 139 |
| Cameroon | 183,591 | 8.1 | 3,479 | 399 |
| Cape Verde | 1,557 | 0.3 | 39 | 140 |
| Central African Republic | 240,376 | 2.2 | 463 | 196 |
| Chad | 495,750 | 4.4 | 590 | 124 |
| Congo | 134,749 | 1.5 | 809 | 502 |
| Egypt | 385,237 | 39.9 | 16,024 | 373 |
| Equatorial Guinea | 10,830 | 0.2 | 114 | 530 |
| Ethiopia | 471,776 | 31.0 | 3,659 | 109 |
| Gabon | 102,317 | 0.6 | 1,779 | 2,760 |
| Gambia | 4,361 | 0.6 | 126 | 195 |
| Ghana | 92,100 | 11.4 | 15,544 | 1,269 |
| Guinea | 94,925 | 5.1 | 716 | 130 |
| Guinea-Bissau | 13,948 | 0.6 | 94 | 147 |
| Ivory Coast | 123,485 | 7.5 | 6,812 | 845 |
| Kenya | 224,960 | 15.2 | 4,779 | 292 |
| Lesotho | 11,716 | 1.3 | 361 | 258 |
| Liberia | 43,000 | 1.7 | 865 | 473 |

| State | Area in[1] sq. miles | Population[2] in millions (1975) | GNP in[2] million (1978) | GNP per capita[2] |
|---|---|---|---|---|
| Libya | 680,000 | 2.8 | 19,513 | 6,487 |
| Madagascar | 226,657 | 8.1 | 1,940 | 223 |
| Malawi | 45,747 | 5.7 | 968 | 158 |
| Mali | 478,652 | 6.3 | 717 | 106 |
| Mauritania | 397,683 | 1.4 | 420 | 279 |
| Mauritius | 720 | 0.9 | 870 | 900 |
| Morocco | 175,050 | 19.8 | 12,197 | 573 |
| Mozambique | 303,079 | 9.8 | 2,062 | 195 |
| Niger | 458,993 | 5.2 | 1,035 | 185 |
| Nigeria | 356,669 | 72.2 | 44,504 | 573 |
| Reunion | 970 | 0.5 | n.a. | n.a. |
| Rwanda | 10,169 | 4.8 | 871 | 169 |
| Sao Tome & Principe | 372 | 0.1 | n.a. | n.a. |
| Senegal | 76,699 | 5.4 | 1,753 | 302 |
| Sierra Leone | 27,699 | 3.2 | 687 | 199 |
| Seychelles | 107 | 0.075 | n.a. | n.a. |
| Somalia | 246,155 | 3.4 | 469 | 128 |
| South Africa | 471,445 | 27.2 | 41,281 | 1,412 |
| Sudan | 967,491 | 17.6 | 5,778 | 305 |
| Swaziland | 6,704 | 0.5 | 311 | 580 |
| Tanzania | 362,821 | 16.8 | 3,835 | 212 |
| Togo | 21,900 | 2.5 | 779 | 290 |
| Tunisia | 63,170 | 6.2 | 5,763 | 865 |
| Uganda | 91,076 | 12.8 | 4,384 | 318 |
| Upper Volta | 105,886 | 6.5 | 669 | 95 |
| Zaire | 905,559 | 27.2 | 5,024 | 172 |
| Zambia | 290,580 | 5.5 | 2,510 | 425 |
| Zimbabwe | 150,820 | 7.1 | 3,200 | 419 |

Sources 1. *Encyclopaedia Britannica,* 1971 edition
2. U.S. Arms Control and Disarmament Agency, *World Military Expenditures and Arms Transfers 1969-1978* (US Government Printing Office, 1980).

the bottom of the list were Cape Verde ($39 million), Guinea Bissau ($94 million) Equatorial Guinea ($114 million) and Gambia ($126 million). In terms of GNP per capita the leading states were Libya ($6 487), Gabon ($2 760), South Africa ($1 412) and Algeria ($1 157). In contrast to these states are eighteen others which comprise more than half of the thirty-one states declared by the United Nations to be the poorest and least developed in the world: Upper Volta (per capita GNP in 1978 of $95), Mali ($106), Ethiopia ($109), Somalia ($128), Chad ($124), Guinea ($130), Guinea Bissau ($147), Burundi ($139), Benin ($191), Cape Verde ($140), Central African Republic ($196), Gambia ($195), Malawi ($158), Niger ($185), Mozambique ($195), Rwanda ($169), Sierra Leone ($199) and Tanzania ($212). Table 2.2 shows the basic data on size, population and GNP for each African State.

The states also differ in the forms and actual operation of

Government, ranging from the socialist single-party system in Tanzania and Libya to the capitalist single-party system in the Ivory Coast, and capitalist multi-party system in Nigeria. The stability and effectiveness of government also varies widely.

These differences in national attributes amount to differences in power capabilities and influence which are reflected in the hierarchy of influence. In Africa, as David Johns (1979: 269–83) has shown, stratification or hierarchy is clearly discernible in the pattern of diplomatic exchanges. Diplomatic missions are the normal channels for conducting international business, but they are expensive to establish both in terms of money and personnel. Ability to establish such missions, then, is a function of the states' resources and political concerns, that is a function of its capabilities and self-image as an actor in the system. The number of missions a state hosts reflects the importance which the states establishing them attach to the host state for the realization of their own goals and objectives. It follows that the number of reciprocal diplomatic exchanges reflect the mutual importance the states concerned attach to each other. The overall pattern of diplomatic exchange is a mirror of the perceived power relationships on the continent.

The Johns study showed that in 1975 certain countries had established disproportionately more missions (10 or more) in other African countries: Egypt (25), Nigeria and Zaire (23); Ghana (15); Sudan (13); Algeria (12); Central African Republic, Ethiopia and Liberia (11); Libya, Senegal and Somalia (10). The same countries (except Somalia and Central African Republic) along with four others hosted ten or more missions from other African States: Egypt (25); Nigeria and Zaire (24); Ethiopia (22); Algeria (19); Ivory Coast (15); Ghana (14); Kenya (13); Libya, Morocco and Senegal (12); Sudan (11); Liberia and Tunisia (10); In terms of reciprocal diplomatic exchanges the same group of states predominated: Egypt and Zaire (21); Nigeria (19); Ghana (12); Algeria and Ethiopia (11); Senegal and Sudan (10).

In contrast to these leading states were those which hosted only one mission (Malawi, Mali, Upper Volta), two missions (Botswana, Burundi, Mauritania and Mauritius) or three missions (Benin, Gambia, Niger, Rwanda and Togo) and, in some cases, none at all (Equatorial Guinea, Lesotho, Madagascar, Swaziland). Mauritius had established no diplomatic missions at all, some had established only one (Botswana, Lesotho, Swaziland), some only two (Benin, Gambia, Malagasy) while a few had established three (Equatorial Guinea, Malawi, Togo, Upper Volta). It is noteworthy that most of the states in these categories are also among the poorest on the continent and in the world.

Another interesting pattern emerged when Johns examined diplomatic exchanges within the sub-regions of Africa – North, South, East, West and Central. Some states were as active diplomatically in their regions as they were in the continent as a whole, some were more active regionally than continentally and some were more active continentally than regionally. In North Africa there was considerable diplomatic activity, with Egypt the most active continentally and also the most active regionally, followed by Algeria and Libya. Sudan was the least active in the region though one of the most active continentally. Sudan, the poorest in the region, with a mixed Arab and black population obviously felt it needed the rest of black Africa to compensate for its regional disabilities.

In West Africa, Nigeria and Ghana were much more active than other states. The Ivory Coast and Sierra Leone were moderately active. Benin, Mali, Mauritania, Togo and Upper Volta were the least active. Senegal, like Sudan, was relatively more active continentally, than regionally. In the Central African region, Zaire which was most active continentally was also the most active regionally. Equatorial Guinea, the least active continentally was also the least active regionally.

The situation in East Africa was somewhat different. There appeared to be no clear leader. Ethiopia which hosted more missions from the region than any other state (8) – largely because Ethiopia serves as the headquarters of the OAU and the Economic Commission for Africa – sent only two missions to the region in contrast to the nine it sent to other parts of Africa. Obviously Ethiopia was not a regional power, had limited regional interests and felt its interests were better advanced on a continental basis rather than in a narrow regional basis. Somalia, by contrast, received two of its total four missions from the East African region while it sent an equal number of missions (5) to the region as outside. Clearly, Somalia felt it needed continental as much as regional understanding of its cause, especially the wars on the Horn of Africa. But it was not a regional leader. Other East African countries except Kenya, Tanzania and Zambia, were even less active regionally. Kenya received five missions but sent only three to other countries from within the region. Tanzania and Zambia each received four but sent two and four regional missions respectively.

In Southern Africa there was no diplomatic exchange in 1975. Since then, with the independence of the former Portuguese territories and Zimbabwe, there have been a spate of activities, with Zimbabwe clearly in the lead.

Four major conclusions can be derived from the pattern of diplomatic exchange. First, there is a clear diplomatic stratification in Africa. Some countries are very active diplomatically both on the continent as a whole and in their respective regions. These countries are Egypt, Nigeria, Zaire, Algeria and Ghana, labelled in this context as the Group I states. Another set of states, Group II, is relatively less active continentally and regionally. Its members include Kenya, Ivory Coast, Libya, Gabon, Sudan, Zambia and Tanzania. Secondly, this stratification reflects inequality of power. The Group I states have the highest GNPs and the largest populations, Group II states have the next highest levels of GNP while Group III (including such countries as Upper Volta, Burundi, Mali, Mauritania and Malawi) are the poorest. The three groups nearly coincide with Tim Shaw's (1975) categorizations of African states based on the nature of principal exports. Shaw classifies Nigeria, Zaire, Algeria, Zambia and Angola as world 'middle' powers with sub-imperial regional roles and a potential for continental dominance. They are also the producers of petroleum and strategic minerals. Kenya, Ivory Coast and Senegal (which are industrial producers) play an active regional role. The rest of the African states, chiefly producers of primary materials, are described as 'subordinates'.

Thirdly, the spread of diplomatic missions reflects also a struggle of *realpolitik* in the African pecking order. In other words, African international politics can be seen as power politics, marked by competition for leadership within regions and on the continent as a whole. Indeed, as Scott Thompson (1969), Ojo (1974), Aluko (1976) and Akinsanya (1976) have variously shown *realpolitik* and not ideological division is the key to an understanding of African international politics in the 1960s and this is still equally true in the 1980s.

Fourthly and finally, the African pecking order system lacks a single dominant power − a 'super power' − to regulate it in the fashion of the 'Pax Britannica' of the nineteenth century, or of the 'Pax Americana' of our day. In the absence of a dominant power two alternatives are open. One is a concert of the regional leaders: the Group I states who, if they can agree amongst themselves are able to claim that their wish is the African wish. The other alternative is for external actors to establish order either by occasional direct intervention or by creating, manipulating and supporting concerts of lesser powers against the regional leaders. The two alternatives are not mutually exclusive, which is why African international politics is much more complex than is commonly supposed. The economic (and therefore military) weakness of nearly all the African states help to entrench external states, especially the former colonial powers and the United States and the Soviet Union, in the role of essential actors in Africa. As we shall see, this weakness makes economic intergovernmental organizations the most important fora for interaction of states, and makes economic issues the primary concern of African international relations.

# The place of international organizations

It is clear that few African states have diplomatic exchanges with more than a small fraction of the total number of states on the continent. Instead of expensive diplomatic missions most states use their membership of international organizations to serve the same ends. As David Kay puts it the African states, 'unable to afford the costs in money and trained manpower needed to maintain diplomatic representation in over a hundred capitals', have enjoined their UN missions to add 'a distinctly new function':

> To use . . . the opportunity provided by the concentration in New York of diplomatic representatives from most members of the international community to complete their diplomatic network. [Thus] the head of a typical mission . . . may find himself also serving

as his country's ambassador to the United States and *de facto* representative to 80 or more other states (Kay, 1970: 12).

The same is true of the OAU. Ethiopia hosts a large number of missions from its region and from the rest of the continent. This is because most African states see the mission to Ethiopia as a mission to the OAU as well, and thus to all the other states represented at Addis Ababa.

Quite apart from supplementing, and in some cases substituting for, diplomatic exchange, international organizations can also be seen as instruments for restraining power struggles. Kant, the eighteenth–century philosopher observed that organization serves peace. International organizations can also serve as instruments for tackling economic inequalities and inequities. In Africa, in fact, most governmental and non-governmental international organizations deal with economic matters.

There has been a proliferation of governmental international organizations in Africa. In 1969 there were twenty-nine . This excludes those organizations that have primarily external membership, such as the UN and the Commonwealth. It excludes also subsidiary institutions so that the OAU, for example is counted but not its several commissions. Of the twenty-nine none was exclusively for physical protection, three were purely political, six purely economic, two had multi-purposes and eighteen were social and technical and of residual public interest. In 1980 there were forty-nine governmental international organizations. The major difference was in the number of economic organizations which had risen from six to twenty-six (Europa Yearbook, 1969; 1980).

The explosion in the number of economic organizations – they number several hundred if we add the various agencies and organs of each main organization – relative to other kinds clearly suggests that political–security matters are secondary to African states. This should be borne in mind in discussions of such issues as the need for an African High Command or whether the OAU should be given 'stronger political teeth'. That political–security organizations play second fiddle to the economic ones may be due to a number of factors. One is that African states are dependent on non-African states for their security and protection. The second is that African states want to avoid involvement in politically sensitive internal affairs. Thirdly, it may be due to faith in functionalism – the idea that co-operation in non-controversial areas leads to the acquisition of co-operative habits and skills that make co-operation in politically sensitive areas possible.

The African intergovernmental economic organizations are as autonomous as the state members want them to be, which is not very much. They have consequences for these state members only insofar as each state accepts the consequences, which is not very often. Often a state's membership in too many organizations means less commitment on the part of that state, resulting in a vicious circle of organizational incompetence. In Africa these organizations remain, at best, important fora for, and powerful influences upon, actors. But they are rarely autonomous actors in their own right.

# Conclusions

African international relations are state-dominant. This has important implications for international problem-solving on the continent. Because the OAU is subordinate to the state system it does not have the teeth to enable it to impose solutions on members. But lack of power, while regrettable on emotional grounds, may paradoxically be one of the organization's strengths. It is utilized, and it has survived. Thus, although African states numerically dominate the UN they nevertheless prefer to 'try the OAU first' for the mediation and peaceful settlement of disputes. To give it 'more teeth', therefore, might scare off states from bringing their cases to it.

Although the African system is state-dominant, the question arises as to the autonomy of the state itself, or at least those who act in the name of the state. It has been argued that in Africa social classes (other than ethnic) are not well formed, that domestic business groups and trade unions are very weak and that other domestic groups with foreign policy concerns are small. The result is that the state in Africa is a more independent actor than it is elsewhere in the world. This is why individual leaders make a particularly strong impact on the formulation and articulation of foreign policy in Africa. Change of leadership can be very consequential for foreign policy: the overthrow of Nkrumah and Obote, for example, had immediate and drastic impacts on the foreign policy of Ghana and Uganda in the late 1960s and early 1970s respectively. According to this view African leaders use foreign policy to manipulate domestic groups and public opinion.

The preferred view, as argued earlier in this chapter, is that there is interdependence between the state and the social groups of which it is composed. it may very well be that the interdependence is unbalanced, with those acting in the name of the state being stronger than social groups or at least appearing to be stronger than the social groups. Providing the relationship between the leadership and the social groups is not excessively unbalanced, the preponderance of the leadership over the social groups is quite reasonable. Without it the state would cease to be a state.

# References

AKINSANYA, ADEOYE (1976) Afro-Arab alliance: dream or reality? *African Affairs* 75.

ALUKO, OLAJIDE (1976) *Ghana and Nigeria 1957-70: a study in Inter-African Discord,* Rex Collings, London.

BLOUNT, B K (1957a) Science as a factor in international relations, *International Affairs.* 33.

BLOUNT, B K (1975b) Science will change the balance of power, *The New Scientist* **32**, June 27.

CAMBON, JULES (1930) The permanent bases of French foreign policy, *Foreign Affairs* **8**.

CHAMBERLAIN, SIR AUSTEN (1931) The permanent bases of British foreign policy, *Foreign Affairs* **9**.

COOPER, RICHARD N (1968) *The Economics of Interdependence,* McGraw Hill, New York.

COPLIN, WILLIAM D (1971) *Introduction to international politics,* Markham Publishing Co., Chicago.

CROWE, SIR EYRE (1950) Memorandum on British relations with France and Germany. In Hans Morgenthau and K W Thompson (eds) *Principles and problems of international politics,* Alfred Knopf, New York.

EMERSON, RUPERT (1960) *From empire to nation,* Harvard Univ. Press, Cambridge, Mass..

ETZIONI, AMITAI (1968) *The active society,* The Free Press, New York.

DUCHACEK, IVO D (1971) *Nations and men,* Holt, Rinehart and Winston, New York.

FALK, RICHARD A (1966) On minimizing the use of nuclear weapons: a comparison of revolutionary and reformist perspectives. In Richard A Falk, Robert C Tucker and Oran Young, *On minimizing the use of nuclear weapons,* Princeton Center of International Studies, Princeton.

FIELD, G, LOVELL (1968) *Comparative political development: the precedent of the west,* Cornell Univ. Press, Ithaca.

HAAS, ERNST B (1958) *The uniting of Europe,* Stanford Univ. Press, Stanford.

HERZ, JOHN H (1957) The rise and demise of the territorial state, *World Politics,* **9**.

HERZ, JOHN H (1959) *International politics in the atomic age,* Columbia Univ. Press, New York.

HERZ, JOHN H (1968) The territorial state revisited: reflections on the future of the nation state. *Polity* **1** (1).

HOFFMAN, STANLEY (1966) Obstinate or obsolete: the fate of the nation state and the case of Western Europe, *Daedalus* **95** (3).

HOPKINS, RAYMOND F and MANSBACH, RICHARD W (1973) *Structure and process in international politics,* Harper and Row, New York.

HUNTINGDON, ELLSWORTH (1915) *Civilization and climate* Yale Univ. Press, New Haven.

JOHNS, DAVID (1979) Diplomatic exchange and state inequality in Africa. In Thomas Shaw and Kenneth A Heard (eds) *The politics of Africa: dependence and development,* Africana Publishing Co., New York.

KAY, DAVID M (1970) *The New Nations in the United Nations 1960–1967,* Columbia Univ. Press, New York.

KISSINGER, HENRY (1969) Domestic structure and foreign policy. In James Rosenau (ed) *International politics and foreign policy,* The Free Press, New York.

KUHLMANN, RICHARD VON (1931) The permanent bases of German foreign policy, *Foreign Affairs* 9 (2).

LIBBY, RONALD T (1976) External cooptation of less developed country's policy-makers: the case of Ghana. *World Politics,* 29.

LIPPMANN, WALTER (1955) *Essays in the public philosophy,* Little, Brown & Co., Boston.

MACKINDER, SIR HALFORD (1919) *Democractic ideals and reality,* Henry Hold & Co., New York.

MILLS, C A (1949) Temperature dominance over human life, *Science,* September 16.

MODELSKI, GEORGE (1968) The corporation in world society, *Yearbook of World Affairs, 1968* Institute of World Affairs, London.

MORGENTHAU, HANS (1962) *Politics among Nations,* Alfred Knopf, New York, 3rd edn.

NOTESTEIN, FRANK W (1951) Population, *Scientific American,* September.

OJO, OLATUNDE (1974) *Nigerian's foreign policy 1960-66: politics, economics and struggle for African leadership.* Doctoral Dissertation, University of Connecticut.

ORGANSKI, A F K (1958) *World politics,* Alfred Knopf, New York.

ORGANSKI, A F K (1965) *The stages of political development,* Alfred Knopf, New York.

ROLFE, SIDNEY E and DAMM, WALTER eds (1970) *The multinational corporation in the world economy,* Praeger, New York.

ROSTOW, W W (1963) *The stages of economic growth: a non-Communist Manifesto,* Cambridge Univ. Press, Cambridge.

SHAW, TIMOTHY M (1975) Discontinuities and inequalities in African international politics, *International Journal* 30 (3).

SINGER, DAVID J (1961) The levels of analysis problem in international relations. In Klaus Knorr and Sidney Verba (eds) *The international system,* Princeton Univ. Press, Princeton.

SMITH, TONY (1979) The underdevelopment of development literature. *World Politics* 31 (2).

SNYDER, RICHARD; BRUCK, H W and SAPIN, BURTON (1962) *Foreign policy decision-making,* The Free Press, New York.

SPROUT, HAROLD and SPROUT MARGARET (1971) *Towards a politics of the planet earth,* D. Van Nostrand Co., New York.

THOMPSON, WILLARD SCOTT (1969) *Ghana's foreign policy 1957-66,* Princeton Univ. Press, Princeton.

VERNON, RAYMOND (1962) *Sovereignty at bay: the multinational spread of U.S. Enterprises,* Penguin, Harmondsworth.

WOLFERS, ARNOLD (1962) *Discord and collaboration,* The Johns Hopkins Univ. Press, Deltimore.

YOUNG, ORAN R (1972) The actors in world politics. In James Rosenau, Vincent Davis and Maurice A East (eds) *The analysis of international politics,* The Free Press, New York.

# 3 Foreign policy and the developing state

The preceding chapter has analyzed in detail the concept of 'actor' or 'actors' in international relations. It has critically examined conceptions pertaining to the various actors that play determinant roles in international relations, focusing more sharply on the state as the actor in these relations. If states are indeed the key actors in international relations, it becomes quite obvious that a crucial task for analysis and theoretical work lies in the elucidation of the dynamic processes that constitute the basis of the exchanges that define interstate relations. These exchanges or interactions − complex, multiple, and, in our highly interdependent world, essentially continual − constitute the domain of foreign policy. If we may define foreign policy very schematically and provisionally as those actions of a state that are designed to achieve particular objectives involving other actors beyond the states' own boundaries, we see clearly that the foreign policies of states are the sinews of international relations. It is difficult to conceive of these relations existing entirely independently of the cross-currents of the foreign policies of state-actors on the international arena.

The concept of foreign policy has been defined in various ways. In these definitions it is possible, however, to discern and distinguish between those that are functional in the sense of focusing on the nature and overall purpose of the actions that constitute foreign policy, and those that view these actions within a broader sociological perspective. An example of the former is George Modelski's definition which views foreign policy as the process whereby a state adjusts its actions to those of other states so as to 'minimize adverse actions and maximize the favourable actions of foreign states' (Modelski, 1962: 3). Policy is seen here not as actions based on some grand design but as a continual process of pragmatic adjustment to the actions of others in the external environment. The purpose of the adjustments is to make the environment more hospitable and favourable or, at least, less hostile and disadvantageous. This conception is no doubt valid as far it goes, but it is too general and too abstract. It lacks the clarity that would highlight both the general and specific character of foreign policy as a mode of state action in international relations.

We thus turn to the sociological definition of foreign policy. A rather elaborate example of this has been suggested by I. D. Levin who asserts:

> Foreign policy is a combination of aims and interests pursued and defended by the given state and its ruling class in its relations with other states, and the methods and means used by it for the

achievement and defense of these purposes and interests. The aims and interests of a state in international relations are realized by various methods and means: first of all, by peaceful official relations, maintained by a government, through its special agencies, with the corresponding agencies of other states; by economic, cultural and other contacts, maintained by state agencies, as well as by public and private institutions (economic, political, scientific, religious, etc.), which provide opportunities for exercising economic, political and ideological influence on other states; finally by using armed forces, ie, by war or other methods of armed coercion (Levin in Farrell (ed), 1966: 213).

This means, then, that the objectives and interests that a state seeks to promote or safeguard as it interacts with other states must be viewed against the background of its internal social structure and the configuration of political power within it. More specifically, the class that controls and wields state power necessarily shapes foreign policy and does so, as might be supposed, in accordance with its own class interests, even though these might be rationalized ideologically as the interests of the entire nation. The latter should not be taken to mean that there are no interests which can be shared by the members of a nation-state in common. Depending on the given political circumstances, defence of state sovereignty, national independence, and the territorial integrity of a country, among other things, all correspond to the interests of the nation as a whole. However, in the majority of cases, foreign policy decisions are not concerned with matters directly related to such 'core' interests or values, as K. J. Holsti has termed them. Rather, routine foreign policy decision-making tends to centre on so-called 'middle-range objectives' (Holsti, 1977: 145–51), such as interstate economic, commercial and political relations, including attempts to influence the behaviour of other states in desired directions. Whilst these actions and objectives may have a bearing on state sovereignty or territorial integrity, the relationship is not an intrinsic one. Hence, one can argue that it is over 'routine' matters of this kind that class interests tend to have a decisive influence on policy-making. It is also in respect of such matters that foreign policy tends to be invested with an overlay of ideological rationalization. Aggressive imperialist adventures – gun-boat diplomacy – have often been rationalized in the name of the defence of 'national' honour and 'national' security. Such 'honour', 'interests', and 'security' frequently turn out, on close examination, to be no more than the honour, interests and security of the ruling regime or dominant class.

The preceding discussion suggests that foreign policy is an extension or complement of domestic policy. The distinction between the two is thus not a matter of substance. Rather it derives from the fact that a state's foreign policy takes account of the relevant attitudes, actions and reactions of other actors whereas its domestic policy is not, in general, burdened with such considerations.

The above definition of foreign policy also refers to the methods and means available to a state in the pursuance of its policy objectives.

Such methods and means obviously determine the extent to which the given policy is likely to be successful. As far as means are concerned, they range from the traditional methods of peaceful diplomacy to the ultimate instrument of coercive action, war. The choice of method or instrument is, in most cases, a function of the resources available to the particular state, the responses and capabilities of other interested or affected states, and the prevailing climate of international 'opinion' at the given time.

It should be clear that the more of the resources and instruments at the disposal of a state, the greater its potential to influence the development of the international system in a direction favourable to itself. In common parlance, the more 'powerful' a state is, the greater is its capacity to influence other states, that is to say, the greater is its ability to achieve the objectives of its foreign policy.

A more comprehensive formulation of the issue of means and capabilities has been made by Silviu Brucan (1978: Ch 3). Brucan suggests that the process of foreign policy formulation derives from five factors; (a) natural-material basics, including size of territory, population, geographic location, resources and the state and level of economic-technological development; (b) societal structure and forces, including social classes, ethnic composition, and cultural and psychological factors at work in the society; (c) contingency and situational factors, including 'political and economic crises, coups d'etat, elections, massive strikes, large-scale violence, military actions and war'. These influence the intensity of social and national 'drives and reactions'; (d) the state system, including the governmental machinery of decision-making; and (e) leadership, which refers to the way in which state power is used by current office-holders and decision-makers.

The five variables cited above clearly all have relevance for policy-making and execution. It is, unfortunately, not possible to assign 'weights' to them indicating *a priori* their relative significance in the policy-making process. Two general observations may, however, be made in regard to them. In the first place, the five variables may be viewed as falling into three broad categories: those which are in the nature of permanent and immutable physical realities which the policy-maker cannot alter at all, or can only alter at great cost in terms of resources and time; those variables which are entirely amenable to manipulation by decision-makers; and those which occur randomly and yet are capable of exerting decisive impacts on the course of events. The first set of variables includes the so-called natural-material basics and societal structure and forces. The second set refers to the state system, including the institutions and agencies of government which can be changed more or less easily by those in power or at their initiative. The third set of variables – contingency/situational factors and leadership – are both unpredictable and also capable of influencing policy-making in sudden and decisive ways. There is no doubt at all, for example, that the coup d'état in Uganda in 1971 and the personality and style of leadership of General Idi Amin significantly affected the substance and direction of Uganda's foreign policy after that coup. Similar examples can be cited from the recent history of other states in Africa and elsewhere.

In the second place the five variables constitute a kind of benchmark against which to measure or gauge the potential and actual capabilities of developing African states in respect to foreign policy formulation and implementation. The question of the capabilities of developing states has been approached from two perspectives. On the one hand is the approach which identifies the observable, and objective deficiencies of these states and the negative impact these have on policy formulation and implementation. David Vital, for example, has cited the 'mental and administrative limitations, economic disabilities, national defence allocation deficiencies, and the general relative vulnerability to external coercion and pressure' of developing countries as critical variables in any assessment of the capabilities of these states in international relations (Vital, 1967: 10–14). On the other hand, the question has also been approached from the point of view of the impact of capability deficiencies on the developing countries. Theories of neo-colonialism are of this kind (Nkrumah, 1965; Leys, 1974; Shaw and Heard (eds), 1979). Here, the emphasis is on the consequences of structural dependency – exploitation, the drain of surplus production, the loss of political control and the virtual nullification of political independence. In this situation political independence is viewed as largely a matter of mere form rather than of substance. Put in more general terms, the greater the external control over the economic resources and processes of a state, the less meaningful is its formal political independence and hence the less it is able to define and pursue an independent foreign policy.

Yet it would be an exaggeration to say that developing countries were incapable of playing a role in international politics because of the low level of development or the inadequacies of their 'natural-material basics' or because of their structural dependency on the world capitalist system. Enough evidence exists in the history of post-war international relations to show that small developing countries can, in fact, exert significant influence on the movement of world politics and thereby achieve their policy objectives. In 1956 Egypt, under Gamal Abdel Nasser, won control of the Suez Canal against the claims of Britain and France who had a seemingly overwhelming military force at their disposal. Since its formation in 1964, the United Republic of Tanzania, has earned under President Julius Nyerere a reputation among Third World states for its steadfast adherence to the principles of anti-colonialism and non-alignment even though Tanzania is classed by the UN among thirty of the least developed countries in the world. Tanzania has upheld these principles even when this was bound to cost the country dearly in material terms: Tanzania's formal recognition of the German Democratic Republic in 1964 led the Federal Republic of Germany to withdraw all its aid and the following year the United Kingdom withdrew its aid after Tanzania broke off diplomatic relations in protest against Rhodesia's Unilateral Declaration of Independence (UDI). More recently, the Frontline States – Angola, Botswana, Mozambique,

Tanzania, Zambia and Zimbabwe – have collectively made significant political efforts to stand up to the vaunted military might and aggressive politico-military activities of the Republic of South Africa as an expression of their commitment to, and support for, the liberation of Namibia and South Africa itself. Indeed, the establishment in 1980 of the Southern African Development Coordinating Conference (SADCC), comprising the six Frontline States plus Malawi, Lesotho and Swaziland, represents a potentially effective riposte against South Africa's destabilization manoeuvres and aspirations to hegemony in the region.

These examples indicate that the undoubted drawbacks imposed by a limited resource base need not incapacitate the exercise of initiative by developing states in regard to matters of importance to them in their foreign relations. Put differently, the ability to exercise such initiative is not invariably a function of the natural-material basics but may depend on such other variables as political leadership – the intellectual capacity, resourcefulness, judgement, imagination and political astuteness of leaders and policy-makers – or, alternatively, the institutional coherence and administrative competence of the political system as a whole. There is no doubt, for example, that Tanzania's generally successful foreign policy can, in considerable part, be explained by reference to the personal attributes and ability of President Nyerere. On the other hand, in Congo (now Zaire) in 1960–1, despite the coherence of his vision for his country and its relations with other states near and far, the former Congolese Prime Minister, Patrice Lumumba, was unable to translate that vision into reality because of a virtually collapsed state machine.

The ability of a developing state to achieve its policy objectives varies in accordance with the given issue or issue-area. It is possible to identify four such issue-areas: high-priority issues or 'core values'; regional issues; continental issues and global issues.

'Core values' are of such importance that states invest vast amounts of resources in order to safeguard them. A country's territorial integrity, for example, is a matter of such crucial importance that governments and nations will normally spare neither effort nor resources to defend it. That is to say, even an economically under-developed and militarily weak state will 'throw everything it has' into defending its territory or independence. It follows, therefore, that the willingness to make supreme sacrifices in the defence of core values will assure even to a developing state a significant degree of influence in the settlement of issues that have a direct bearing on such values.

Developing states also normally have a significant ability, or at least potential, to affect the outcomes of issues of a purely regional or local character. Neighbouring states are likely to deal effectively with such matters as trade, territorial boundaries, and movement of persons across national boundaries through established bilateral or regional mechanisms or institutions. Examples of these include SADCC and the Economic Community of West African States (ECOWAS). The ability of developing states to affect outcomes in matters of a local or regional character arises not only from the intensity of their interest in such matters, but also from the fact of their greater knowledge of, and familiarity with, the issues involved.

It should, however, be noted that in the contemporary era of heightened superpower competition for spheres of influence, even so-called local or regional issues can, and often do, assume a global character as a result of superpower intervention. Territorial disputes in the Horn of Africa, the Civil Wars in Chad and in Nigeria and the political conflict between Libya and Egypt, have all in their turn attracted a more or less pronounced measure of superpower intervention. Such external intervention not only bedevils the search for solutions to the issues involved, it also diminishes the capacity of the developing states concerned to influence the settlement of the issue or issues.

The capacity of the individual African state to exert influence on the course of events tends to decline as one moves from local or regional issues to continental and global issues. This is so partly because such issues tend to be too remote from the immediate pre-occupations of the states concerned; partly because of the inadequacy of the information on the basis of which policies could be formulated; partly because of lack of resources to tackle the issues involved; and partly because many other actors may by their prior or more intensive involvement have reduced the possibilities of effective African involvement. It is perhaps illustrative of the situation that at both the continental and global levels the African states' principal mode of participation is multilateral. Continentally, the OAU is the main mechanism for tackling the problems that the African states face in common. Globally, the African states have found it useful to work in close collaboration with other developing countries in seeking solutions to the problems these states face in common, particularly the so-called North–South economic problems – trade, technology transfers, commodity prices, terms and conditions of international aid (Erb and Kallab, 1975.) Examples of institutionalized collaboration among developing countries include the Non-Aligned Movement, the 'Group of 77' and the African–Caribbean–Pacific (ACP) grouping of states. These institutions and other similar ones are designed to enhance the bargaining power of the developing countries vis-à-vis their developed interlocutors. In other words, their existence reflects, in part at least, the awareness of the developing countries that the objectives of those of their foreign policies that have a global dimension cannot be fully achieved through individual efforts or intiatives. Collective diplomacy is here seen as a potentially more efficacious instrument. It can, therefore, be assumed that as the scope of their involvement in global issues increases, developing states will both expand and strengthen the institutional mechanisms that serve to express and champion their collective interests.

Yet multilateralism in foreign policy, of which institutions such as the above are the expression, is not without problems of its own. First, the divergent aims of the developing states themselves render effective co-operation among them difficult. Such co-operation is often difficult to achieve even in areas where broadly shared goals otherwise exist. For example, all African states share the aspiration of developing their economies rapidly and of doing so – in part at least – by importing or inviting foreign capital and technology. However, there is a wide divergence of views on whether, for example, transnational corporations (TNCs) are the appropriate agencies for effecting the transferrence of such capital and technology. Thus, whereas socialist Tanzania is suspicious of the activities of TNCs, 'free-enterprise' Ivory Coast pursues an open-door policy with regard to these corporations. However, the two states are partners in the Group of 77, the ACP grouping, and in other multilateral institutions for Third World co-operation. This divergence of views or perspective, which stems from factors such as the structure and ideology of regimes, often means that Third World co-operation is achieved at the lowest common denominator of agreement. As a result, observers tend to become cynical about intergovernmental organizations which proclaim grandiose objectives but somehow fall short of translating these into concrete accomplishments. The cynicism is, however, not justified in so far as it fails to take full account of the factor of individual state interests which tend to override collective or multilateral interests. Yet pursuit of collective interests cannot be regarded as méaningless, because the task of identifying, and working towards the realization, of these interests is itself a learning process. Thus, it can be said that the act of participating in multilateral institutions affords states the opportunity to develop the confidence necessary for them subsequently to appreciate the benefits that close co-operation can yield.

Second, multilateral co-operation is rendered difficult by the inability or reluctance of states to surrender any significant portion of their sovereignty in order to facilitate the achievement of collective goals. This inability or reluctance is often explicitly enshrined in the charters or constitutions of intergovernmental organizations. Thus, although inspired by the desire for African continental unity, the OAU Charter, as drafted in Addis Ababa in 1963, gives special emphasis to the following cardinal principles: the sovereign equality of member states; non-interference by member states in each other's internal affairs; respect for state sovereignty and territorial integrity of each member state; and the condemnation of political assassination and subversion perpetrated by one member state against another (Cervenka, 1969: 15, 34). These principles, which merely represent an elaboration of the concept of state sovereignty, can be viewed as being in some way in contradiction with the policy of seeking interstate unity as a vehicle for achieving collective goals. For, to be effective, such a vehicle would need to be strengthened by at least the partial surrender to it of the sovereignty of the constituent states.

Finally, Third World multilateral co-operation has to contend with the divisive tactics of the great powers. Since one of the main purposes of this co-operation is to redress the existing global imbalance of wealth and power so as to benefit the developing countries, it is inevitable that those powers that benefit from the current lop-sided distribution of these resources would resist the effort to change it. One method for achieving this end is that of 'divide and rule'. This, in part, explains the frequency with which great powers intervene in conflicts of a purely local character involving Third World states.

Despite these drawbacks, intergovernmental organizations will no doubt continue to play a vital role in synthesizing and promoting the objectives of the foreign policies of developing countries. To this extent the foreign policies of these states will tend to reflect the multilateral dimension that has historically been generally absent from the foreign policies of older states.

# References

AKINYEMI, BOLAJI (1974) *Federalism and foreign policy: the Nigerian experience,* Ibadan Univ. Press, Ibadan.

BRUCAN, SILVIU (1978) *The dialectic of world politics,* The Free Press, New York.

CERVENKA, ZDENEK (1960) *The Organisation of African Unity and its Charter,* F A Praeger, New York.

ERB, GUY F and KALLAB, VALERIANA (eds) (1975) *Beyond dependency: the developing world speaks out,* Overseas Development Council, Washington, D.C.

FARRELL, R BARRY (ed) (1966) *Approaches to comparative and international politics,* North Western University Press, Evanston.

FRANKEL, JOSEPH (1967) *The making of foreign policy,* Oxford Univ. Press, Oxford.

HOLSTI, K J (1977) *International politics: a frame-work for analysis* (3rd Edn.) Prentice Hall: Englewood Cliffs, New Jersey.

IDANG, G J (1973) *Nigeria: internal politics and foreign policy,* Ibadan Univ. Press, Ibadan.

LEGUM, COLIN and LEE, BILL (1977) *Conflict in the Horn of Africa,* Africana Publishing House, New York.

LEYS, COLIN (1974) *Underdevelopment in Kenya: the political economy of neocolonialism, 1964–1971,* California Univ. Press, Berkeley.

McKAY, VERNON (1966) *African diplomacy: studies in the determinants of foreign policy,* Pall Mall, London.

MODELSKI, GEORGE (1962) *A theory of foreign policy,* Pall Mall, London.

NKRUMAH, KWAME (1965) *Neocolonialism: the last stage of imperialism,* Nelson, London.

NNOLI, OKWUDIBA (1978) *Self-reliance and foreign policy in Tanzania,* NDK, New York.

ROSENAU, J N (1967) *Domestic sources of foreign policy,* The Free Press, New York.

SHAW, TIMOTHY M and HEARD, KENNETH A (eds) (1979) *The politics of Africa: dependence and development,* Longman, London.

TANDON, YASHPAL (ed) (1974) *Readings in African international relations* (2 vols.) East African Literature Bureau, Nairobi.

THIAM, DOUDOU (1965) *The foreign policy of African states,* F A Praeger, New York.

THOMPSON, W SCOTT (1969) *Ghana's foreign policy, 1957–1966,* Princeton Univ. Press, Princeton.

VITAL, DAVID (1967) *The inequality of states: a study of the small power in international relations,* The Clarendon Press, Oxford.

ZARTMAN, I WILLIAM (1966) *International relations in the new Africa* Prentice Hall, Englewood Cliffs, New Jersey.

ZARTMAN, I WILLIAM (1971) *The politics of trade negotiations between Africa and the European Economic Community: the weak confront the strong,* Princeton Univ. Press, Princeton.

# 4　Africa and the global economy

Attention has been drawn in the preceding chapters to the critical importance of economics in African international relations and foreign policies. It was suggested that economics is both an independent and a dependent variable in these relations and policies, and that African states are engaged in a struggle for economic survival and economic independence in order to increase their chances of preserving their sovereignty and political independence from internal and external threats. If economics is indeed basic to African, and any other, international relations and foreign policies, it is obviously critically important for us to understand the nature and the dynamics of the dominant capitalist global economic system; the ways in which it makes African states dependent and underdeveloped; and the impact of this dependency and underdevelopment on both inter-African state relations and African relations with the rest of the world. Only such an understanding of the capitalist world economic system and Africa's historical and contemporary relations with it can realistically inform political and economic policies and strategies in the African struggle.

We first examine the extent of African poverty and under-development relative to the rest of the world before we look at the major theories explaining this state of affairs.

## African poverty and underdevelopment

Although Africa is well endowed with human and material resources it is an incontestable fact that the continent has been, and continues to be, the poorest and the most underdeveloped region of the world. Africa has about the highest hydro-electric potential in the world. By one count (Bissell, 1979) Africa also produces approximately 55 per cent of the world's cobalt, a strategic mineral indispensable for the production of high-strength, high-temperature alloys essential to aircraft and space industry as well as for the production of permanent magnets. Zaire alone produces about 47 per cent of this mineral and Zambia produces a further 8 per cent. Bauxite, another important mineral is abundant especially in Guinea (Conakry) which produces 13 per cent of the world output, making it the second largest producer. About 15–20 per cent of the world's copper is produced in Zambia and Zaire, 4 per cent of the world's tin in Nigeria and Zaire and about the same proportion of the world's iron ore is mined in Liberia and Mauritania, and of petroleum in Nigeria, Angola, Gabon and Zaire, excluding the North African production.

Although nature has not been very kind in terms of weather and soil quality for agricultural production (note the Sahelian drought and the sandy Sahara desert which is expanding at an estimated 0.01 per cent per annum), Africa nevertheless produces the bulk of certain important agricultural raw materials. Cocoa and palm produce are predominantly produced in Africa, while the continent contributes a significant world production of coffee, rubber, timber, groundnuts and sisal.

Despite these resources and great potential in others, African states remain poor and underdeveloped. By underdevelopment we mean that there are inadequate social and economic structural changes to give the economy a balanced, integrated and self-sustaining growth in the Gross Domestic Product (GDP). More disturbing, the poverty and under-development of African states relative to the rest of the world is increasing. As we noted in Chapter 2 African states have an average per capita Gross National Product (GNP) of less than $330 per annum, about twenty have per capita GNP of between $330 and $759, seven between $760–$3 249 and three between $3 250 and $7 600 (World Bank Atlas, Washington D.C. 1981). The average per capita GNP for the continent as a whole is less than $400. To reach an average of $500 by the year 2000, the growth rate, presently averaging 5 per cent per annum, will have to increase to about 7 per cent but even this will not reduce the gap between Africa and the rest of the world.

More significant is the fact that less than 10 per cent of the Gross Domestic Product (GDP) derives from manufacturing. Of the total world manufacturing output, Africa contributes only about 0.6 per cent, and it has been estimated that at the very best Africa might contribute 2 per cent of world manufacturing production by the year 2000. The meagre manufacturing so far is heavily concentrated in the area of light industry, especially in the food/beverage and textile/clothing sectors. Even these are unevenly distributed among regions and within regions. North Africa produces the bulk of African manufactures and within that region production is concentrated in Egypt. The rest of African manufactures are concentrated in particular areas: in West Africa it is concentrated in Nigeria and the Ivory Coast and within those states in Lagos and Abidjan; in East and Central Africa manufacturing is concentrated in Zaire and Kenya and within those states in Kinshasa and Nairobi (Adedeji, 1976).

Heavy manufacturing plants – petro-chemicals, chemical, basic mineral and fabricated mineral product industries and steel production – remain miniscule in Africa both absolutely and in terms of world production. Per capita consumption of these products as well as energy is also the smallest in the world.

A more disturbing fact is that there is hardly any African country that produces enough food to feed its population. Most spend considerable foreign exchange to import food. Nigeria, a relatively wealthy country and heavily endowed with agricultural resources has, for example, in recent years been spending over $1.5 billion on food imports. And it has been estimated that in spite of its operation 'Feed the Nation' and the 'Green Revolution' programmes it will be importing nearly 16 millions tons of food at the cost of between $6 and $11 billion by the year

2000 (Oculi, 1979; Hughes and Strauch, 1981). Since all African countries rely on agricultural export receipts for their imports of food as well as capital and manufactured consumer items and since they are competing in the production of these export crops for a world market that is increasingly finding synthetic substitutes, the future economic prospects are extremely bleak. Most of the countries have a monocultural economy producing crops which are beset by hazardous fluctuations in production and prices. The harvest of a bumper crop by one or two countries can depress prices disastrously, as the case of the

**TABLE 4.1 Some data on indices of development among the three 'castes' of the international economic order**

**Table i**
GDP per capita in US dollars

| | 1960 | 1970 | 1975 |
|---|---|---|---|
| Upper caste [a] | 1743 | 2668 | 5515 |
| Middle caste | 340 | 436 | 1111 |
| Lower caste | 130 | 220 | 380 |

**Table ii**
Rate of illiteracy

| | 1960 | 1970 |
|---|---|---|
| Upper caste | 4.6% | 3.2% |
| Middle caste [b] | 52.7% | 44.1% |
| Lower caste | 81.0% | 73.7% |

**Table iii**
No. of persons per tractor in use

| | 1965 | 1970 | 1975 |
|---|---|---|---|
| Upper caste | 73 | 68 | 65 |
| Middle caste | 2074 | 1880 | 1444 |
| Lower caste | 1236 | 1067 | 1003 |

**Table iv**
Crude petroleum production in metric tons per capita

| | 1960 | 1965 | 1970 | 1975 |
|---|---|---|---|---|
| Upper caste | 0.65 | 0.78 | 1.0 | 1.1 |
| Middle caste | 0.26 | 0.34 | 0.45 | 0.53 |
| Lower caste | 0.05 | 0.35 | 0.83 | 0.60 |

**Table v**
Cement manufacturing in metric tons per capita

| | 1960 | 1965 | 1970 | 1975 |
|---|---|---|---|---|
| Upper caste | 0.28 | 0.37 | 0.43 | 0.48 |
| Middle caste | 0.04 | 0.04 | 0.06 | 0.16 |
| Lower caste | 0.03 | 0.04 | 0.05 | 0.06 |

**Table vi**
Energy production per capita in metric tons of coal equivalent

| | 1960 | 1965 | 1970 | 1975 |
|---|---|---|---|---|
| Upper caste | 3.64 | 4.20 | 4.96 | 5.30 |
| Middle caste | 0.71 | 0.76 | 0.96 | 1.12 |
| Lower caste | 0.24 | 0.70 | 1.41 | 1.14 |

**Table vii**
Energy consumption per capita in metric tons of coal equivalent

| | 1960 | 1965 | 1970 | 1975 |
|---|---|---|---|---|
| Upper caste | 3.95 | 5.00 | 5.76 | 6.22 |
| Middle caste | 0.40 | 0.42 | 0.56 | 0.67 |
| Lower caste | 0.25 | 0.29 | 0.31 | 0.39 |

**Table viii**
Steel consumption per capita in metric tons

| | 1960 | 1965 | 1970 | 1975 |
|---|---|---|---|---|
| Upper caste | 0.34 | 0.42 | 0.48 | 0.48 |
| Middle caste | 0.03 | 0.03 | 0.05 | 0.06 |
| Lower caste | 0.02 | 0.02 | 0.03 | 0.04 |

**Table ix**
Passenger-kilometres flown in 1 000 million

| | 1960 | 1965 | 1970 | 1975 |
|---|---|---|---|---|
| Upper caste | 113 | 211 | 406 | 578 |
| Middle caste [c] | 11 | 21 | 46 | 100 |
| Lower caste | 2 | 5 | 9 | 17 |

**Notes**
a Excludes USSR
b Excludes China, Korea & S. Vietnam
c Excludes China

Source: United Nations, *World Statistics in Brief*, New York, 4th edn. 1979.

bumper cocoa harvests of Ghana, Ivory Coast and Nigeria demonstrated in the early 1960s.

One way of expressing the African poverty and underdevelopment relative to the rest of the world is to say that Africa is at the bottom of the international economic order. Ali Mazrui (1977: 4–13) has likened the international economic system to a caste system in which heredity (race), rigid and permanent separation (geographical, social and physical factors), and a division of labour (primary producers versus secondary and tertiary producers) produce a hierarchy determining rank and status. The white race, generally concentrated in the northern hemisphere, by a hierarchical division of labour continues along the path of industrial and post-industrial development. They may be termed the upper caste. The black race, generally concentrated in Africa, are, by contrast, 'the hewers of wood and drawers of water' in the hierarchical division of labour. Economic and technological disabilities condemn Africans to a permanent position as the lower caste. The races of the northern hemisphere with technological and organizational superiority are permanently the upper caste. One might add a middle caste – the 'yellow' races of Asia and Latin America. Without necessarily accepting the implicit assumption of economic and technological disabilities based on race and the implied fatalism of a permanent lower caste position with no hope for upward mobility, Mazrui's analogy is basically a valid description of Africa's contemporary place in the international economic system. The illustrative data in Table 4:1 on selected indices of development among the three 'castes' etch a picture of the reality.

# Theories of underdevelopment

There are two broad theoretical schools to explain underdevelopment. One is based on neo-classical economics and is generally known as the developmental school. The other is the dependency school which, as Caporaso (1978) defines it 'seeks to explore the process of integration of the periphery (i.e. Third World countries) into the international capitalist system and to assess the implications for development.' Frederick Cooper (1981) identifies a third school – the Marxist theorists – but it has much in common with the dependency school as both proceed from a structuralist paradigm, stressing structures of production, exchange relationships, international capital and class formation and class conflicts. Indeed, dependency theory can be seen as 'an expansion of Marx's interpretation of history, an extension of his method and central ideas to a problem which, on a world scale, was still in embryo at his death' (Leys, 1975: 7).

## The neo-classical school

This school is so-called because it derives from the conventional, textbook economics based on the teachings of classical Western theorists from Ricardo to Keynes. This is the school that emphasizes both the free-market economy and the comparative advantage and the advantages of external trade. Modern disciples of this school see development in terms of evolution, of a movement of 'individual productive units' from 'meagre self-sufficiency' to 'prosperous interdependence as producers . . . integrated into a national network of markets, information flows, and social institutions' (Johnson and Kilby, 1975). Since the developed societies are characterized by 'prosperous interdependent producers integrated into a national network', the task in Africa (or any developing nation) is to recreate the socio-economic factors that brought about development in the West.

There was a broad consensus that certain deficiencies accounted for economic backwardness in Africa and other Third World countries. Notable among these deficiencies are inadequate savings and capital formation, inadequate infrastructures, lack of entrepreneurial skills and technical know-how, lack of diversity in the economy and lack of achievement motivation due to what Kussum Nair called 'limited aspirations'. The last factor has now been discredited as Africans are now recognized as highly motivated economically and highly responsive to changes in the economic market (Hopkins, 1973). Neo-classical analysists argued that the removal of these deficiencies would be enough to assure development. Foreign technical assistance and foreign private investment were seen as a partial, if critical, solution to the problem of inadequate savings, lack of capital and lack of entrepreneurial skills and technical know-how. Economic planning was seen as a partial solution to integrating and diversifying the economy and as a means of inculcating achievement motivation.

Experts were not agreed, however, on what were the best policies and strategies of economic development planning to employ (Hirschman, 1958). W. Arthur Lewis (1954, 1958) stressed export-led growth because of its foreign exchange earnings and multiplier effect. He was supported by those who, like Theodore Schultz (1964), urged the transformation of traditional agriculture. A debate ensued on the nature of the transformation as to whether commercial farmers or the peasants should receive encouragement to increase the scale of their operations. Other experts stressed industrialization, precipitating arguments over whether heavy industries should take priority over light industries; whether the modern industrial sector should draw resources from the backward sectors or whether priority should rather go to rural self-sufficiency and 'cottage industries'; and finally whether the urban informal sector should be favoured over the rural or the modern industrial sectors.

Given these arrays of policies and strategies of development it is not surprising that planning in Africa in the decade of the 1960s was so disastrous. Apart from the confusion of the varieties, development strategies and policies failed more fundamentally because they were based on false assumptions. In the first place the explanation of underdevelopment was tautological in a dual sense. As Ake (1981: 6–8) correctly observes: 'On analysis, it is soon clear that the things offered . . . as causes of underdevelopment are in fact symptoms of underdevelopment'. Moreover 'the explanation is highly biased in that it suggests that development presupposes capitalism'. In so far as capital accumulation, commodity exchange (external trade in this context), acquisitive drive (achievement motivation) and skills (technological and entrepreneurial) have an organic unity in a distinctive capitalist mode of production, the explanation is a tautology in a second sense, 'because it amounts to suggesting that a society is not developed because it does not have the characteristics of a developed society.' In the second place, the explanation begs the question of why the identified deficiencies in African developmental process are prevalent in Africa but nowhere else. Certainly it is not by sheer coincidence that such differentials exist between Africa and the rest of the world, particularly the industrialized part of it.

It is because of these inadequacies of the neo-classical school and the empirical failings of the policies it inspired that academicians and some political leaders have turned attention to alternative explanations and strategies.

## The dependency school

The dependency school focuses on the historical origins and the subsequent 'development of underdevelopment'. Sometimes it is referred to as a 'world systems theory' because of its basic tenet that all contemporary societies are integrated into a single world economic system, the capitalist system, and no concrete contemporary socio-economic formation can be understood except as a part of this one world-system (Amin, 1974: 3; Wallerstein, 1974a and 1974b; Frank 1972). Originally a Latin American preserve, seeking to explain why the goal of autonomous capitalist development had eluded policy-makers despite the existence of a substantial indigenous bourgeoisie (Leys 1975: 15), dependency theory is now embraced by increasing numbers of Africanist writers (both Western and Afro-Caribbean). Notable among these are Immanuel Wallerstein, E. A. Alpers, Peter C. W. Gutkind, and Steve Langdon for the West; Walter Rodney, H. Brewster and N. Girvan for the Caribbean; and Samir Amin (Egyptian) and Claude Ake (Nigerian) for Africa.

While there are substantial disagreements within the school as well as significant differences of emphasis, modifications and refinements of interpreted positions, the following, simplified basic tenets of the school can generally be agreed upon:

1  African states, indeed all underdeveloped states, are dependent on the capitalist world for technology, capital, finance and monetary systems, and for trade. This is because the capitalist world has a virtual monopoly over the 'means of production'.

2  Dependence and monopoly mean control and exploitation. 'All countries named as underdeveloped in the world are exploited by others and the underdevelopment with which the world is now preoccupied is a

product of capitalist, imperialist and colonialist exploration' (Rodney, 1974: 21–2).

3    This dependency relationship is the product of the incorporation of Africa and underdeveloped countries into the capitalist system. Incorporation started way back in the seventeenth century and was completed, in three or four stages, by the opening decade of the twentieth century (Wallerstein, 1976; Amin, 1972: 503–24; Rodney, 1974).

4    Incorporation resulted, under the aegis of imperialism and colonialism, in the disarticulation of transport as roads and railways were built not for the integration of the colonial country's economy, but to facilitate exportation of raw materials to the capitalist core – Europe – and to bring manufactures to the capitalist periphery – Africa – and other colonial territories. Incorporation also resulted in the disarticulation of export commodities; African states acquiring a monocultural economy or relying on a few export commodities for foreign exchange and development funds. Similarly, in consequence of the imports of manufactures from the core to the periphery, incorporation resulted in the disarticulation of the manufacturing sector of the African states. Incorporation also encouraged monopolistic tendencies, ultimately leading to the emergence of multinational corporations with headquarters at the core which dominate and control the leading sectors of the economy of the periphery. The end-product of disarticulation and monopolistic tendencies was the segmentation of the economy of the periphery. This is reflected in the fact that there is little or no interconnection among the productive sectors while the economies of the periphery became orientated towards the core, developed technological inequalities vis-a-vis the core and came under greater institutional control of the multinationals (Ake, 1981; Furtado, 1967; Brewster, 1973; Girvan, 1973).

Underdevelopment was and still is generated by the exploitations attendant upon the incorporation of African countries into the world capitalist system via imperialism and colonialism. It can therefore be understood only as an aspect of imperialism past, present and future. This explains why the political kingdom which Kwame Nkrumah thought would lead to economic freedom and development has proved to be a pious hope. In his book, *Neocolonialism: The Last Stage of Imperialism* (1966) the first President of Ghana adopted in virtually identical terms the definition of neo-colonialism adumbrated by the 1961 All-African Peoples Conference at Cairo as an explanation of the dashed hopes. The Cairo conference defined neo-colonialism as 'the survival of the colonial system in spite of the formal recognition of political independence in emerging countries which become the victims of an indirect and subtle form of domination by political, economic, social military or technical means' (Legum 1962: 254). For Nkrumah, the 'essence of neo-colonialism is that the State which is subject to it is, in theory, independent and has all the outward trappings of international sovereignty. In reality its economic system and thus its political policy is directed from outside.' Neo-colonialism is an instrinsic aspect of dependency theory. But dependency goes beyond neo-colonialism to show how class formation and consciousness are shaped by the incorporation of a segment of the periphery into the global capitalist economy.

The nature of incorporation of African states' economy into the global capitalist system results in new class formation, class consciousness and class struggles (Ake 1978, 1981; Sunkel, 1973; Leys, 1975). To the wealthy classes which had survived from the colonial times or which were created under colonialism, a new class is added. This is the petit-bourgeoisie and the educated salary earners created by new economic activities – overseas trade, commerce, teaching, mining, cash crop production, public service. In time these become the national bourgeoise who resist colonialism and inherit state power at independence. They are, however, a derived middle class because they do not own the means of production, but are rather 'comprador elements' – the intermediaries between the metropolitan bourgeoisie and the local economy.

There is yet another class. It comprises the relatively recent class of urban factory workers under colonialism as well as those such as peasants and craftsmen engaged in traditional occupations. Together, these might be labelled the proletarian class. In marxist terms a dual contradiction and dual class struggle arise from this class structure. On the one hand the contradiction between the metropolitan international bourgeoisie who own the means of production and the comprador national bourgeoisie results in a class struggle as the latter seeks to overthrow the former and acquire for itself control over the means of production. This aspect of the struggle was reflected symbolically in the struggle for independence and, since then, in the struggle for what is now termed a New International Economic Order (NIEO). On the other hand there is a contradiction and class struggle within each peripheral country: the national bourgeoisie and governing class – the segment of the population most integrated into the world economy – is pitched against the national proletariat, the urban workers and peasants who are only marginally integrated if they are integrated at all into the global economy.

The class structures and class struggles attendant upon incorporation make African states, like alcoholics and drug addicts, literally 'hooked', to borrow Tony Smith's analogy. 'They cannot exist without their dependence, but they also cannot exist with it' (Smith, 1979: 249) They cannot develop with their dependence because their vertical link into the global system inhibits their industrialization beyond limited import-substitution industries. The economy is largely relegated to the less dynamic forms of growth associated with agriculture and extractive industries. But they also cannot do without their dependent status because the national bourgeoisie is sustained by it. The contradiction between the national bourgeoisie and the proletariat of their countries makes it impossible to mobilize the latter for a revolution against the international bourgeoisie. 'Economic stagnation and desperate poverty deprive the governing classes of Africa of the chance of maintaining even a veneer of legitimacy'. Only their vertical economic links with the bourgeoisie of the capitalist core sustain what little legitimacy they have (Ake, 1978: 30).

This explains the importance of economic and military aid, the penchant for allowing foreign military bases and foreign troops on African soil, and the frequent military intervention by the core states in order to maintain puppet regimes in power. There are sanctions (what Richard Olson (1979) calls 'Invisible blockade') to be brought against a governing class which chooses to transgress against the basic rules of the game. The core states simply agree amongst themselves on a policy to bring the recalcitrant peripheral governing class to order. The subtle economic weapons at their disposal include 'declines in investment, either in new funds or for expansion; delays in the delivery of spare parts and in other areas of trade; snags in licensing or other technology transfers; dwindling bilateral and multilateral loans and grants, refusal to refinance existing debts; drying up or outright elimination of credit lines' (Olson, 1979). Ghana, in the last years of Nkrumah's rule (1963–5) and under Busia (1968–71) faced some of these sanctions which, in each case, led to military coups against the regime (Thompson, 1969; Libby, 1976).

The African governing classes, as Tony Smith correctly paraphrases the dependency position have 'structured their domestic rule on a coalition of internal interests favourable to the international connection . . . The basic needs of the international order must therefore be respected if this system is to continue to provide services that the local elites need in order to perpetuate their rule in their turn'. Thus despite the fact that the African governing classes are in a struggle against the governing classes of the capitalist core, the interests of the two classes coincide in some respects, and the two classes are, in effect, in alliance. In the course of time a symbiotic or patron-client relationship has developed, in which 'the system has created its servants whose needs dictate that its survival be ensured whatever the short-term conflicts of interests may be' (Smith, 1979: 251). In sum, as Ake (1978: 65) put it, 'the ruling classes in Africa are an integral part of the structure of imperialism and of the syndrome of imperialist exploitation'.

Until quite recently, the dependency theorists were unanimous in their assessment of the developmental implications of the incorporation of the periphery into the international capitalist core as all agreed that there cannot be development in the peripheral capitalist states. But the implicit counsel of despair in this verdict together with the evidence that some countries that were once peripheral capitalist states have developed successfully and that 'as a general rule the countries most integrated into the world economy have tended to grow more quickly over a longer period than those that are not' (Smith, 1979: 250) have all led to a division between the orthodox dependency theorists and those who now see possibilities, albeit limited, of development in some but by no means all peripheral capitalist states (Wallerstein, 1974c: 26). The specific question which should logically follow – 'which kind of countries, and under what conditions, *can* develop?' – is hardly ever asked. Rather, attention is focused on the more practical and general question of what to do in order to liquidate dependency and achieve development. On this question there appears to be a consensus – there must be a reorientation of production. Generally a reorientation of production is deemed to involve two inter-related ideas, namely self-reliance and socialism.

Self-reliance is defined as a deliberate process or strategy for ending dependence and promoting development. Biersteker (1980) has shown it to have three analytically distinct components. The first is a partial disengagement of the economy from its traditional pattern of relations with the international system. This is accomplished primarily by a policy which reduces the proportion of trade, investment and monetary/technical assistance and transactions with the capitalist core, while attaining self-sufficiency in basic needs such as food, clothing, energy and national defence. The second component of self-reliance is the restructuring of the pattern of relationships with the international system. This is done partly through 'collective self-reliance', that is, through increased trade, investment, monetary/technical transactions, and the development of politico-economic co-operative institutions and relations with other Third World countries. It is also partly achievable through deliberate fiscal, monetary and incomes policies that alter consumer values and consumption patterns, engender decentralization for maximum mass participation, and restructure the existing domestic class relations. The third and final component of self-reliance is reassociation with the international system on a changed basis.

Clearly, self-reliance does not mean autarchy i.e., exercising one's absolute sovereignty in such a way as to cut off all intercourse, trade, borrowing of capital, skill and technology with the rest of the world, in short isolationism par excellence. But it does mean using simpler home-made technology to manufacture purely for the domestic market or the markets of other underdeveloped countries (Leys, 1975: 16–17). It is a strategy which requires mass markets for less sophisticated goods. Such markets can only be created by a radical redistribution of purchasing power which in turn requires a different kind of political leadership. In short it implies radical social changes at the periphery.

It is in its call for radical redistribution of purchasing power that self-reliance can be seen as the other side of the socialist coin. Socialism not merely aims to redistribute purchasing power radically, it revolutionizes the social relations of production by placing ownership of the means of production in the hands of the workers and thus ending exploitative relations of production. The internal linkages of Africa's incorporation into the global capitalist system provide the dynamics which result in socialism. Ake argues that:

> The global struggle will exacerbate and radicalize the major contradiction in the relations of production of the African nations, the contradiction between the African bourgeoisie and the African proletariat, and by so doing hasten and effect its resolution in the form of a socialist revolution.

By maintaining neo-colonial dependence, which lies behind Africa's underdevelopment, the African bourgeoisie deepens and radicalizes the contradictions in existing relations of production and hence promotes its own revolutionary liquidation (Ake, 1978: 25, 55)

Self-reliance through socialism − that is the solution to dependence and underdevelopment.

## Criticisms of the dependency school

The dependency school is widely acclaimed for its contribution to our understanding of the mechanism of poverty and underdevelopment. It alerts us to the complexity and intensity of the interaction between the centre and the periphery of the global capitalist system, the impact on the internal dynamics of change and development in the periphery and, thus, of the nature of its politics. It clearly reveals how external factors shape domestic segmentation in the structure of production and block broad social transformation and economic development. However, despite the acknowledged contribution to our understanding of the mechanisms of poverty and underdevelopment, the dependency school has been criticized on several grounds.

First it has been criticized for its circular reasoning (the chicken or egg argument) and what Gerald Helleiner (1979: 224) has termed 'the fallacy of misplaced concreteness'. The circular reasoning argument is based on the problematic question of explaining the relationship between underdevelopment and the material base for development. Are African states dependent because of their small size, their extreme poverty, their limited power in international markets and international resource organizations or vice versa? In other words are they dependent because they are underdeveloped or are they underdeveloped because they are dependent? Jinadu (1977) has rightly observed that 'while it is argued that it is the paucity of capital that makes capitalist penetration and hence underdevelopment possible, it is also usually argued that paucity of capital is due to capitalist penetration and underdevelopment' and it is not clear whether 'neo-colonial dependence results in underdevelopment' or 'underdevelopment . . . leads to neo-colonial dependence'. A related problem is whether dependency as a structural phenomenon and as a relationship of asymmetrical interdependence 'adds anything to one's understanding of the Third World's essential dilemma of poverty and powerlessness'. As Helleiner (1979: 223) puts the case: 'If dependence is defined as a state in which developmental experience is substantially affected by developments in the metropoles of the international (capitalist) economy, then it is little more than a synonym for "under-development" . . . (and) calling upon African countries to reduce their "dependence" amounts, then, to advising them to give up their poverty and/or powerlessness'.

But even more fundamental is the 'fallacy of misplaced concreteness'. For example, underdevelopment is seen to proceed with certain inevitability unless and until state power becomes vested in an 'independent' class or group. But when once a 'progressive' or independent government comes to power, the advice about breaking dependence appears no longer to be appropriate. On the contrary, the paraphernalia of dependence no longer seem as pernicious and can be permitted, provided the regime shows an 'attitude of mind' reflective of its wish to be self-reliant. Thus the concept of an 'independent regime' and what constitutes 'breaking dependency' becomes subjective. Tanzania, for instance, whose dependence on exports and foreign finance is as great today as it was before its declaration of socialism and self-reliance as a policy-goal in 1967 is thus seen to be less dependent than, say, the Ivory Coast, a country equally dependent but whose leaders have not self–consciously proclaimed a self-reliant policy. (Helleiner, 1979: 233–6).

Closely related to this argument is the criticism that dependency is too theoretical and abstract (Martin, 1980) while some of its theoretically logical conclusions are empirically unsubstantiated and of dubious validity. In particular it ignores praxis (the unity of theory and practice), it exaggerates the 'all-pervasive and self-perpetuating character' of the core capitalist power with respect to the periphery, reducing virtually everything that happens in Africa to a capitalist conspiracy. It thus ignores the relative autonomy of the peripheral state as well as the integrity, specificity and particularity of its local history which is independent of its membership in the global whole (Smith, 1979). Because of these failings, a product of the proclivity to 'totalize' in order to see the tyranny of the totality over the parts, dependency theory is almost totally irrelevant to the critical question of how a particular African state might go about liquidating its underdevelopment. Dependency does no more than indicate what global obstacles must be overcome in order to obliterate underdevelopment. But how? This leads us to the final criticism of the dependency theory – its advocacy of a revolutionary break with the global capitalist system.

One aspect of the revolutionary break, self-reliance, is a logical impossibility and a call for suicide if it means autarchy. Fortunately it does not. But its definition as selective disengagement is a contradiction in terms, self-defeating and practically impossible of attainment. This is in part because of the very structural constraints of the international system which the theory identifies and in part because of the nature and weakness of the national bourgeoisie, the only class capable technically and culturally of gaining and exercising power in the foreseeable future.

Biersteker (1980) and Ojo (1985) have discussed the elusiveness of self-reliance in the Tanzanian and Nigerian experience. If anything, selective self-reliance appears to deepen dependence and incidentally underdevelopment, providing a mere cloak for dividing spheres of interest between the national bourgeoisie and the metropolitan capitalists without coming to open conflict. Indigenization, an aspect of selective disengagement, has for instance, merely expanded the size of the respective national bourgeoisies in the countries practising it while rationalizing the relationship between this bourgeois class and its patron, international capitalism, in a manner that tempers the inherent conflict between them. As Ake observes in respect of Nigeria's indigenization:

The [indigenization] decree limits the chances of conflict by a clearer demarcation of spheres. It reserves a sphere of influence for Nigeria's marginal capitalists, and international capitalism is to refrain from interfering in this sphere. Such restraint is clearly necessary to contain the potentially dangerous economic nationalism of the petty bourgeoisie. [Indigenization) integrates the Nigerian bourgeoisie with international capitalism by involving them in business partnerships to a greater degree than ever before (Ake, 1978: 49).

In any case drastic reduction or elimination of foreign aid, technical assistance, engineering and management contracts (which a truly self-reliant strategy calls for) would cause a sharp drop in living standards precipitating a revolution against the bourgeoisie. Understandably the latter refuses to commit suicide. Immanuel Wallerstein's conclusion, in an early theoretical discourse is inescapable: self-reliant development is a 'myth' (Wallerstein, 1974c).

There are similar difficulties with the other strand of the revolutionary break or radical reorientation of production – socialism. It has been said that a socialist revolution is not logically deducible from dependency theory itself or from its view of the inherent incapacity of capitalism to bring about a transformation of the economy (Leys, 1975: 20). The one exception – Claude Ake's *Revolutionary Pressures in Africa* – which attempts a theoretical link between dependency and a socialist revolutionary situation contains logical inconsistencies. For, to the extent that the national bourgeoisie is structurally linked to the powerful international bourgeoisie, and to the extent that the global system is an indivisible whole, to that extent will national proletarian revolution be impossible. The logic of the structure alliance points, rather, to a global socialist revolution in which proletarians of all nations unite against the combined forces of a national/international bourgeoisie. This is why Wallerstein (1974c) observed that true socialism, when it occurs, will be world-wide. But he adds that this is not possible for at least a century or two, a reality with which the erstwhile Communist International – which also aimed at a global socialist revolution – has had to come to terms.

But even if a national proletarian socialist revolution were logically deducible from the dependency theory, there would still be the question of its practical feasibility. The hostility of the international bourgeoisie, who would naturally oppose such a challenge to the existing structure, is only one aspect of the problem. Dependency theorists themselves acknowledge that the international structure has so locked Third World countries into the capitalist system that nothing appears capable of changing it (Dos Santos, 1973). More basic is the question of the revolutionary consciousness and potential of the national proletariat. Hyden (1980) has argued that there are no social forces to carry through socialist transformation. Peasants cannot do the job. Other writers, such as Langdon (1981), Leys (1975) and Martin (1980) do not believe that the urban proletariat has much revolutionary potential either. This probably explains why attempts at socialist transformation have failed in many countries. Where there has been some initial successes – Zimbabwe, Angola, Mozambique, for example – the countries have had a leadership that has been nurtured in a colonial revolutionary struggle that is not replicable elsewhere on the continent. And the ability even of this leadership to follow a socialist revolution through to the end is becoming increasingly doubtful. Some countries, like Tanzania, have succeeded in socializing distribution but not production while others have merely brought about state capitalism which is dubbed 'Socialism'. But the fundamental problem for most African states (except maybe Zimbabwe and the Republic of South Africa) is that there is often little or nothing to socialize and insufficient honest, efficient and nationalistic technicians and administrators to make socialism economic. Frederick Cooper of Harvard University has observed that 'little capital formation can come from a peasantry that is both poor and uncaptured', while Réné Dumont wonders how there can ever be socialism in the face of corruption, opulence and reliance on foreign capital skill and technology (Cooper,1981: 66; Dumont, 1969, 1973). Another way of stating the case in Marxist terms is to say that the existing capitalist mode of production and, therefore, the forces of production have not developed to the stage where it is possible to talk concretely of their being ripe for transformation.

Given the foregoing arguments, Colin Leys' verdict appears inescapable: 'It would be dogmatic and mechanical to assert that neo-colonialism and underdevelopment must inevitably lead to revolutionary change as a result of inevitable social and economic crisis' (Leys, 1975: 274). Indeed Ake himself, in his more recent *A Politcal Economy of Africa,* has soft-pedalled on revolutionary socialist change. He now argues that 'the state of productive forces in Africa threatens to turn socialism into a caricature even with the best intentions . . . We must avoid the common error of seeing socialist revolution as the panacea for the problems of Africa, including underdevelopment' (Ake, 1981: 188). The path to socialist transformation is strewn with numerous obstacles, not the least of which is power of the state which is weak in relation to states of the capitalist core, but which is strong relative to the domestic society. Ake concludes that 'the present state of economic stagnation will continue, deepening class contradictions and causing governmental instability but not necessarily sparking off [socialist] revolution in the forseeable future . . . Facism – that is the reality staring us in the face in much of Africa' (Ake, 1981: 180).

There appears to be a consensus that neither domestic nor international capital can, separately or conjointly, bring about a capitalist transformation in Africa. Socialist transformation is also problematic. In short neither a fundamental capitalist nor socialist transformation will occur in Africa. The present governing classes are incapable of engineering such a fundamental transformation, for to do so would amount to political suicide, nor will the international structure permit such a transformation. In lieu of such changes African leaders often adopt radical slogans to which they pay lip-service to appease the masses, but eschew real changes in the structure of production. In the end, as Leys (1975: 18) puts it, what happens is that 'a new industrial enclave' is established in the economy, 'but without any tendency to set in motion a chain reaction of investment and employment which will eventually make it burst out of the enclave and transform the economy as a whole. On the contrary, the society [is] "locked into" its subordinate role in the international capitalist system by new means'. Indeed empirical studies, notably of Kenya and the Ivory Coast, have shown that despite the existence of local classes of accumulating capitalists, capitalist transformation has proved elusive. 'These capitalists merely reproduce multinational dependent industrialization with its limited spread effects and linkages [while] structural relationships within the economy generate foreign exchange crises as investment accelerates and chokes off on-going capital accumulation' (Langdon, 1981: 9).

There also appears to be an emerging consensus that despite the general implications of dependency theory for underdevelopment, there can be pockets of development, but it will be a dependent, as opposed to independent or self-reliant, development. Langdon's empirical studies have shown increasing numbers of a local class of accumulating capitalists capable of bringing about multinational dependent industrialization. Immanuel Wallerstein (1974c) for his part has argued that transformation is marginally possible under limited conditions which are available to a few peripheral states at different times but not to all peripheral states at the same time.

The pockets of development may be seen as products of two factors: hierarchy of capitalist interests, and product life cycle. The first argues that in the Third World in general and Africa in particular the core capitalist states have varying interests in the various regions depending on the strategic and economic values of the areas. The greater the value, the higher the core state's interest in preventing the growth of strong politico-economic systems independent of capitalist hegemony. In Africa, Southern Africa is clearly the most important region, followed by countries and regions that have strategic mineral resources such as Zaire and Nigeria, or which are strategically situated such as Kenya and the Horn of Africa. Such priority regions have larger quantities of resources, particularly capital and technology, transferred to them, and such transfers are enough to permit modest dependent capitalist development. They are, so to speak, 'allowed to develop' but their development is by invitation only.

A second and closely related factor explaining pockets of development in Africa and the Third World is what is termed the product life cycle theory. According to this theory, a product is at first produced at the metropole and sold there. Later it is produced at the centre (metropole) but sold at the periphery. Later still, when its technology has become routinized, the uncertainties are small and savings from cheap labour are immense, the product is produced at the periphery and sold there. Savings from labour are immense because wages are kept low, and additional profits are made in the inflated prices of parts which must be imported from abroad and in the inflated costs of the accompanying technology in the form of technical experts, patents etc. Because of the imported in-puts the production lacks the multiplier effect, the forward and backward linkages that spur self-reliant development. It is this kind of dependent development that has taken place in Brazil, and which is beginning to occur in pockets in Africa (Evans, 1979).

The preceding propositions have far-reaching implications for development strategies and foreign policies of African states. In terms of foreign policy, African states find themselves in a situation where they have constantly to pressure the capitalist core to transfer larger quantities of resources to Africa to spur development there. Basically this is what the so-called North–South dialogue over a New International Economic Order (NIEO) is all about.

## North–South dialogue

North–South dialogue is a term that has gained currency since the early 1970s to describe the discussions, negotiations and confrontations between the underdeveloped countries (South) and the industrialized world (North) over the former's demand for the establishment of a New International Economic Order. Although NIEO is itself a new term which came into existence during the sixth special session of the United Nations general assembly in 1974, its essential concerns have deeper roots within and outside the United Nations fora. It is, in a sense, a formal comprehensive and systematic articulation of those fears, desires and demands of the underdeveloped countries (in respect of their place in the global economic system) which have increasingly come to the fore since the realization that political independence did not necessarily bring with it economic development. NIEO seeks the restructuring of international trade with a view to shifting the terms of trade in favour of the Third World countries. It seeks to promote processing and manufacturing in the Third World and to secure a guaranteed market for some of the products. Above all NIEO seeks the transference of real resources to the Third World via indexing, technical assistance and technology transfer.

The strategy employed for the realization of the goals of NIEO is multifarious. There is, first, pure dialogue in the form of exchange of views and proposals and issuing communiques at summit conferences such as occurred in Cancun, Mexico in 1981. Secondly, there are strict negotiations of the conference type of diplomacy. This is the kind of diplomacy characteristic of the United Nations Conference on Trade and Development (UNCTAD) where the Group of 77 – the underdeveloped countries – confront and reach agreements with the industrialized countries on favourable economic packages (Mandeley, 1976). It is the kind of diplomatic negotiations involved in the EEC agreements with the African, Caribbean and Pacific (ACP) countries, known as the Lomé Conventions (Gruhn, 1976). The agreements established a scheme for stabilizing the underdeveloped countries' export earnings (Stabex), a similar scheme for mineral product earnings (the so-called 'son of Stabex'), and a foreign aid package.

A third strategy is the type characteristic of trade unionist activism, leading labour unions and the management to engage in collective bargaining over better working conditions and better production returns. Elements of this are found in UNCTAD where the Group of 77 can be said to engage in collective bargaining with the industrialized capitalist core which owns the means of production and may thus be seen as the 'management' or the employer. But the trade union strategy goes beyond collective bargaining to outright confrontations where the underdeveloped countries use the threat of withholding their natural resources as weapons to extract political and economic concessions from the industrialized core. This is the strategy of OPEC. It is the strategy being urged upon other international resource organizations such as the Inter-Governmental Council of Copper Exporting Countries (CIPEC), the International Tin Council (ITC), the Association of Iron-Ore Exporting Countries (AIOEC), the International Bauxite Association (IBA) and the Union of Banana Exporting Countries (UBEC). However, several difficulties stand in their way and the success of OPEC has not been easy to reproduce (Bissel, 1979; Mikdashi, 1976). The Non-Aligned Movement has, since the 1970s, shifted its concerns and strategy from keeping out of military alliances and ideological issues and securing as much foreign aid as possible. Now the Movement consciously utilizes its natural resources and its increasing organizational size to extract economic concessions or, as in its support of African liberation movements, as a political lever (Mazrui, 1977: 5–6, 21).

There is, finally, the strategy of collective self-reliance in the North–South Dialogue over NIEO. This is the so-called South–South linkage involving increased trade, aid and, where possible, economic co-operation and integration among underdeveloped countries.

The achievements of the North–South dialogue have been little more than window-dressing. It could hardly be otherwise, given the nature of interests involved. The North is unlikely to yield more than marginally to the South partly because its nationalism and racism 'are unlikely to tolerate what must look like a reckless generosity towards real or potential enemies' and partly because its imperialist competitions 'lead to immense expenditure on armaments', leaving a mere pittance to be transferred to the South (Ake, 1978: 185). And yet the South lacks the power to force the hands of the North because it lacks productive resources or the instruments of labour. Even the vaunted OPEC depends entirely on the North's technology to drill oil in the first place. And since the North has a monopoly on this technology it is 'able to redeem the petro-dollars and to pass on the burden of OPEC's price hike to the [South's] countries as import inflation' (Ake, 1978: 24–5). There is, in addition, a conflict of nationalisms in the South which the North exploits in a divide-and-rule fashion to further weaken Southern power. Immediate national self-interests often conflict with long-term group interests, resulting in conflicting stands and policies over specific economic and political issues. These conflicts and co-operation will be seen, in the ensuing chapters, to pervade African relations with the super powers, their activities in the United Nations and their regional integrative efforts on the continent.

Apart from its implications for foreign policy (as epitomized in

NIEO and North–South dialogue), the analysis of Africa's place in the global economy presented here also has practical and theoretical implications for realistic development strategies. The analysis suggests that in the foreseeable future only modest reform is possible in Africa. As we have noted, neither the international capitalists nor the national bourgeoisie wants to see radical transformations in which obviously, they would have much to lose. This is why, as Ake has argued, both sides have elevated the concept of development into an ideology with the slogan 'partnership in development'. This ideology creates the illusion of an identity of interest in change which masks their objective interests in the status quo (Ake 1978: 20–1). But because of economic pressures from the masses, some changes would have to be made.

How much change or reform is possible depends largely on the national bourgeoisie, on the organization of the state and on the skill and sophistication with which the national bourgeoisie uses the state to overcome political and technical problems involved in achieving development (Seidman, 1978; Smith, 1979; Cooper, 1981). In this context the relative autonomy of the African state gives the leadership considerable leeway even within the constraints of dependency. Accordingly, law, for example, could be harnessed to change behaviour for, after all, 'any social formation is at bottom a product of the way people behave and development must involve changes in behaviour.' (Seidman cited in Martin, 1980: 318). Alternatively bureaucratic changes and policy shifts could be employed to foster a better redistribution of domestic resources, to ameliorate the harsh lives of some peasants and urban workers, or to curtail the privileges of foreign and local capitalists; in short to reduce mass poverty. Such reforms of a redistributive kind are perhaps the best that are realistically feasible, given the pessimistic outlook of the dependency perspective with its unenviable choices that it leaves the underdeveloped countries. If transforming the capitalist mode of production is not as yet practicable, we should then perhaps welcome its reform in the direction of redistribution. The alternative to this will be total paralysis, if not decay (Langdon, 1981).

If reform of a redistributive kind is the best that is realistically feasible then theories of underdevelopment, in addition to analyzing general causes and prescribing general and unrealistic solutions of underdevelopment, must also engage in finding ways of overcoming particular instances of underdevelopment in order to bring about immediate and practicable development. Such a theory would entail combining the perspectives of the dependency school with the insights of the neo-classical theorists – to continue their views on alternative rural development strategies, industrial policy choices, ways of shaping redistribution so as to reach specific groups, and what the alternatives are to reliance on foreign capital, technology and markets. Such a synthesis of elements of the two perspectives was the direction Langdon and others urged the Africanists that gathered at the 1981 Conference of the African Studies Association to pursue. It is as yet too early to see what theoretical progress has been, or can be, made in this direction and what its implications will be for political practice.

# References

ADEDEJI, ADEBAYO (1976) 'Collective self-reliance in developing Africa: scope, prospects and problems'. Keynote address at the International Conference on ECOWAS. Lagos: Nigerian Institute of International Affairs, 23-27 August, 1976.

AKE, CLAUDE (1978) *Revolutionary pressures in Africa,* Zed Press, London.

AKE, CLAUDE (1981) *A political economy of Africa,* Longman, London.

ALPERS, E A (1975) *Ivory and slaves in East-Central Africa,* Univ. of California Press, Berkeley.

AMIN, SAMIR (1972) Underdevelopment and dependence in black Africa: origins and contemporary forms, *Journal of Modern African Studies* **10** (4).

AMIN, SAMIR (1974) *Accumulation on a world scale: a critique of the theory of underdevelopment,* Monthly Review Press, New York.

BIERSTEKER, THOMAS J (1980) Self-reliance in theory and practice in Tanzanian trade relations, *International Organization* **34**, (2).

BISSELL, RICHARD E (1979) African power in international resource organizations, *The Journal of Modern African Studies* **17** (1).

BREWSTER, H (1973) Economic dependence: a quantitative interpretation *Social and Economic Studies* **22** (1).

CAPORASO, JAMES (1978) Introduction: dependence and dependency in the global system, *International Organization* **32** (1).

COOPER, Frederick (1981) Africa and the world economy. Paper commissioned by the Social Science Research Council for presentation to the African Studies Association Annual Meeting, Bloomington, Indiana, October 1981.

DOS SANTOS, TEOTONIO (1970) The structure of dependence, *American Economic Review* **60** (5).

DOS SANTOS, TEOTONIO (1971) Théorie de la crise économique dans les pays sous-développés. In A Abdei-Malek (ed), *Sociologie de l'impérialisme,* Anthropos, Paris.

DOS SANTOS, TEOTONIO (1973) The crisis of development theory and the problem of dependence in Latin America. In Henry Bernstein (ed) *Underdevelopment and Development: the Third World Today,* Penguin, Harmondsworth.

DUMONT, RENE (1969) *False start in Africa,* Praeger, New York.

DUMONT, RENE (1973) *Socialisms and development,* Andre Deutsch, London.

EVANS, PETER (1979) *Dependent development,* Princeton Univ. Press, Princeton.

FRANK, ANDRE GUNDER (1972) The development of underdevelopment. In James D Cockcroft et al *Dependence and underdevelopment: Latin America's political economy,* Anchor Books, New York.

FURTADO, C. (1967) *Development and underdevelopment,* Univ. of California Press, Berkeley.

GIRVAN, N. (1973) The development of dependency economics in the Caribbean and Latin America: review and comparison, *Social and Economic Studies* **22** (1).

GRUHN, ISEBILL (1976) The Lomé Convention: inching towards interdependence, *International Organization* **30** (2).

HELLEINER, GERALD K (1979) Aid and dependence in Africa: issues for recipients. In Thomas Shaw and Kenneth A. Heard (eds) *The politics of Africa: dependence and development,* Africana Publishing Company, New York.

HIRSCHMAN, ALBERT O (1958) *The strategy of economic development,* Yale Univ. Press, New Haven.

HOPKINS, ANTHONY G (1973) *An economic history of West Africa,* Longman, London.

HUGHES, BARRY B AND STRAUCH, PATRICIA A (1981) The future of development in Nigeria and the Sahel: projections from the World Integrated Model (WIM). In Timothy M. Shaw (ed) *Alternative futures for Africa,* Westview Press, Boulder.

HYDEN, G (1980) *Beyond Ujamaa in Tanzania,* Heinemann, London.

JINADU, ADELE (1977) A review essay of revolutionary pressures in Africa *Nigerian Journal of Economic and Social Studies* **19** (2).

JOHNSTON, BRUCE AND KILBY, PETER (1975) *Agriculture and structural transformation: economic strategies in late-developing countries,* Oxford Univ. Press, New York.

LANGDON, STEVEN W (1981) A commentary on Africa and the world economy: theoretical perspectives and present trends. Paper presented to the Annual Meeting of the African Studies Association, October, 1981.

LEGUM, COLIN (1962) *Pan-Africanism: a short political guide,* Pall Mall, London.

LEWIS, ARTHUR W (1954) Economic development with unlimited supplies of labour, *Manchester School* **22.**

LEWIS, ARTHUR W (1958) Unlimited labour: further notes, *Manchester School* **26.**

LEYS, COLIN (1975) *Underdevelopment in Kenya: the political economy of neo-colonialism 1964-1971,* Univ. of California Press, Berkeley.

LIBBY, RONALD T (1976) External cooptation of less developed country's policy-making: the case of Ghana, *World Politics* **29.**

MANDELEY, JOHN (1976) The Third World pressures at Nairobi: the political economic significance of UNCTAD IV, *Round Table* **264.**

MARTIN, ROBERT (1980) The use of state power to overcome underdevelopment, *The Journal of Modern African Studies* **18** (2).

MAZRUI, ALI (1977) *Africa's international relations,* Heinemann, London.

MIKDASHI, ZUHAYR (1976) *The international politics of natural resources,* Cornell Univ. Press, Ithaca.

NKRUMAH, KWAME (1966) *Neo-colonialism: the last stage of imperialism,* International Publishers, New York.

OCULI, OKELLO (1979) Dependent food policy in Nigeria, 1975-1979, *Review of African Political Economy* **15/16.**

OJO, OLATUNDE J B (1983) Self-reliance as a development strategy. In Claude Ake (ed) *A political economy of contemporary Nigeria,* Longman, London.

OLSON, RICHARD S (1979) Economic coercion in world politics with a focus on North-South relations, *World Politics* **31** (4).

RODNEY, WALTER (1974) *How Europe underdeveloped Africa,* Howard Univ. Press, Washington D.C.

SCHULTZ, THEODORE W (1964) *Transforming traditional agriculture,* Yale Univ. Press, New Haven.

SEIDMAN, ROBERT B (1978) *The State, Law and Development,* St Martins Press, New York.

SUNKEL, O (1973) Transnational capitalism and national disintegration in Latin America, *Social and Economic Studies* **22** (1).

SMITH, TONY (1979) The underdevelopment of development literature: the case of dependency theory, *World Politics* **31** (2).

THOMPSON, WILLARD SCOTT (1969) *Ghana's foreign policy 1957–1966,* Princeton Univ. Press, Princeton.

WALLERSTEIN, IMMANUEL (1974a) The rise and future demise of the world capitalist system, *Comparative Studies in Society and History* **16.**

WALLERSTEIN, IMMANUEL (1974b) *The modern world system,* Academic Press, New York.

WALLERSTEIN, IMMANUEL (1974c) Dependence in an inter-dependent world: the limited possibilities of transformation within the capitalist world economy, *African Studies Review* **17.**

WALLERSTEIN, IMMANUEL (1976) The three stages of African involvement in the world economy. In Peter C W Gutkind and Immanuel Wallerstein (eds) *The political economy of contemporary Africa,* Sage, Beverly Hills.

# 5    The search for African unity

## From London to Addis Ababa

In May 1963 nearly sixty-three years after the first Pan-African Conference convened in London on 23 July, 1900, thirty-one African heads of state and government met in Addis Ababa. There, between the 23 and 25 May, they debated the issues of African unity, independence and the sovereign rights of states. On 25 May they signed a charter creating an all-African body − the 'Organization of African Unity' (OAU). The name was, indeed, appropriate. No unity had been achieved; only a declaration to work for it. This work has yet to be accomplished.

The idea of African unity originated in the black diaspora. The two movements − Pan-Negroism and Pan-Africanism − developed in the West Indies and North America. Pan-Negroism was concerned with the dignity of all black peoples, while Pan-Africanism began both as a cultural and political movement to group together blacks in diaspora and to mobilize blacks both in diaspora and in Africa against white domination, oppression and racial discrimination (Mazrui, 1965: 1; Mazrui, 1977a: 26−7; Shepperson, 1960). In political terms it was a movement for a united black world.

For continental Africa, Pan-Africanism nurtured the idea of African brotherhood and solidarity. It inspired the struggle for political independence and the call for African unity. Pan-Africanism laid the basis for African nationalism (macronationalism) and was the mother of the concept of continental unity (Padmore, 1956; Holworth, 1961; Shepperson, 1960; Nkrumah, 1963; Mboya, 1963; Makonnen, 1973; Woronoff, 1970). Pan-Africanism became an expression of the indigenous African quest for continental unity following the 1945 Manchester Congress (Odede, 1968; Macyo, 1968).

The Manchester Congress marked a turning point in the quest for African continental unity. While Pan-Africanism nurtured the idea of continental unity, the Manchester Congress betrayed the idea. Before 1945 sentiments among the Pan-Africanists leaned heavily towards a continental nation-state, but after the Manchester Congress attitudes began to shift away from the idea of an all-African state. The explanation for this development rests in the outcome of the 1945 congress.

Firstly, the Manchester Congress did not draw up a concrete programme of action to bring about continental unity. It failed to organize a continental political party. Instead, the congress unleashed micronationalist forces upon the continent when it urged all Africans living in the diaspora to return to their respective colonial territories in order to fight for the independence of individual African colonies (Makonnen, 1973; 168). Local territorially based political activities quickly fell prey to the trappings of state nationalism and its accompanying inter-state power struggles.

Secondly, the emphasis of the Manchester Congress shifted from continentalism to West African regionalism. The West African National Secretariat was established in London in 1946 in place of the Pan-African Secretariat which Nkrumah had advocated. In 1947 the West African Secretariat organised the West African Congress. Both the Secretariat and the Congress pledged themselves to achieve self-government for West African territories, to create a federation of independent West African states and to use the West African federation to work towards African unity (Thompson, 1969: 89–90, 133; Legum, 1965; 153–4). Finally, the Manchester Congress injected into African international politics the concept of 'economic and social development by co-operation' (Thompson, 1969: 133). Whether this suggests that the Pan-Africanists already saw functionalism, that is a belief in international economic integration as a prerequisite for political integration, as a basis for eventual political integration cannot be verified. All that seems clear is that the Manchester Congress relegated continental political unity to the cause of regional unity. George Padmore, one of the fathers of Pan-Africanism, wrote in 1956 that 'the Pan-Africanist perspective embraces the federation of regional self-governing countries and their eventual amalgamation into a united states of Africa' (Padmore, 1956; 376).

Pan-Africanism has, however, remained very important to African international politics. Ever since the 1945 Manchester Congress African leaders have favoured some form of inter-African integration. Their views have varied from federalism to functionalism to neo-functionalism. But in the continuing search for African unity federalism and neo-functionalism have been the dominant concepts.

Neo-functionalists approach the problem of international integration from the perspective of economic functionalism. They emphasize regional functional integration as a prerequisite for international integration. Neo-functionalism, associated mainly with Ernst Haas, derives from the principle of economic determinism (Haas, 1967). Its basic proposition is that 'step-by-step economic decisions are superior to crucial political choices' (Lieber, 1972: 42). Hence the first step to international integration is the achievement of regional functional integration. It argues further that functional regional institutions lead to increased regional exchanges. As these exchanges become intensified, greater pressure will be exerted on regional functional institutions. The centre of economic activities will shift to the regional level, with entrepreneurs also transferring their allegiance from the nation-state to the regional organs. As a result, demands on the regional institutions would increase significantly and would warrant the establishment of regional political machinery capable of mediating conflicting interests at the regional level. The process eventually leads to the emergence of a dominant supra-national authority. Once regional integration has been achieved, a similar pattern of development should take place at the international level (Haas and Schmitter, 1966: 259–99; Haas, 1964; 1968).

Federalism refers to a political organization in which two or more states agree to form a union government with central authority, while retaining local autonomy. A federal system of government entails the writing of a constitution which spells out clearly the powers of the central government and of the constituent units. In the international system federalism has been advocated by the proponents of world peace. Since the formation of the United States of America following the 1787 Philadelphia constitutional convention, federalists have looked to the United States as an example of how best men could unite to form a world government. Federalists thus call for a written constitution and the establishment of world political, legal and military institutions to take over the functions currently performed by national governments (Kuehl, 1969; Divine, 1967; Haas, 1974: 205; Lieber, 1972: 39–40). At a regional level federalism is the call for the coming together of independent nation-states to form a federal regional government. Federalists attach greater emphasis to political institutions than to economic and social factors which functionalists believe are essential in the gradual process of international integration.

Until 1965 the head of state most in favour of federalism was the late President Kwame Nkrumah of Ghana. But in his struggle for continental unity he stood alone against a majority of African leaders who tended to favour a neo-functionalist approach, because federalism involved constitutional or legal obligations while functional integration calls only for moral commitments.

In April, 1958, the first ever Conference of Independent African States convened in Accra, Ghana. It had been called by Nkrumah and it brought together all eight independent African states. The Union of South Africa was excluded. The conference considered the issue of African unity, the questions of imperialism and colonialism, African economic development and apartheid in South Africa.

African unity had always been at the heart of Nkrumah's African policies. He probably expected the conference to support a United States of Africa. But, guided by national interest, the independent states asserted the principle of the inviolability of national independence, sovereignty and territorial integrity. To guarantee the right of African states to exist, the countries pledged not to 'interfere in the internal affairs of another country' (Legum, 1965: 42).

Nkrumah was not contented with the conference's resolution endorsing African unity and solidarity without any commitment to a United States of Africa. Through his initiative, the first All African Peoples' Conference was convened in Accra in December, 1958, just eight months after the first Conference of Independent African States. Uninhibited by national interest considerations, the All African Peoples' Conference called for 'a Commonwealth of African states' (Legum, 1965: 43), a Commonwealth without racial or tribal boundaries (Mazrui 1965: 1; Mboya, 1963: 231). Tom Mboya of Kenya, who had been elected chairman of the conference, declared they had gathered in Accra to 'announce African unity and solidarity' (quoted in Mazrui, 1977b: 5). The delegates went further and drafted a constitution with a provision for 'a United States of Africa' (Legum, 1965; Appendix 22: I.B. pp 241–3).

Clearly the views taken by the two conferences diverged. African nationalists who had not yet won independence for their territories on the whole supported the idea of a United States of Africa in the hope that it would speed up the liberation of areas still under colonialism. Delegates representing independent national governments feared that such a development would destroy the nation-state.

The second Conference of Independent African States, held in Addis Ababa, Ethiopia from 15–24 June, 1960, highlighted the point. The conference revealed two diametrically opposed positions. The Ghanaian delegation took the position that the delegates should decide on the establishment of a 'Union of African States'. It proposed that the conference should recommend the establishment of 'a committee of experts with specific terms of reference to work out details of the Union of African States'. According to the Ghanaian Foreign Minister, Ako Adjei, Nkrumah, Tubman and Sékou Touré had, at their meeting in Sanniquillie, Liberia on 19 July, 1959, agreed on the principles of a Union of African States (Legum, 1965: Appendix 10: 188–9). The leader of the Nigerian delegation, Y. M. Sule, objected. Having accepted Pan-Africanism as 'the only solution to our problems in Africa', Sule observed that 'at the moment the idea of forming a Union of African States is premature'. The union should come gradually. Expressing the majority sentiment, Sule declared that 'At the moment we in Nigeria cannot afford to form union by government with any African states by surrendering our sovereignty' (Legum, 1965: Appendix 11: 190–2).

The Addis Ababa conference was another defeat for Nkrumah who had hoped to persuade African states that a union government was necessary. But Nkrumah received consolation from the second All African Peoples' Conference (Tunis, 25–30 January, 1960). The conference amended the 1958 constitution but it retained the provision for 'a United States of Africa' (Legum, 1965: Appendix 22: IC 243). The third All African Peoples' Conference (Cairo, 23–31 March, 1961) maintained the tempo by resolving to mobilize the African masses to work for the emergence of a union state (Legum, 1965: Appendix 22: iv, 265–6). While the resolutions of the All African Peoples' Conferences implied mass interest in African unity, achievement of unity depended upon the nation-states themselves. But they were not ready to surrender their sovereignty. This fact explains why interest in federalism both at the regional and continental level failed to produce federal governments in Africa.

It seemed briefly that federalism might be more successful at the regional level. In the late 1940s leaders in the Maghreb began to discuss the possibility of forming a federation and by 1958, at a time when the newly independent states of Morocco and Tunisia were supporting Algeria's struggle for independence, enthusiasm for the federation was high. But in the end neither the Algerian war nor the later Arab–Israeli conflict were sufficient to overcome the differences within the Maghreb, and the federation was stillborn.

The Union of Nile States, formed by Egypt and Sudan and which anticipated the inclusion of Uganda, was motivated by the importance of the River Nile to both Egypt and Sudan. The union collapsed in 1955, because Sudanese nationalists could not accept Egypt's interference in Sudan's internal affairs. The widely talked of East African Federation never materialized because of nationalism, particularly in Kenya. In the end, Kenya, Tanganyika (now Tanzania) and Uganda settled for functional integration in the form of the East African Community which lasted from 1967 to 1977.

The nearest any group of independent African states came to closer political integration was the establishment of the Ghana–Guinea union in November 1958. Mali joined the union in December the following year. As conceived by Nkrumah and Sékou Touré, the union was to start as a confederation. Nkrumah and Sékou Touré declared in May 1959 that membership of the union would be open to all interested independent African states and that citizens of member states would be granted dual citizenship. The member states would jointly decide what elements of their national sovereignty to surrender to·the union. National flags, anthems and mottos were to exist side by side with those of the union and each state in the union would maintain its national army and diplomatic representation (Legum, 1965: 205-6, Appendix 6: 178–9).

When Mali joined the union in December, 1959 it looked as if the confederal arrangement might attract more membership. Given the determination of states to uphold their sovereignty and national identity, confederacy seemed the best political option that the federalists could offer in the hope of winning support for continental political integration. The Union of African States Charter drawn up in Accra on 1 July, 1961 by Nkrumah, Sékou Touré and Modeibo Keita was a well tailored document which took into account both Nkrumah's enthusiasm for a tangible Union of African States and the concern of less enthusiastic confederalists for the preservation of national identity. Section I (Article II) of the charter stated that the Union of African States would serve 'as the nucleus of the United States of Africa'. It thus gave Nkrumah the hope that a confederal system would, in the future, develop into a federal system embracing the entire continent. Article V of the same section created 'the supreme organ of the the Union of African States' made up of the heads of state of member countries. Although Section 1 (Article IV) and Section 4 (Article VII) provided for a joint defence system, member-states maintained their respective national armies. The charter, on the whole, left national independence, sovereignty and territorial integrity intact (Legum, 1965: Appendix 14: 201-4).

However, the Union of African States failed to attract any additional countries after Mali. The failure reflected widespread hostility to federalism on the continent. Between 1960 and 1962 Africa became polarized into two political blocs known as the Brazzaville–Monrovia Group, on the one hand, and the Casablanca Group, on the other

(Legum, 1965: 50–2; Nyangira, 1980: 4–5; Thompson, 1969: 161–75). The division arose from many factors – ideological differences, personality of leaders, national interest considerations and having just achieved independence, many leaders were reluctant to surrender any of their power to a new confederal authority. (Legum, 1965; El-Ayouty, 1975; Thompson, 1969; Woronoff, 1970).

The Brazzaville–Monrovia Group, which became the Lagos Group in 1962, consisted of twenty conservative and moderate African states. It had its origin in the December, 1960 Brazzaville Conference of twelve conservative former French colonies opposed to the support of African states for Patrice Lumumba's government in the former Belgian Congo. The Brazzaville twelve also opposed the political union of African states. They favoured functional integration. A larger group met in Monrovia in May, 1961. Like the Brazzaville twelve, it rejected the idea of a continental political union and endorsed inter-African functional co-operation (Legum, 1965: 50–3; Nyangira, 1980: 4; West Africa Pilot, 6 May, 1961; Italiaander, 1961: 196).

The Casablanca Group arose in response to the Brazzaville twelve whose opposition to Lumumba's government, recognition of Mauritania to which Morocco laid claim, failure to recognize the Algerian Liberation Front and whose rejection of a contemplated union of African states antagonized a section of African states. The group consisting of seven countries with diverse interests met in Casablanca in January, 1961. Morocco wanted support for its opposition to Mauritania's independence and admission to the United Nations. Nasser saw the group as a chance of increasing Egyptian influence in Africa and to gain the support of African states against Israel. For Sékou Touré the enlarged group provided a badly needed political support against France and the former French colonies that had ostracized him for refusing to remain within France's sphere of influence. To Modiebo Keita and Nkrumah the group offered a forum for projecting a collective African view on the Congo crisis and for advancing the idea of a union of African states (Legum, 1965: 51)

The Casablanca Conference decided to reject the idea of drawing up a constitution for an African union. A constitution is a legally binding document. and its provisions are enforceable by court of law. Wade and Phillips have defined a constitution as 'the rules which regulate the structure of the principal organs of government, their relationship to each other and determine their principal functions'. (Wade and Phillips, 1977: 5). Professor Dicey adds that a constitution defines 'The rules of a country which determine the form of its government, the respective rights and duties of the government towards its citizens, and the citizens towards the government.' The Casablanca Conference understood the implications of a binding constitution. It would create a new political system and a government which stood above the existing nation-states. It was consequently felt to be unacceptable.

Instead, the conference participants drew up a charter which they called 'The African Charter of Casablanca' (Legum, 1965: Appendix 15). A charter is a document establishing 'a loose international organization based upon voluntary co-operation of [member] states' (Cervenka, 1969: 80). It is not legally binding. Compliance with its provisions is voluntary and depends largely on moral force and goodwill. Above all the organization which is created by a charter remains surbordinate to the nation-state.

'The African Charter of Casablanca' established an association of African states willing voluntarily 'to preserve and consolidate our identity of views and unity in international affairs, to safeguard our hard won independence, the sovereignty and territorial integrity of our states, to reinforce peace in the world by adopting a policy of non-alignment'. On African unity, the charter provided for the establishment of an African consultative assembly, but only when conditions permitted. In the meantime, the charter created a political committee to co-ordinate foreign policies, an economic committee to promote economic co-operation, a cultural committee and a joint African High Command to co-ordinate defence. (Legum, 1965: Appendix 15: 205–6; Thompson 1969: 173). During the months following the signing of the charter and especially after the heads of state approved the protocol for the implementation of the provisions of the charter in June, 1961, the Casablanca states attempted to make the three committees and the Joint High Command operational. However, the actual operation of these organs remained at conference and diplomatic representation levels only (Cervenka, 1969; 140, 144–5).

The importance of the African Charter of Casablanca is twofold. First, in the quest for African unity, it provided a political and industrial framework. Ingrained in the charter was Nkrumah's 'belief that political unity should come first, as the necessary prelude to the creation of an extended field for which integrated economic and social development plans could be worked out'. Nkrumah maintained this approach to the May, 1963 Addis Ababa summit meeting (Cervenka, 1969: 139–40, 80–1). Second, it introduced the charter system into inter-African politics. The Casablanca Charter was the precursor of the Monrovia Charter (12 May, 1961), the Lagos Charter (30 January, 1962) and the Organization of African Unity Charter (26 May, 1963).

The document which came out of the Monrovia conference was only a draft charter, but it laid the basis for the Organization of African Unity. It expressed the views of all those opposed to a political union. First and foremost, the Monrovia draft charter emphasized the absolute equality and sovereignty of African states. Without mentioning names it cautioned Ghana and Morocco against attempting to annex other states. (Ghana had laid claim to Togo on the grounds that the colonial boundaries that divided the Ewe between Ghana and Togo were illegitimate, while Morocco had claimed Mauritania on historical grounds and religious affinity). The draft charter further stressed the principle of non-interference in the internal affairs of sister states and prohibited the harbouring of dissidents from other African states. The document registered strong opposition to racial policies in Southern Africa and it pledged support for African liberation movements. The Monrovia draft charter, unlike the African Charter of Casablanca, laid out a functionalist and non-political approach to African unity. It proposed that 'The Unity that is aimed to be achieved at the moment is not the political integration of sovereign African states, but unity of aspirations and action considered from the point of view of African social solidarity and political identity' (Cervenka, 1969: 140–1). The Monrovia document moved towards inter-African functional integration by calling for economic, educational, cultural, scientific and technical co-operation (Legum, 1965: Appendix 17, 216–7; Thompson, 1969: 172–3; Cervenka, 1969: 141).

The Monrovia Conference had only produced a draft charter. Its ratification, however, had to await the proposed Lagos Conference which, the Monrovia group hoped would be attended by the Casablanca powers. But when the Lagos Conference convened on 25 January, 1962, all the Casablanca states declined the invitation to attend. Of the twenty countries present all had belonged to the Brazzaville–Monrovia group, except Tanganyika (Tanzania) and Congo (Zaire). Thus at the close of ths conference on 30 January, the twenty countries agreed to ratify the Monrovia draft charter in principle only and gave it the title 'The Charter of Inter-African States and Malagasy Organization'. The charter left the door open for other African states to suggest changes and to sign it. One thing that should be noted about the Lagos Charter is the fact that it omitted African unity. The reason for this is contained in Article III of the Charter which, among other matters, emphasized the principle of 'the sovereign equality of the African and Malagasy states, whatever may be the size of their territory, the density of their population or values of their possession' (Cervenka, 1969: 225).

There were two main innovative features of the Lagos Charter – the creation of a general secretariat to act as the central administrative organ of the Inter-African States and Malagasy Organization and consideration of mechanisms for resolving inter-African disputes. Both features were to find their way into the OAU Charter.

Despite all the divisions between the various African blocs the cause of African unity had made considerable progress since the Manchester Congress. First, and most important, by 1963 the majority of African states had become independent. Second, there was widespread agreement on the need for some form of continental unity, although, as we have seen, radicals such as Nkrumah were isolated in their wish for a Pan-African government. Third, there was universal condemnation of the racist apartheid regime of South Africa. Lastly, all the conferences held between 1958 and 1963 passed resolutions in support of national liberation struggles on the continent. All these sentiments were neatly expressed in the final declaration of the 1958 Conference of Independent African States:

> We resolve to preserve unity of purpose and action in international affairs which we have forged among ourselves in this historic conference; to safeguard our hard won independence, sovereignty and territorial integrity; and to preserve among ourselves the fundamental unity of outlook on foreign policy so that a distinct African

personality will play its part in co-operation with other peace-loving nations to further the cause of peace.

# The Organization of African Unity

In his welcoming address to the delegates attending the opening session of the Addis Ababa summit meeting the host, Emperor Haile Selassie, echoed the 1958 resolution:

> What we still lack despite the efforts of the past years, is the mechanism which will enable us to speak with one voice when we wish to do so and to make important decisions on African problems when we are so minded.

He told the heads of state and government that Africa needed

> a single organization through which Africa's single voice may be heard and within which Africa's problems may be studied and resolved. We need an organization which will facilitate acceptable solutions to disputes among Africans and promote the study and adoption of measures for common defence and programmes of co-operation in economic and social fields (OAU, 1963).

The apparent general consensus among African states that they needed a forum for the expression of the African personality did not prevent the existence of disagreement in Addis Ababa in May, 1963 (Wolfers, 1976: 1–4; Nyangira, 1980: 7–8; Cervenka, 1969: 2–5, 9–15). Early in March, 1963 the idea of holding a summit meeting of African heads of state and government from 23 to 26 May, 1963 had largely been accepted. A preparatory secretariat was subsequently set up in Addis Ababa to work out the details of the summit conference. Then a conference of foreign ministers convened in Addis Ababa on 15 May to work out the agenda for the heads of state and government meeting scheduled to open on 23 May.

During the foreign ministers' conference four divergent approaches to African unity emerged. First, there was the view that Africa needed only a single all-African states charter, which would replace the African Charter of Casablanca and the Monrovia–Lagos Charters. Its proponents envisaged a charter which would lay out a 'Declaration of Principles' for inter-African conduct. All African states would be expected to subscribe to these principles without surrendering any of their sovereignty. This position was held by Libya and Sudan and was based on the 1941 Atlantic Charter signed between Britain and the United States (Divine, 1967: 41; Cervenka, 1969: 2). The second proposal added to the idea of a declaration of principles the concept of 'a loose association of African states' which would be set up within the framework of an All-African Organization'. Its leading advocate was Liberia, along with other states which felt that the Organization of American States provided the best model for African conditions. The third view was a mixture of functionalist and regional federalist views. Nigeria ruled out the possibility of an organic unity of African states. It favoured inter-African economic co-operation. It also thought that efforts towards organic unity should be a step-by-step process, starting with regional co-operation and finally extending to the whole continent. This posture was held also by Ethiopia, the Brazzaville Group, and Tanganyika which advocated the federation of East African states. Finally, there was the view, held mainly by Ghana, that the Addis Ababa summit meeting should produce a Union of African States, with a Union Government, an African Civil Service, an African High Command and a Court of Justice (Cervenka, 1969: 2–3; Nyangira, 1980: 7–8; Matthew, 1977).

The heads of state and government summit meeting paralleled the foreign ministers' conference. Nkrumah went to Addis Ababa determined to persuade the assembled heads of state and government to accept his proposal for an All-African Union Government. Tafawa Balewa of Nigeria had already become fully convinced that political integration was completely unacceptable. Zdenek Cervenka remarked that 'In the course of the speeches, what had formerly been thought different views on the concept of African Unity . . . were reduced to a subtle political duel between Ghana on the one hand and Nigeria on the other' (Cervenka, 1969: 9).

What lay behind this political duel? First, most African states did not want a political unification of Africa, and Nigeria had assumed the leadership of the group opposed to African federation. Second, the United States government had convinced key African leaders, among them Tafawa Balewa, William Tubman and Haile Selassie, that a united African government would be led by the 'socialists and pro-Soviet' Nkrumah and Nasser. The United States Department of State wrote to their allies in Africa warning them that such a union would introduce communism to Africa. The United States suggested instead a regionalist approach to inter-African integration*. Third, on the eve of the summit meeting, there was a concerted international effort to depict Nkrumah as a ruthless and power-thirsty Pan-Africanist who would use any means including political assassination to achieve his goal. This image of Nkrumah was accepted by many West African leaders (*Time*, 20 May 1963; *Newsweek*, 20 May 1963; Cervenka, 1969: 6–7) and it set the stage for confrontation at the founding of the Organization of African Unity.

On 24 May Nkrumah put before the assembled heads of state and government his proposal for a political and institutional approach to African unity, the same proposal that had resulted in disagreement

* The documents referred to above were written during the Kennedy administration and are available on microfiche published under the title *The Declassified Documents* by the Carrollton Press, Inc., Washington, D.C., 1976–7.

during the foreign ministers' conference. Nkrumah, who in his book *Africa Must Unite* had warned that the choice before African states lay between unity and survival on the one hand and disunity and collapse on the other (Nkrumah, 1963: 189), submitted to the conference that 'African unity is above all a political kingdom which can only be gained by political means'. He proposed the establishment of three commissions: one to be charged with the task of writing a constitution for a union government of African states, a second to draw up a plan for a continental economic and industrial programme (to include the possible creation of an African common market, monetary zone and central bank) and a third commission to work out details of a common foreign policy (*Proceedings of the Summit Conference,* Mimeo). It should cause no surprise that Nkrumah's proposals were not adopted by the conference; Milton Obote was his only supporter.

Tafawa Balewa accepted African unity as a goal to be sought. However, such a unity could not be at the expense of the sovereignty of African states, regardless of their size. Balewa agreed that an African common market was a good idea, but it was 'a very complicated matter'. The most practical approach to African integration would be to start with regional groupings. He proposed the division of Africa into three regional groups – North Africa (including Sudan), West Africa (extending down to the River Congo) and East Africa (incorporating most of the central African states). The end result of this approach would be the eventual development of an African common market.

This was the view held by nearly all heads of state and government, except Nkrumah and Obote. Both Modiebo Keita and Sékou Touré favoured functional co-operation and they now only vaguely talked of a future political unity. Nasser who, like Modiebo Keita and Sékou Touré, belonged to the radical Casablanca Group, declared that organic unity could not be achieved overnight. President Philibert Tsiranana of Madagascar (Malagasy Republic) registered a strong objection to any form of continental political arrangement – a federal plan presupposed 'an important surrender of national sovereignty' and a confederal formula was unacceptable 'because the authority we set above the state might impose directives unacceptable to some of us'. Presidents Habib Bourguiba of Tunisia and Senghor of Senegal expressed similar sentiments. President Julius Nyerere of Tanganyika, who supported the proposed East African Federation, stood somewhere between the continental unitarists and the functionalists. He believed that political integration ought to start at the regional level.

The summit meeting underlined the existence of strongly divergent views on African unity. The Casablanca Group broke rank over the issue. The Brazzaville–Monrovia–Lagos Group were more united than ever in their opposition to a Union of African States. Yet, Ghana, with the support of Uganda, was determined to insist that the summit meeting agree to a political and institutional integration of Africa.

This kind of stalemate could have aborted the creation of the OAU, and this fear was expressed by Haile Selassie (Wolfers, 1976: 16, 19). But African heads of state and government buried their differences and united on the issue of decolonization. Cervenka, writing in 1974, observed:

> It was the common stand on colonialism and racial oppression that brought the representatives of 31 African states to a summit conference of heads of state and government of independent African states in Addis Ababa during the period of 23–26 May, 1963, where they signed the Charter of the Organization of African Unity. The assembled leaders expressed reservation about the charter and the character of the organization. However, no objection was strong enough to justify abstention. *To do so would have been to risk being named as a dissident in Africa's united stand against colonialism and apartheid* (Cervenka, 1974: 326; 1969: 12).

The repulsive nature of colonialism and racialism in southern Africa had united African states under one organization. It is this fact that led Dodou Thiam to remark that 'decolonization is undoubtedly the subject which commands the greatest measure of unity between the various African countries' (Thiam, 1965). Cervenka confirms the pre-eminence of the decolonization factor in the founding of the OAU. 'The unanimous assertion by the assembly of heads of state and government of the OAU at Rabat that the time has come to declare war on Portugal as a first step towards the final liquidation of colonialism in Africa has made African states more united than ever before' (Cervenka, 1974: 326).

It is true that in Addis Ababa heads of state and government of independent African states came close to failure. However, Ben Bella's emotional speech calling for a unified African support for liberation movements buried the strong differences that characterized the debate on African unity. But it does not do justice to the founding fathers to assert that they established the OAU for the sole purpose of fighting colonialism. If this view is accepted then the collapse of the OAU must be expected as soon as Namibia is liberated and apartheid defeated in the Republic of South Africa.

Decolonization and racialism have always been a major concern of Pan-Africanism. But the founding of the OAU was 'a compromise, which is usually how large groups of states set up international organizations' (Wallerstein, 1967: 66). There was a definite feeling among African leaders in 1963 that the OAU would 'promote unity [of purpose] and solidarity of African States' (Cowan, 1968: 156). Furthermore, there were many African heads of state and government who wanted a single continental body to put to an end the existence of opposing blocs (Zartman, 1966: 34–5). Those concerned with the rights of individual states saw in the OAU the best organ for establishing 'legitimacy among members' (Thompson and Bissell, 1972: 22). In addition to legitimization of the nation-state, the OAU was expected 'to partly increase the bargaining power of African states in vital economic, financial and commercial areas' (Ndongko, 1982: 3–4). Thus the OAU meant different things to the thirty-one heads of state and government who founded it (Marasinghe, 1982: 1–14). The OAU Charter was designed to cater for most of these diverse views and, as a result, reflected the politics of compromise (Elias, 1965: 245; Nyangira, 1980: 8).

## Principles and aims of the OAU

The preamble of the OAU Charter outlines the principles and aims of the OAU, while Article III of the Charter enumerates these principles. The founding fathers are said to have devoted almost half of their time to discussing the preamble (Elias, 1965: 246; Cervenka, 1969: 30). This was because of their desire to accommodate most of the divergent views prevailing in Addis Ababa in order to enable unanimous agreement.

The preamble consists of twelve paragraphs, five of which deal with fundamental human rights such as the inalienable right of all peoples to self-determination, the recognition of the historical demands by African peoples to freedom, equality, justice and human dignity and the acceptance of the United Nations Declaration of Human Rights as forming the basis for international peace, without which neither international nor inter-African co-operation would be possible. Four paragraphs were devoted to control and consolidation of African resources 'for the total advancement of our peoples'. The final three paragraphs cover all forms of inter-African unity. It is interesting to note that mention of colonialism, which it has been said motivated the founding of the OAU, is made in only one paragraph (seven), which contains a general discussion of the right of all African states to independence, sovereignty and territorial integrity. In the minds of African leaders the elimination of colonialism was associated with peace and security.

Article III of the Charter declares that member states resolve to respect the sovereign equality of all states, agree not to interfere in the internal affairs of other states, and honour each state's sovereignty and territorial integrity. These three principles form the basis of the legitimacy of the state. The fourth principle, which provides for the peaceful settlement of disputes by negotiation, mediation, conciliation or arbitration, must be read as a rejoinder to the first three. A commitment to 'a policy of non-alignment with regard to all blocs' is a device for protecting the state and the continent against extra-continental super-power domination. Another principle established in Article III denounced 'political assassination as well as subversive activities on the part of neighbouring states or any other state', and was designed to promote the policy of good neighbourliness, since there had been suspicion among many West African states that Ghana had engaged in subversive activities against neighbouring states. The most important principle to note is the pre-eminence of the nation-state.

The aims of the OAU, outlined in Article II of the Charter, reflect the organization's principles. The primary aim is 'the unity and solidarity of African States' (to be realized by co-operation in the fields of politics, diplomacy and defence), commitment to national sovereignty, territorial integrity and independence, and determination to eradicate 'all forms of colonialism from Africa'. Economic goals include the promotion of inter-African functional co-operation in the fields of education, health-care, science, technology, transport, communications and the economy in general.

# The OAU and international politics

International political objectives of the OAU can be discussed under two sub-headings – intra-continental politics by which is meant inter-state interactions among African states and extra-continental policies which refers to interactions between Africa and the wider international community (Saenz, 1970: 206–11).

At independence African states had to develop norms and procedures for inter-state conduct. They also had to face inter-state problems generated by statehood. One such problem was the number and size of the newly independent states. They were many and small and their boundaries were of colonial origin. Politically and militarily they were weak and very susceptible to external interference. Modiebo Keita observed in 1961 that 'the African countries can never achieve full independence as long as they remain small and each concentrates on itself alone' (Modiebo Keita, 1961: 435–6). President Julius Nyerere warned that the 'security' of Africa's 'freedom' and 'real economic prosperity' could not be achieved until 'the present multitude of small states are replaced by one internationally sovereign authority' (Nyerere, 1968: 195).

The OAU is the African body responsible for seeking this larger unity of African states. Its existence provides hope for a future union government. More importantly, the OAU Charter incorporates the idea of unity of purpose and solidarity. This aspect of unity has been exampled in the more or less unanimous resolve to help liberate the whole continent from colonialism and the solidarity that African states have shown with colonial peoples and victims of apartheid in South Africa.

The OAU serves as the channel for inter-African relations. It provides a framework for problem-solving (Zartman, 1967). It has already been noted that one of the main fears of African leaders was a further balkanization of the continent. The OAU has and continues to act as a stabilizing institution by resisting attempts to redraw African boundaries. The resolution of the 1964 Cairo assembly of heads of state and government on African boundaries gave legality and legitimacy to the existing borders (Cukwurah, 1973, 176–206). Furthermore, it has been the policy of the OAU members states not to recognize secessionist movements. President Milton Obote recently invoked the 1964 resolution in response to the crisis caused in the OAU by the admission of the Western Sahara as the fiftieth member of the OAU. *(Weekly Review*

(Nairobi) 30 April, 1982). It has been said that the OAU 'represented a practical response to the balkanised conditions of Africa at the end of its colonial experience, when the leaders of independent governments inherited many sensitive border problems' (Legum *et al,* 1979: 36).

The principle of non-interference in the internal affairs of member states has largely been observed and this has helped to minimize conflicts among African states. Of course, the adherence to the principle can be blamed for the OAU's inability to deal with such murderous régimes as Idi Amin's Uganda, Bokassa's Central Africa Empire and Micombero's Burundi (Nyangira, 1980: 13–14), but such restraints have enhanced continental peace. From the perspective of inter-African politics, the OAU promotes 'normalization of relations' among African states (Mathew, 1977: 3–8).

The OAU has also attempted to internalize inter-state conflicts in Africa by establishing and seeking to implement the principle of peaceful resolution of disputes on the basis of African solutions for African problems. The procedure for the settlement of inter-African disputes is set down in Articles III and XIX of the Charter and in the 1964 OAU protocol on mediation, conciliation and arbitration. Although Article III lists negotiations as one of the methods for the resolution of inter-state conflict, negotiation is left out in Article XIX of the Charter and in the operational protocol. Therefore conflict resolution through negotiation remains only a principle of the OAU.

## Peace settlements of disputes and national sovereignty

Article XIX of the OAU Charter, which established the commission on mediation, conciliation and arbitration, commits 'Member states . . . to settle all disputes among themselves by peaceful means'. The Article, therefore, 'establishes a legal obligation binding all member states to settle their dusputes peacefully' (Cervenka, 1969: 85).

Both Article XIX of the OAU Charter and the protocol on the commission of mediation, conciliation and arbitration offer the member states three alternative methods for peaceful settlement of disputes – mediation, conciliation and arbitration. Only the last method involves legal obligations. Conciliation entails the clarification of issues and endeavours to bring about agreement between the parties by mutual consent. Terms proposed to the parties by the conciliation commission are nothing more than recommendations for the parties' consideration. Conciliation therefore does not impinge on national sovereignty, as its recommendations are not obligatory. Surprisingly African states have not resorted much to this procedure. However, the commission set up to deal with border problems between Ethiopia and Sudan and between Ethiopia and Kenya operate on the basis of conciliation.

The arbitration tribunal is a court. It bases its conclusions on the rule of international law and its conclusions are legally binding on the parties, but the consent of the parties is required before a dispute can be put to arbitration. Arbitration touches on national sovereignty because its decisions are, in theory, legally enforceable. In reality, however, the effectiveness of arbitration is compromised by the absence of a powerful agency to ensure compliance with the tribunal's decisions. African states have not often gone to arbitration. Two points may explain this reluctance. First, national sovereignty and honour might be compromised, especially in a situation where one of the disputants is designated to enforce the tribunal's decision. Under international law states can use force to ensure compliance with international obligations on their own behalf. The second explanation seems to rest in the fear that arbitration might require the use of non-African institutions which might apply non-African standards. The evolution of and the apparent adherence to the principle that 'disputes between Africans should be settled by Africans alone' illustrate this point. Conflicting parties have, therefore, been more willing to seek the good office of the OAU in efforts to settle their differences, than to make use of such institutions as the UN.

The method most resorted to is mediation. Under Article XXI of the protocol the role of the mediation commission is 'confined to reconciling the views and claims of the parties' in dispute. The commission's written proposals to the disputants become protocol only after both parties have accepted them. The sovereignty and honour of the nation-state is further protected by the confidentiality of the proceedings and the advisory character of the mediator's proposals. Thus African states have found it the more acceptable procedure.

Since the founding of the OAU, African states have resorted to mediation whenever disputes have arisen among them. In October 1963 when fighting broke out between Morocco and Algeria over a territorial dispute, the OAU offered to mediate. Emperor Haile Selassie and President Modiebo Keita acted on behalf of the OAU. During the Congo crisis in October–November 1964 the OAU appointed an *ad hoc* committee under Jomo Kenyatta to try to find a peaceful solution to the problem. During the second half of the 1960s the OAU mediators contained the conflict between Ethiopia and Kenya on the one hand and Somalia on the other. In 1966 President Hamani Diori of Niger mediated a border dispute between Chad and Sudan. More recently, the OAU under the chairmanship of President Daniel Arap Moi of Kenya attempted to mediate a peaceful resolution of the Western Sahara conflict and the civil war in Chad.

Some of these mediation efforts have succeeded while others have failed. Mediation between Ethiopia and Somalia did not prevent an all-out war between the two OAU member states in 1978. While the OAU succeeded in resolving the 1972 Tanzania–Uganda conflict, it failed to prevent them from going to war in 1978. The OAU's attempts at mediation failed during the Nigerian civil war. But these failures underline the position of the OAU as a political actor in inter-African affairs and reflect its structural weakness.

Although the OAU renounced the use of force in the settlement of disputes, it resolved to use force when necessary to promote decolonization and to dislodge apartheid in South Africa. Through the OAU's liberation committee and liberation fund, member states joined hands with liberation fighters by providing financial, moral and diplomatic support. The Front Line states acted on behalf of the OAU by providing military bases for liberation fighters in Southern Africa. They were also active in handling liberation discussions with non-continental powers, especially in the discussions that preceded the independence of Zimbabwe and in the delicate negotiations on Namibia's independence. Finally, the OAU successfully removed South Africa from all African international organizations in an effort to force the apartheid regime to reform itself by granting the African majority their political, legal and social rights.

## The OAU and extra-continental politics

Another dimension of the political role of the OAU relates to the co-ordination of a collective foreign policy. At the founding of the organization, member states resolved that, in addition to supporting intra-continental liberation movements, they would also undertake diplomatic action to persuade the international community to isolate colonial powers and South Africa. Thus since 1963 the OAU member states have made concerted efforts to ostracize South Africa. Within three months of the summit meeting, a delegation of the OAU foreign ministers went to the UN to persuade non-African governments to break diplomatic ties with, and impose sanctions on, Portugal, which was still then a colonial power, and South Africa. While this approach did not work with Portugal, the OAU has scored significant diplomatic successes against South Africa.

In 1963 alone two UN Security Council special meetings were held to discuss the demand of African states that South Africa and Portugal be expelled from the UN because of their attitudes to decolonization and to racial equality. In August 1963 the UN Security Council passed a resolution calling on UN member states to halt the sale of military material to South Africa and in December 1963 the Security Council passed another resolution widening the scope of international embargos against South Africa. In May 1964 a UN expert group on South Africa recommended economic sanctions against South Africa. Although economic and military sanctions have not been successful against South Africa, their imposition by an international organization attests to the OAU's role as the co-ordinator of African diplomacy and foreign policy.

More importantly, while a collective African attempt to bar South Africa from the UN has not been successful, African states have succeeded in removing South Africa from the UN Economic Commission for Africa and from the Commission for Technical Co-operation in Africa. South African ships and aircraft have been banned from African ports and airfields. It has been forced to withdraw from UNESCO, the International Labour Organization (ILO), the World Health Organization (WHO), the Food and Agriculture Organization (FAO) and from the International Olympic Games. Although this apparent diplomatic isolation is not the decisive factor, it has a bearing on the current willingness of South Africa to discuss Namibia's independence.

## The OAU and non-alignment

The policy of non-alignment is embodied in Article III (section 7) of the OAU Charter. This section commits African states to the policy of non-alignment with regard to the great powers. Non-alignment is a foreign policy orientation in which states refrain from committing their military forces in a conflict between two antagonistic alliances. It is a relatively recent development and although it has received political acceptance it has yet to be tested under international law in a real war situation. Thus, unlike neutrality which has been legally recognized since 1815, non-alignment has not been accorded legal status.

Non-alignment seeks to achieve several aims. Firstly, it seeks to promote world peace by preventing the intrusion of superpower politics into areas outside the traditional 'spheres of influence' of the USA and the Soviet Union. Secondly, non-aligned states have, themselves, great interests of self-preservation in the policy. This is why Nkrumah appealed to the African states to be non-aligned for he realized that the security of African nation-states and of the continent as a whole would be jeopardized if Africans allowed superpowers to establish bases on African soil. Thirdly, by making a collective stand on external affairs, the non-aligned states enhance their international power and prestige. It has been said that non-alignment is 'a manifestation of Africanism' and 'is closely related to African nationalism and Pan-Africanism and the fear of neo-colonialism and balkanization' (McKay, 1966: 16). Furthermore, in joining together with other non-aligned states outside Africa, African states are able to achieve a collective strength which can be used to promote common political and economic interests (Holsti, 1967: 104–5; Burton, 1967: 265; Hadsel, 1970: 434; Emerson, 1970).

## The OAU and African economic development

Economic conditions in Africa at the time of independence left much to be desired. Writing in 1963 Tom Mboya observed that 'In the colonial era, Africa was stamped as a producer of raw materials, and after independence, one of our immediate tasks is to transform Africa into manufacturing and producing countries . . . Africa cannot continue to trade with other nations without trying to put herself in a position to compete effectively with the highly industrialized world today' (Mboya, 1963: 183).

In 1958 the UN had established the Economic Commission for Africa (ECA) whose purpose was to co-ordinate international economic and technical assistance to stimulate viable economic and social development in Africa. By 1963 the ECA had done a lot of work in collecting and analyzing data, but the application of research findings had yet to be effected. Between 1963 and 1964 African states in the UN pressured the organization to move beyond paper work. In 1963 the ECA established the African Institute for Economic Development and Planning (IDEP) in Dakar. Its function was to provide technical training for government officials, to conduct research on factors impeding economic development of African states with a view to suggesting practical ways of overcoming them and to provide 'advisory services on economic development' (Akpan, 1976: 122). In 1964 the ECA established the African Development Bank (ADB) in Abidjan in order to promote the economic development of African states. Since then the ADB has established three affiliate financial institutions – the International Finance Corporation Investment and Development Fund (1972), the African Development Fund (1973) and the Special Relief Fund 1976). These institutions are designed to co-ordinate and distribute both African and international resources for the economic and social development of African states. Since the mid-1960s, the OAU and the ECA have collaborated in their search for ways and means of promoting African development (Andimicael, 1976; Akpan, 1976; 122–4; Cervenka, 1977: 177–80).

Although the African states recognized the valuable role the UN, through the ECA, could play in encouraging development in Africa, the founding fathers of the OAU felt that their own organization would do more in helping African states overcome economic underdevelopment (Magee, 1970: 7; EL-Ayouty, 1975: 214–20). Article XX of the OAU Charter created five specialized commissions with the aim of promoting and co-ordinating inter-African economic and social development. The five commissions have now been merged into two – the Economic and Social Commission and the Educational, Scientific, Cultural and Health Commission.

The Economic and Social Commission underlined the importance that the OAU member states attached to co-operative development efforts. Functionally, the commission aims at studying the problems relating to the economic and social development of African states. The commission was, and still is, expected to create a free trade area among African states, to establish a common external tariff for Africa's exports and a common fund for raw material price stabilization and to promote inter-African trade. Its other areas of activities include the restructuring of Africa's international trade by setting up an African payment and clearing union and by establishing an African monetary zone. The commission also has responsibility for harmonizing current and future development plans in Africa and for promoting integrated inter-African transport and communication systems (Andimicael, 1975: 218).

Successive summit meetings of the OAU have restated the need for a co-ordinated African economic policy and for the unification of African economies. These have culminated in the Lagos Plan of Action, issued in April 1980, and in the Preferential Trade Area for Eastern and Southern Africa, created in Lusaka in 1981. These are both joint OAU–ECA plans for enhancing inter-African trade and promoting both continental and regional integration.

African states today, as in 1963, believe that political co-operation through the OAU is best for development efforts (Legum et al, 1979: 37). Today, as in 1963, the OAU represents Africa's determination to attain peace and security, freedom and justice, economic and social development 'through common efforts among African states'

(Andimicael, 1975: 9). The OAU is expected, as in the field of politics, to provide the basis for African co-operation in order to promote the economic and social development of the continent. (Emerson, 1970: 7). Obviously the OAU has been assigned a very difficult task. We may ask how successful has it been in accomplishing those tasks?

Both political stability and economic development need an authoritative agency, equipped with all the necessary legal means, including the use of legitimate force, to mediate, arbitrate and control conflicting interests within the society. The OAU lacks that quality. It is a voluntary association whose authority lies in moral suasion and consensus of opinion. The member states have yet to recognize that the benefits to be derived from inter-African integration should outweigh their determination to preserve the individual sovereignty of each state. The African states have refused to allow themselves to be superceded by a higher and stronger authority capable of implementing the objectives they set for themselves in 1963.

First, the OAU represents Africans' desire to 'speak with a single voice'. However, as before 1963, Africa continues to be divided by ideological and personality differences and by the pursuit of conflicting national interests (Adelman, 1980: 9). This fact is underlined by the division that arose over the questions of the Western Sahara and of dialogue with the apartheid regime of South Africa (Matthew, 1977: 313–4; Cervenka, 1974: 337).

Second, the OAU commits African states to complete the decolonization of the continent. However, efforts have been borne largely by nationalists. African states have often been divided over the question of collective military action against colonial regimes and white supremacy. Even on the issue of material support, where there is a general consensus, very few African states co-operate and contribute to the liberation fund.

Third, the OAU has not been able to maintain inter-African peace. For example, when the OAU failed to mediate the territorial dispute between Tanzania and Uganda, Nyerere reacted by calling the OAU 'a trade-union of tyrants' adding that 'When African nations find themselves incapable of collectively punishing a single country, then each country must look after itself' (Adelman, 1980: 9). More recently, Nyerere's sentiment was echoed by the Chadian government, which was disillusioned by the OAU's first ever attempt at inter-African peace-keeping, a programme destined to fail from the start. The OAU has also been spurned by the Western Sahara Liberation Front (POLISARIO) which discarded the OAU plan for an internationally supervised referendum in the disputed area.

Fourth, after nineteen years inter-African functional integration remains unrealized. Finally, the OAU has not preserved Africa as a non-aligned continent. More and more of its members have become entangled with the super powers contrary to the policy of non-alignment. The Soviets are today in Ethiopia after having been expelled from Somalia. In the latter they have been replaced by the Americans who have also gained 'access to military facilities' in Kenya, Egypt, Sudan and

Morocco. Egypt, Somalia and Sudan have even gone to the extent of holding joint military exercises with the United States on African soil. Nyerere has aptly observed that Africa is daily 'humiliated by outside powers. . . . Our interests are ignored, our opinions brushed aside, and warnings disregarded. And this happens because the African states are disunited – for no other reason than that'. It would therefore seem that for the OAU to be able to perform its functions fully and effectively it will have to be transformed from a functional organization to a political authority enjoying the sort of powers which other supra-national authorities enjoy.

# References

ADELMAN, KENNETH (1980) *African realities.* New York.

ANDIMICAEL, B (1970) *The OAU and the UN: relations between the Organisation of African Unity and the United Nations,* Africana Publishing Co., New York.

AKPAN, MOSES E (1976) *African goals and diplomatic strategies in the United Nations,* North Quincy, Mass.

CERVENKA, ZDENEK (1969) *The Organisation of African Unity and its Charter,* Frederick A Praeger, New York.

CERVENKA, ZDENEK (1974) Major policy shifts in the Organisation of African Unity. In K. Ingham (ed) *Foreign Relations of African States,* Butterworths, London.

CERVENKA, ZDENEK (1977) *The unfinished quest for African unity,* Uppsala.

COWAN, C (1968) *The dilemnas of African independence,* New York.

CUKWURAH, A O OYE (1973) The Organisation of African Unity and African territorial and boundary problems, *Indian Journal of International Law,* **XIII.**

DIVINE, A ROBERT (1967) *Second chance: the triumph of internationalism in America during World War II,* Aithineum, New York.

ELIAS, T O (1965) The charter of the OAU, *American Journal of International Law,* **LIX** (2).

EL-AYOUTY, A (1975) *The Organisation of African Unity after ten years,* Frederick A Praeger, New York.

EMERSON, RUPERT (1970) Pan-Africanism. In Irving Leonard Markoritz (ed) *African Politics and society,* The Free Press, New York.

HAAS, ERNST B (1964) *Beyond the nation state: functionalism and international integration,* Stanford Univ. Press, Stanford.

HAAS, ERNST B (1967) The uniting of Europe and the uniting of Latin America, *Journal of Common Market Studies,* **5.**

HAAS, ERNST B (1968) Technocracy, pluralism and the new Europe. In Joseph Nye Jr. (ed) *International regionalism,* Little, Brown & Company, Boston.

HAAS, ERNST B and SCHMITTER, PHILIPPE (1966) Economies and differential patterns of political integration; projections about unity in Latin America. In Amtai Etzioni (ed) *International political communities,* Garden City, New York.

HAAS, MICHAEL (1974) International integration. In Michael Haas (ed) *International system: a behavioural approach,* New York.

HOFMEIER, ROLF (1982) Regional economic integration: the rise and fall of the East African Community. A paper presented at the International Conference on the Law and Economy in Africa. University of Ife, Nigeria, 15-20 February, 1982.

HOLWORTH, M (1961) Soviet writings on Africa, *Contact.*

ITALIAANDER, ROLF (1961) *The new leaders of Africa* (trans J. McGovern) Prentice-Hall, London.

JACQUES, FREYMOND (1965) The European views of neutralism, *Annals of the American Academy of Politics and Social Services,* **CCCLXII.**

KEITA, MODIEBO (1961) The Foreign Policy of Mali, *International Affairs* **XXXVII (IV)** (October).

KUEHL, WARREN F (1969) *Seeking world order* Vanderbilt Univ Press, Vanderbilt.

LEGUM, C (1965) *Pan Africanism: A Short Political Guide,* Frederick A Praeger New York.

LEGUM, C (1979) Communal Conflicts and International Intervention in Africa. In Colin Legum *et al. Africa in the 1980s: a continent in crisis.* New York.

LIEBER, ROBERT (1973) *Theory of world politics,* George Allen and Unwin, London.

MACHYO B S (1968) Pan Africanism. Makerere Adult Studies Centre, Pamphlet No 3.

MATTHEW K (1977) The Organisation of African Unity, *India Quarterly* **XXX.**

MAKONNEN, R (1973) *Pan-Africanism from within,* Oxford Univ. Press Nairobi.

MAZRUI, A A (1976) *African international relations and diplomacy of dependence and change.* London.

MAZRUI, A A (1977) The legacy of Kwame Nkrumah in Africa: from Kenyatta and Mboya to Nyerere and Amin, *Historical Association of Kenya Annual Conference Papers.*

MAZRUI A A (1965) Pan-Africanism in the Cold War, *East African Institute of Social Research Conference Paper.*

MARASINGHE, M L (1982) A review of regional economic integration in African and other developing countries. A paper presented at the International Conference on the Law and Economy in Africa. University of Ife, Nigeria.

McKAY, V (1966) International conflict patterns. In V. McKay (ed) *African Diplomacy,* Frederick A Praeger New York.

NKRUMAH, KWAME (1961) *I speak of freedom,* Heinemann, London.

NKRUMAH, KWAME (1963) *Africa must unite.* London.

NKRUMAH, KWAME (1966) *Challenge of the Congo.* London.

NDONGKO, WILFRED A (1982) Regional economic integration of French-speaking countries in Africa: the case of the West African Economic Community. A paper presented at the International Conference on the Law and Economy in Africa, University of Ife, Nigeria.

NYANGIRA, N (1980) Regional organisation and integration: the case of the OAU. Seminar paper given in the History Department of the University of Nairobi.

ODEDE, S O (1969) *Nigeria in the Context of Pan Africanism, 1945–1966.* Mimeograph, Nairobi.

OAU (1963) *Proceedings of the Summit Conference.* Mimeo, Addis Ababa.

PADMORE, G (1956) *Pan-Africanism or communism: the coming struggle for Africa.* London.

ROTHCHILD, DONALD (1968) Experiment in functional integration, *African Review* **XIII.**

SAENZ, PAUL (1970) The OAU in the subordinate African regional system. *African Studies Review,* **VIII** (2).

SHEPPERSON, G (1960) Notes on Negro American influence on the emergence of African nationalism, *Journal of African History,* **I** (2).

THIAM, DOUDOU (1965) *The foreign policy of African states.* New York.

THOMPSON, V B (1969) *Africa and unity: the evolution of Pan-Africanism,* Longman, London.

WADE, E C G and PHILLIPS, G G (1977) *Constitutional and administrative law* (7th edn), Longman, London.

WOLFERS, MICHAEL (1976) *Politics in the Organisation of African Unity.* New York.

WALLERSTEIN, IMMANUEL (1967) *Africa, the politics of unity,* New York.

WORONOFF, J (1970) *Organisation of African Unity,* Meruchen NJ.

YOUNG, ORAN (1972) The Actors in World Politics. In James Rosenau, Vincent Davis and Maurice A East (eds), *The analysis of international politics,* New York.

ZARTMAN, WILLIAM (1966) *International Relations in the new Africa* Prentice Hall, New Jersey.

ZARTMAN, WILLIAM (1967) Africa as a subordinate state system in international relations. *International Organisation,* **XXI.**

# 6    African states and the superpowers

## Introduction

The relations between African states and the superpowers – the Soviet Union and the United States – like all other inter-state relations are guided in a large measure by considerations of national interest. In these relations, individual African states and the superpowers pursue their own interests. An African state judges 'the policies of the superpowers by the degree to which they advance or harm its own perceived interests' (Legum, 1978: 7). The same can also be said to be true of the superpowers. However, the superpowers, because of their dominant power position vis-a-vis the African states, are better placed to extract greater advantages from their relationships with the African states.

The Soviet Union and the United States are called superpowers because they are sufficiently powerful to maintain international peace and order anywhere in the world (Fox, 1980: 417–8; Fox, 1944). They are said to have special responsibilities. Hedley Bull has observed 'To say that a state is a great power is to say not merely that it is a member of the club of powers that are in the front rank in terms of military strength, but also that it is regarded by other members of the society of states as having special rights and duties' (Bull, 1980: 437). Even though Hedley Bull uses 'great power' instead of superpower, he agrees with Fox that only the Soviet Union and the United States are 'fully capable of playing the role of great power' (Bull, 1980: 438–9).

After the Second World War the Soviet Union and the United States emerged as the most powerful states in the world. Their rights and duties came to be recognized not only in their respective spheres of influences – the Soviet Union in Eastern Europe and the United States in the Western Hemisphere – but also beyond these geopolitical areas. They have sufficient military and economic strength to make their influence felt throughout the world. What takes place in the international system must therefore, take into consideration their existence and attitudes.

As world powers, the Soviet Union and the United States seek to spread their influence beyond their borders. This explains, in part, their involvement in Africa. Of the two, the latest arrival on the African political scene is the Soviet Union. Before the 1960s, its only attempt to gain a foothold on the continent occurred immediately after the Second World War, when it demanded the right to control Libya and Massawa in Eritrea. Both Libya and Massawa have strategic locations; Libya on the Mediterranean and Massawa on the Red Sea (St. John, 1982: 131). Although this early Soviet interest was thwarted, the United States had more success. After the end of the war the United States entered into a military agreement with Liberia by which the United States promised to come to the defence of Liberia in case of an external attack. In 1949 it signed a military and nuclear co-operation pact with South Africa and by the middle of the 1950s it had acquired military bases in Libya and Morocco and had built military communication facilities in Ethiopia (Orwa, 1983a).

In spite of these early involvements, the deepening of interactions and exchanges – diplomatic, cultural and commercial – between African states and the superpowers is a consequence of the collapse of colonialism throughout the continent. Once the former colonies attained statehood and sovereignty, they could enter into diplomatic relations with any other sovereign states of their choice. Hence, nearly all independent African states, have diplomatic relations with the superpowers. But why?

## U.S. and Soviet economic assistance

African governments have duties and responsibilities. It is the duty of African states to ensure the security and well-being of their citizens and this requires the utilization of a large quantity of resources. Because of economic underdevelopment it is unlikely that individual African states left to themselves are able to meet their obligations. This is, at least, the attitude of the ruling elite and it has been encouraged by policy-makers from the developed countries (Orwa, 1983a). The Soviet Union and the United States have surplus resources of capital, technology and skilled manpower all of which are in short supply in Africa. Aid is a particularly valuable source of capital in view of the high interest rates charged by commercial banks. Loans from government assisted institutions such as the World Bank, its affiliate the International Development Agency (IDA) and the International Monetary Fund (IMF) carry a low rate of interest and allow for a longer period of grace for repayment than commercial banks allow. Aid is also given in the form of grants and gifts. In addition to aid, African states also expect to find markets for their products in the Soviet Union and in the United States in order to reduce their traditional dependence on their former colonial masters.

Both the Soviet Union and the United States have been responsive to requests for economic assistance. Between 1955 and 1976 the Soviet Union provided $3 259 million in economic aid to African countries. $1 019 of this amount was provided between 1970 and 1976. The communist states of Eastern Europe supplied a further $2 162 million worth of aid between 1955 and 1976. Until 1973 the single largest recipient of bilateral Soviet economic aid was Egypt which received more than 40 per cent of total Soviet aid (Albright, 1980: 17; Nielson, 1969: 206–7).

The United States began to give economic assistance to independent African states soon after the end of the Second World War. The early beneficiaries were those countries which had oil or had given the United States military bases or facilities. Between 1953 and 1961 the United

States gave $1 105.8 million in aid. Grants amounted to $740.2 million while loans totalled $365.6 million. Morocco received $290.3 million, Tunisia $241 million, Libya $173.1 million, Ethiopia $84.4 million and Liberia $29.2 million. For the eight year period 1962–1970 United States bilateral economic assistance to Africa totalled $3 297.9 million (Orwa, 1983a). Since 1970 these figures have jumped tremendously, especially when aid given through multilateral bodies and UN agencies is included (USAID, 1978). Most of the money has gone into the development of essential infrastructure such as roads, railways, electric power plants, hospitals and schools.

In the area of trade the Soviet Union initially offered better concessionary trade terms (Albright, 1980: 16). However, African states were slow in taking advantage of trade opportunities in the Soviet Union. In 1966 the most important of the Soviet Union's trading partners were Ghana, Algeria, Malagasy Republic, Guinea, Morocco and Somalia. (Ghana, Algeria, Guinea and Morocco belonged to the radical Casablanca Group). But only Ghana had a significant export trade with the Soviet Union (Nielsen, 1969: 210–4).

The ideology of individual African states and the reaction of the West to that ideology have in the past determined whether or not states need to establish close links with the Soviet bloc. Radical regimes, out of favour with the West and especially the United States, have looked to the Soviet Union for aid, military support and protection against their western detractors. Egypt, until the death of Nasser in 1972 depended on the Soviet Union for its military needs. Nasser's radical Pan-Arab ideology and his opposition to Israel were viewed with great suspicion by the West. During the first half of the 1960s Ghana and Guinea were likewise closer to the Soviet Union because the West ostracized them for pursuing socialist policies. Between 1969 and 1977 the military government in Sudan was close to the Soviet Union. Since 1969 Libya has purchased a large quantity of Soviet made military hardware. In the fiscal year 1974–5 alone Libyan arms purchases from the Soviet Union were estimated to be worth $1 billion (St John, 1982: 134). Ethiopia is said to have received a similar amount of arms during the 1977–8 Ogaden war (Albright, 1980: 3). Since winning their independence both Mozambique and Angola have signed friendship treaties with the Soviet Union, and during the civil war in Angola in 1975–6 the Angolan government relied heavily on Soviet military aid. During the Nigerian civil war of 1967–70 the Soviet Union supplied the Federal government with the weapons that helped to ensure the defeat of the secessionists. Finally, Soviet military aid helped to keep Idi Amin in power in Uganda. In total it is estimated that Soviet military assistance to Africa between 1955 and 1976 was worth $5 472 million (Albright, 1980: 17).

It should be said, however, that many of the alliances between Africa and the Soviet Union have been marriages of convenience. Somalia remained close to the Soviet Union between 1969 and 1977 as long as the Soviets supported Somalia's design for a 'Greater Somalia'. When the Soviets changed their minds in 1977 they were unceremoniously kicked out of Somalia. Egypt treated the Soviet Union in the same way after it opposed Egyptian plans for the 1973 Arab–Israeli war. The Soviets suffered a similar fate in Ghana and Guinea in the late 1960s.

Soviet relations with the Sudan provide a case-study of the highly volatile nature of many of the alliances between African states and the Soviet Union. In the mid-1960s a military coup brought a group of army officers led by General Mahgub to power in Sudan. In 1968 Mahgub's government signed an agreement with the Soviet Union. The agreement involved a major arms transaction, the cost of which was put at $50 million. The overthrow of Mahgub's government by General Gaafa Numeiry in 1969 initially did not threaten the growing Russo–Sudanese relations, as the visit by General Numeiry to Moscow in November 1969 attested. The visit, coming six months after he took over the government, suggested the importance the new government put on Russo-Sudanese co-operation. The following year Sudan received the first consignment of Soviet arms, including fighter planes. But this apparent friendship was not to last.

In 1972 a group of Sudanese communists attempted to overthrow Numeiry's government. Numeiry accused the Soviet Union of involvement in the coup attempt and relations began to cool down, with Numeiry turning increasingly toward the West for both military and economic assistance. The years 1976–7 marked the end of the courtship between Sudan and the Soviet Union. The first major incident occurred in 1976 when a Libyan backed group attempted to overthrow Numeiry's government. Libya, which receives most of its military material from the Soviet Union, was thought to be working on behalf of the latter. Numeiry's suspicion of the Soviet Union was increased in 1977. First came the Shaba invasion by Zairian rebels operating from Angola. Then Ethiopia and Somalia went to war and the Soviet Union which had been a close ally of Somalia since 1969, shifted its support to Ethiopia. Finally, came the Egypto–Libyan border war. Numeiry subsequently became convinced that Sudan's neighbours, Ethiopia and Libya, were intent on invading Sudan with the help of the Soviet Union. Therefore on 12 May, 1977 Numeiry cancelled the 1968 agreement, expelled Soviet military experts and ordered the reduction of the Soviet embassy staff.

The volatility of relations between African states and the Soviet Union can be explained by a number of factors. First, although many African leaders profess to be socialists, their version of socialism differs from that of the Soviet Union (Padmore, 1956; Mboya, 1963, 1970; Senghor, 1964; Nyerere, 1969). Secondly, cultural, economic and political ties between the Soviet Union and Africa are very recent. African political and economic institutions and organizations are based on Western models. Official languages in Africa are, with a few exceptions, European ones, inherited from the former colonial powers. As a result most African leaders are opposed to communism as a system of socio-economic and political organization. The democracies of Western Europe and Northern America, with whom African states have close historical links, are viewed more sympathetically and with greater understanding by African states. Finally, and perhaps more importantly, because the currency of the Soviet Union is non-convertible the Soviet Union has been unable to penetrate Africa commercially (Albright, 1980: 16).

The West has been more successful in the commercial penetration of Africa. As a result Africa has become integrated into and dependent upon the capitalist world economy. The West, and especially the United States, have sought to protect their interests in Africa through the provision of extensive military aid. Ethiopia received $170 million in military assistance and $240 million in economic aid from the United States between 1953 and 1970 (Abir, 1972: 9). This aid and assistance was given to help the decaying Ethiopian monarchy maintain internal stability, to ward off the threat from Somalia and as payment for permission to install a military communications system in Ethiopia. After Ethiopia moved to the Soviet bloc the United States provided Somalia with military assistance which in 1980 was worth $44 million. Immediately after the Camp David Accord the United States extended $2.5 billion in economic and military aid to its new ally, Egypt. In 1976 Kenya received twelve F5 fighter planes at a cost of $76 million. In 1982 Kenya was expected to receive $53 million in military assistance and $42 million in economic aid. Military assistance to Kenya, Sudan and Liberia increased by 178 per cent from 1981 to 1982 (Coker, 1982: 124).

All African states except Egypt and South Africa have to import all their military requirements. Defence comes high on the list of spending priorities in most African states; per capita military expenditure on the continent varies from $9.4 in Tanzania to $163 in Libya, and in 1981 total military expenditure by African states was between $14 billion and $16 billion (*Africa Now,* July 1982, *Africa Guide,* 1981). The amount involved is staggering, especially in the continent which has twenty-one of the world's poorest countries, the highest mortality and illiteracy rates and the lowest GNP per capita in the world. Clearly African states cannot afford to buy such large amounts of arms and so they depend on credits and grants as well as direct supplies of arms from the superpowers.

The superpowers also provide African states with technical personnel, training facilities and logistical support. During the 1975–6 civil war in Angola the Soviet Union trained Angolan forces, provided them with logistical support and transported the Cuban shock troops who were to play a vital part in the MPLA victory over its rivals and the South African invasion forces (Legum, 1978: 41; Connel-Smith, 1979; Aluko, 1981). Soviet personnel and Cuban troops helped Ethiopia to defend its territorial integrity against Somalia's invasion in 1977–8.

In the past the superpowers have maintained unpopular governments in power. For example, in 1964 the United States, in conjunction with Belgium, sent paratroopers against nationalist forces in Stanleyville and helped to organize mercenaries in the Congo in order to maintain in power a government which seemed on the point of collapse in the face of a popular uprising (Kamitatu, 1971). In 1977–8 the United States, Belgium and France all intervened in Zaire to protect the Mobutu regime.

African states may find that the cost of foreign aid outweighs the perceived benefits. The inability of African countries to develop viable domestic sources of investment capital, the more or less permanent state of economic underdevelopment and the demand for social justice perpetuate the ruling classes' reliance on external sources for assistance, since such assistance helps them to allay domestic unrest. However, this dependence on foreign aid makes African ruling elites vulnerable to blackmail by the aid donors. More often than not the donor reaps greater advantages than the recipient. For example, in return for economic and military grants and favourable trade and loan terms the recipient country might be forced to compromise vital national interests, such as allowing the establishment of foreign military bases on its soil and the virtual surrender of the right to pursue independent domestic and foreign policies.

## Superpower interests in Africa

The superpowers, when they offer to help African states, do so in pursuit of their own interests. Since 1960 the United States, Belgium and France have maintained Mobutu in power but not because Mobutu is the most able political figure in Zairian politics. They are aware that his regime is an authoritarian one, in addition to being one of the most corrupt governments in Africa. However, Mobutu is a dependable anti-Communist and pro-West leader in Africa and he can be counted on as a protector of massive Western investment in Zaire. This is particularly important when it is recognized that between 1960 and 1978 Belgian direct investment in Zaire increased from $3.5 billion to $6 billion, that of the United States from $20 million to $800 million, that of Britain from slightly less than $20 million to between $600 million and $800 million while French direct investment stood at $20 million in 1978 (Connel-Smith, 1979; Orwa, 1983b).

The superpowers come to the assistance of African states in order to further their own interests. Foreign aid can be used as a device for gaining influence. As J. Berliner correctly observes: 'The economic aid appears to be a prominent component of a broader foreign policy designed to expand influence in the underdeveloped countries' (Berliner, 1958: 17). Economic aid and its military counterpart is usually 'structured to influence the role played by the state in the economic development of underdeveloped societies in Africa, Asia and Latin America' (Wood, 1980: 1), in such a manner that the development is conditioned by developments in the dominant centre (Europe, North America and the Soviet Union). The consequences are almost always to the disadvantage of the underdeveloped societies (Coker, 1980: 127; Wood, 1980: 2).

The Soviet Union and the United States give aid in order to win client states. In Africa, where the departure of the colonialists left a power vacuum, both the Soviet Union and the United States have sought politically and ideologically friendly countries to provide diplomatic support in international forums. Africa is used by the superpowers to consolidate their positions of global power (Payne, 1978; Aluko, 1981; Ogunbadejo, 1980).

The Soviet Union and the United States both also have economic and strategic interests in Africa. The Soviet Union is less fortunate in the economic sphere but it is planning to expand its import–export trade with the continent (Kanet, 1975; Payne, 1978). The Soviet Union is also interested in having access to Africa's strategic minerals from which a combined European and American dominance has traditionally excluded it. W. Scott Thompson suggests that if the Soviet Union was able to get a foothold in certain African countries, such as Zaire and South Africa, which are rich in strategic minerals it would probably attempt to secure the minerals exclusively for itself. He adds that the presence of the Soviet Union in the countries within the proximity of the sea lanes would enable the Soviet Union to prevent the supply of minerals from Africa and oil from the Middle East from reaching the West (Thompson, 1980: 217). This policy is known as the 'strategy of denial' (Janke, 1978; Kudryavtsev, 1976). It is a strategy which attempts to deny Western Europe, Japan and, to a limited extent, the United States strategic minerals, thus disrupting their domestic economies. Although it would be extremely difficult to implement the 'strategy of denial' the possibility of it represents a real threat to the United States and its allies.

The United States has very good reason to be concerned by the prospect of possible Soviet dominance in Africa. Since the end of the Second World War the United States has assumed the responsibility of protecting Western Europe from the communist threat. This involves protection of interests in Europe and in any other part of the world where Western European interests may be at risk. Africa is one such area where European interests are deeply entrenched. Foreign direct capital investment in Africa is predominantly Western European. Much of Africa's foreign debt comes from North America and Western Europe (World Bank, 1980, 1981). The West is also dependent on Africa's mineral resources. Since the closure of the Suez Canal, the flow of oil to Western Europe through the sea lanes surrounding the African continent has arisen by 3 600 per cent (Thompson, 1980; Thompson and Silvers, 1975). Finally, it is estimated that 87 per cent of Africa's international trade is with Western Europe and North America (Cervenka, 1974).

In spite of its self-sufficiency in most strategic minerals the United States still depends on Africa for the supply of some of the most critical industrial minerals. Cobalt: the United States imports 99 per cent of its requirements from Zaire. 50 per cent of world cobalt production comes from Zaire and 10 per cent from Zambia. Industrial diamonds: over 50 per cent of world production comes from Zaire. Manganese: the United States needs to import 98 per cent of its requirements and the bulk of this is supplied by Gabon and South Africa. Platinum: the United States needs to import 88 per cent of its requirements and 55 per cent of this comes from South Africa. Chromium: the United States needs to import

91 per cent of its requirements, and South Africa and Zimbabwe are its leading suppliers. Petroleum: 40 per cent of United States imports are from African states (Algeria, Angola, Congo, Libya and Nigeria) and Nigeria alone accounts for 20 per cent of United States petroleum imports. In 1979 petroleum imports were mainly responsible for the United States trading deficit of $11 000 million with Africa (Oude and Clough, 1980: 82–4; Shafer, 1982: 154–7; Adelman, 1980: 17–19). Finally, it is interesting to note that if the Soviet Union were able to control South Africa it would be able to exercise a near monopoly on gold, platinum, vanadium, manganese and chrome (Janke, 1978: 5).

Africa's geographical location also makes it of great strategic importance. It is surrounded by major international waterways all of which are crucial to the global strategic and military calculations of the superpowers. Both the Mediterranean and the Red Seas are not only critical for the defence of Western Europe and the Middle East but they are also crucial to the protection of oil fields in the Middle East and in the Persian Gulf. As a result, North Africa and the Horn of Africa occupy an important place in the calculations of American and Soviet strategists.

The situation is similar in West, East and Southern Africa. West Africa, with its North Atlantic coastline, figures in the calculations of military strategy. A large fleet of Soviet fishing vessels are found in this area. The Soviet Union needs naval facilities along the West African coast in order to protect Soviet fishing vessels and to counter the presence of NATO warships in the North Atlantic. Secondly, long range Soviet surveillance aircraft taking off from points along the West African coast are able to reach the Caribbean. With air facilities in West Africa, the Soviet Union might not have to depend on Cuban facilities in order to monitor United States naval activities in the Caribbean.

The strategic importance of Southern Africa lies in the fact that the Cape is the gateway for naval ships and submarines moving between the South Atlantic and the Indian Oceans. The Cape is, therefore, important for the United States South Atlantic fleet. The Cape is also on shipping routes to both Australia and Brazil from which the bulk of the United States South Atlantic fleet operates. The presence of the Soviet Union in the Cape would threaten the movement of United States warships as the Soviet Union would be able to monitor the movement of the South Atlantic fleet. Finally, Soviet submarines, if deployed in the area, would interfere with shipping around the Cape to Western Europe and Japan.

Most of the largest ocean-going tankers, which transport most of the oil from the Middle East and the Persian Gulf, pass through the Indian Ocean. It is, therefore, a major commercial shipping area for Western Europe and Japan. The Indian Ocean is also close enough to the Soviet Union for missiles, such as the Trident missiles, to reach the Soviet Union. It has irregular underwater currents with thermal layers good for baffling listening devices. This makes the Indian Ocean 'an attractive place' to hide SLBM submarines (Adelman, 1980: 19–20; Kemp, 1978; Schwab, 1978: 6–19).

Until the 1970s, the West held key strategic points in and around the continent. France had, and continues to have, military bases in Djibouti in the Horn of Africa, Mayotte and Comoro in the Indian Ocean and on several islands in the Mozambiquean straits. In West Africa France has bases in Ivory Coast, Gabon and Senegal. Britain signed a secret military treaty with Kenya in 1963. Britain also had a naval base on Diego Garcia on the Indian Ocean but after 1968 it was leased to the United States. The Portuguese controlled both Angola and Mozambique. South Africa falls informally within the NATO defence system.

Early Soviet attempts to acquire naval and air bases in Africa failed. Egypt, the Soviet Union's closest ally in Africa until 1972, never granted the Soviet Union any bases in the country. Soviet efforts to acquire naval and air bases in Ghana and Guinea during the 1960s also failed. For Nasser, Nkrumah and Sékou Touré were the leading advocates of the policy of 'no external military bases in Africa'. This, however, did not discourage the Soviet Union to get a foothold in Africa.

The Soviet Union's response was partly in reaction to developments in the Indian Ocean. The United States took advantage of early European dominance in East Africa and the Horn of Africa to establish a military presence in the Indian Ocean. In addition, the United States positioned its Trident and Poseidon inter-continental ballistic missiles in the Indian Ocean. The number of its naval ships and submarines also increased in the Ocean. Given the proximity of the Indian Ocean to the Soviet Union, its role as the main waterway between European and Asian parts of the Soviet Union and the growing number of Soviet fishing vessels in the Indian Ocean, the Soviet Union perceived a threat to its vital national interests. In response, the Soviet Union increased the number and the presence of its warships. This development, in turn, created the need for communication routes, both naval and air. Communication lines became necessary through the Red Sea to the Indian sub-continent in order to guarantee ship and aircraft movement. Hence naval and air facilities had to be found along the African coast (Legum, 1979: 50).

The Soviet Union obtained its first major military base in Africa in the early 1970s when Somalia granted the Soviet Union a naval and air base at Berbera, which was held by the Soviet Union until 1977. Berbera provided a strategic base at the centre of East Africa and the Horn of Africa. The importance of Berbera was elevated by the Soviet acquisition of another coastal base, in Aden, South Yemen. The two bases are directly opposite and overlook each other with the Port of Aden lying at the point where the Indian Ocean and the Red Sea meet. The presence of the Soviet Union in Ethiopia may also be explained by the desire to gain access to Massawa on the Red Sea. The Soviet Union has also entered into treaties of friendship and co-operation with Angola and Mozambique. Although it has not been granted any military bases in Libya the Soviet Union has maintained close relationships with Libya since 1969. Finally, Soviet interest in Guinea has not waned in spite of the rebuffs in the 1960s.

Since 1977 the United States has moved to forge military alliances with African states within the Horn of Africa. It has replaced the Soviet

Union at the Berbera base. In 1980 it obtained military and naval facilities at Mombasa in Kenya, and signed a military agreement with Sudan. In the south the United States has increased contacts at an official level with the South African authorities (Coker, 1982; Crocker, 1981; El-Khawas and Cohen, 1976). Egyptian military bases, like those of Sudan, Kenya and Somalia, are available for use by the recently created Rapid Deployment Force (RDF) attached to the Fifth Fleet. The objective of the RDF is to move quickly and intervene anywhere in the Middle East, the Persian Gulf or Africa if internal or regional developments appear to threaten vested western interests. The most important of the American military bases is on Diego Garcia, and the African bases are seen as supplementary to it (Lewis, 1976; Makinda, 1982).

# Conclusions: the paradoxes of inter-state relations

A number of conclusions can be reached from the preceding discussion. First, African states are involved with the superpowers in pursuit of what African policy-makers view as vital national interests. Second, American and Soviet policy-makers, like their African counterparts, are neither moralists nor idealists. They are realists guided in these interactions by considerations of national interest. As a result Africa and the superpowers may be said to be interdependent.

However, the nature of the relationship between the superpowers and Africa is also a cause of conflict both within Africa itself and also between Africa and the superpowers. In this chapter we have seen how, for example, superpower involvement in the Horn of Africa has evolved and how it has changed the nature of the conflict within that region. The conflicts between the superpowers in the Indian Ocean and the Horn of Africa together with the superpowers deeper involvement in some strategically placed African states are seen as a threat to the security of the whole of the African continent. African states, fearing that they are being sucked into the nuclear zone, have called for the demilitarization of the Indian Ocean. In their relationships with the superpowers African states have, therefore, to make a complicated calculation, balancing the advantages of economic and military aid against the disadvantages of a possible loss of national sovereignty and the risk of being drawn into a global conflict between the superpowers.

# References

ABIR, MORDECHAI (1972) The contentious Horn of Africa. *Conflict Studies* (24).

ADELMAN, KENNETH L (1980) *African Realities,* Crane, Russak and Co., New York.

ALBRIGHT, DAVID E (1980) 'Introduction' to *Africa and international communism,* Macmillan Press, London.

ALUKO, OLAJIDO (1981) African responses to external intervention in Africa since Angola, *African Affairs,* **LXXX** (319).

BERLINER, J S (1958) *Soviet economic aid: the new aid and trade policy in underdeveloped countries,* Praeger, New York.

BULL, HEDLEY (1980) The great irresponsible? The United States, the Soviet Union and world order, *International Journal,* **XXXV** (3).

CATTAGNO, A A (1972) The Horn of Africa and the competition for power. In A J Scottrell and R N Burrell (eds). *The Indian Ocean: Its political and military importance,* Praeger, New York.

CERVENKA, ZDENEK (1974) Major policy shifts in the Organisation of African Unity. In K Ingham (ed) *Foreign relations of African states,* Butterworths, London.

COKER, CHRISTOPHER (1982) Reagan and Africa, *The World Today,* **XXXVII.**

CONNEL-SMITH, GORDON (1979) Castro's Cuba in world affairs 1959-1979. *The World Today* **XXVI.**

COPSON, RAYMOND W (1977) East Africa and the Indian Ocean: a 'Zone of Peace', *African Affairs,* **LXXVII,** (304).

CROCKER, CHESTER (1980-1) South Africa: a strategy for change, *Foreign Affairs,* **LIX,** (2).

EL-KHAWAS, MOHAMED AND COHEN, BARRY (eds) (1976) *The Kissinger study of Southern Africa,* Lawrence Hill and Co., Westport, Conn.

FOX, WILLIAM (1980) The superpowers then and now, *International Journal,* **XXXV,** (3).

FOX, WILLIAM (1944) *The Superpowers: The United States, Britain and the Soviet Union,* Harcourt Brace, New York.

GROESBECK, MAJOR WESLEY A (1976) To a US Naval Strategy in the Indian Ocean, *Military Review* (June).

HARTMANN, JEANETTE (1981) Tanzania and the Indian Ocean, *Journal of East African Development and Research,* **II.**

JANKE, PETER (1978) The Soviet strategy of mineral denial, *Soviet Analyst* **VII** (22).

KAMITATU, CLEOPHAS (1971) *La grande mystification du Congo-Kinshasa: les crimes de Mobutu,* Francois Maspero, Paris.

KANET, ROGER E (1975) The Soviet Union and the Developing Countries, *The World Today* XXXI, (8).

KEMP, GEOFFREY (1978) US strategic interests and military options in sub-Saharan Africa. In Jennifer Seymour Whitaker (ed) *Africa and the United States: vital interests,* New York Univ. Press, New York.

KUDRYAVTSER, I (1976) Plot Against Africa, *Current digest of Soviet Press* **XXVIII.**

LEGUM, COLIN (1979) Communal conflicts and international intervention in Africa. In Colin Legum, et al *Africa in the 1980s: a continent in crisis,* McGraw-Hill Book Co., New York.

LEGUM, COLIN (1980) African outlooks towards the USSR. In David E Albright (ed) *Africa and international communism,* Africana Publishing Co., London.

LEGUM, COLIN (1980) Crisis in the Horn of Africa: the international dimensions of the Somali-Ethiopian conflict. In Colin Legum (ed) *Africa Contemporary Record, 1978–79,* Africana Publishing Co., London.

LEGUM, COLIN and LEES, BOB (1978) *Conflict in the Horn of Africa,* Africana Publishing Co., London.

LEWIS, WILLIAM H (1976) How a defence planner looks at Africa. In Helen Kitchen (ed) *Africa: from mystery to maze,* Vol. XI. Lexington Books, Lexington, Mass.

MAKINDA, SAMUEL M (1982) Conflict and the superpowers in the Horn of Africa, *Third World Quarterly,* **IV** (1).

MARCUM, JOHN A (1976) Southern Africa after the collapse of Portuguese rule. In Helen Kitchen (ed) *Africa: from mystery to maze,* Vol. XI. Lexington Books, Lexington, Mass.

MBOYA, TOM (1963) *Freedom and after,* Andre Deutsch, London.

MBOYA, TOM (1972) *Challenge of Nationhood,* Andre Deutsch, London.

MORISON, DAVID L (1980) Soviet and Chinese policies in Africa in 1978. In Colin Legum (ed) *Africa Contemporary Record, 1978–79,* Africana Publishing Co., London.

NIELSON, WELDAMAR (1969) *The Great Powers and Africa,* Pall Mall Press, London.

NITZE, PAUL H. (1980) Strategy in the decade of the 1980s, *Foreign Affairs,* **LXXIX** (4).

NYERERE, JULIUS (1968) *Ujamaa: essays on socialism,* Oxford Univ. Press, Oxford.

OGUNBADEJO, OYE (1980) Soviet policies in Africa, *African Affairs,* **LXXIX.**

ORWA, D KATETE (1983a) The evolution of US economic policy for Africa, 1950–1960, *Hekima,* **I** (3).

ORWA, D KATETE (1983b) *The Congo betrayal: The UN-US and Lumumba,* Kenya Literature Bureau, Nairobi.

OUDE, BRUCE and CLOUGH, MICHAEL (1980) The United States' Year in Africa. In Colin Legum et al *Africa in the 1980s: a continent in crisis,* McGraw-Hill Book Co., New York.

PADMORE, GEORGE (1956) *Pan-Africanism or communism: the coming struggle for Africa,* Dobson, London.

PAYNE, RICHARD J (1978) The Soviet/Cuban factor in the United States policy in Southern Africa, *The World Today,* **XXV.**

SCHWAB, PETER (1978) Cold War in the Horn of Africa, *African Affairs* **LXXVII** (306).

SENGHOR, LEOPOLD SEDAR (1966) *On African socialism,* Frederick A Praeger, New York.

SHAFER, MICHAEL (1982) Mineral myth, *Foreign Policy* (47).

STEVENS, CHRISTOPHER (1976) *The Soviet Union and Black Africa,* Holmes and Miers, New York.

ST JOHN, RONALD BRUCE (1982) The Soviet penetration of Libya, *The World Today,* **XXXVII.**

THOMPSON, W SCOTT (1980) African-American nexus in Soviet strategy. In David E Albright (ed) *Africa and international communism,* Andre Deutsch, London.

THOMPSON, W SCOTT and SILVER, BRETT (1979) South Africa in Soviet strategy. In Chester Crocker and Richard Bissel (eds) *South Africa in the 1980s,* Westview Press, Boulder, Colo.

USAID (1979). *US overseas loans and grants and assistance from international organisations, 1945-1978.* Government Printer, Washington D.C.

WOOD, ROBERT E (1980) Foreign aid and the capitalist state in underdeveloped countries, *Politics and Society* **XX** (1).

WORLD BANK (1980) *Annual report.* Washington, D.C.

WORLD BANK (1981) *Accelerated development in Sub-Saharan Africa: an agenda for action.* Washington, D.C.

# 7 Africa and the former colonial powers

Relations between newly independent African states and the former European colonial powers have remained remarkably close and generally cordial despite the conflicts – some of which were violent – that accompanied the process of transition to independence. Both the closeness and cordiality have proved resilient so that although, with independence, most African states have greatly diversified their external relations as a matter of deliberate policy, their links with their former colonial overlords continue to reflect a 'special' character.

These relations are particularly sharply articulated at the politico-diplomatic and broad economic levels. They manifest themselves politically in various ways: for example, in the form of regular processes of diplomatic consultation; in the existence of more or less formal institutions that facilitate multilateral diplomatic exchanges, such as the (British) Commonwealth of Nations and the Francophone grouping of states; and, in some instances, in formal agreements whereby the former colonial powers are granted exclusive concessions in Africa. An example of the latter are military agreements such as those between Britain and Nigeria (1960–1962) and between France and several of its former West and Equatorial African territories including the Ivory Coast and Gabon, wherein the former colonial power was granted military bases or permission to station its military personnel on the territory of the given African state. Similarly, agreements have often been agreed between African states and their respective former colonizers in respect of such matters as cultural exchanges, immigration and citizenship. For example, in former British East Africa thousands of resident 'Asians' and whites were, by mutual agreement, permitted to retain their British nationality at independence in the early 1960s despite the fact that there was little expectation that they would eventually actually all emigrate to England. Indeed, when in 1972 the former Ugandan ruler Idi Amin forcibly expelled from Uganda all 'Asians' – British citizens and non-citizens alike – the expressed wish of the British government was for the hapless 'Asians' to be resettled elsewhere and not in Britain itself. However, the original agreement on citizenship between Britain and the East African states might be taken as symbolizing the spirit of mutual understanding and solidarity between that country and its former colonies.

These relations show considerable variation in that some African states are more heavily dependent on their former colonial overlords than others. There is little doubt that in general former French colonies in Africa have remained linked to France by tighter institutional arrangements than those states previously ruled by other European powers. Not only did most of the former French colonies conclude direct military-security agreements with France as part of the independence bargain, but they also at the same time accepted economic, technical and financial arrangements that formally institutionalized French control of their development as newly independent states. An example of this is the French government's decision at independence to create two multilateral central banks as a mechanism to group and control the economies of its former colonies in West and Equatorial Africa. These banks – the Banque Centrale des Etats de l'Afrique de l'ouest (grouping Senegal, Ivory Coast, Upper Volta, Dahomey (now Benin), Niger and Mauritania), and the Banque Centrale des Etats de l'Afrique Equatoriale et du Cameroun, later renamed the Banque des Etats de l'Afrique Centrale (grouping Congo, Gabon, the Central African Republic, Chad and Cameroun) – created a uniform currency tied to the French franc and were placed under the overall control of the French treasury. Operationally, whilst the two central banks regulate the currencies of the countries mentioned above, each of the countries maintains a separate account with the French treasury for purposes of its international financial transactions, including the financing of its trade. The overall effect of this system is to give France a large hand in determining the monetary, financial and general economic policies and relations of the African states grouped under these banks (Nkrumah, 1965: Ch. 16).

These institutional ties are only a part of the intricate web that binds many French-speaking African states to the former 'mother country'. Equally notable are the ties based on French private investment, aid, trade and technical and cultural exchanges involving the former colonies. It is significant that these ties and relations have survived the political transition in France from the rule of the Gaullists and their conservative allies to that of the French Socialists under Francois Mitterrand.

The question which immediately arises is why the newly independent African states have preserved something of the umbilical cord tying them to the former 'mother countries'. One line of argument would suggest that this relationship is in some way linked to the process of socialization of the African elite during colonialism. This thesis has been propounded and elaborated by, among others, Tevoedjre (1965) and Singer (1972). Its central claim is that leaders formally and informally schooled under colonialism evince a 'love-hate' attitude towards their former colonizers. Besides, institutional networks, either inherited from the colonial era or established as part of the independence bargain, tend to persist over time despite an official rhetoric that may suggest their illegitimacy. Bureaucratic mechanisms and procedures based on British and French models persist long after independence has been gained. Armies continue to be commanded by officers trained at Sandhurst or St Cyr. The former colonizer's language, being itself very often an indispensable tool of international or even internal communication – including communications among African states – must be fostered rather than discarded. This same language, among other things, enormously facilitates communications with the former colonial power, and this has many political, diplomatic and, more broadly, cultural implications. Hence, high-level manpower tends to be trained in the former metropolis because educational systems are at least comparable and sometimes identical. As the students imbibe a British, French, Portuguese or Spanish education they naturally must to some considerable degree reflect the cultural attributes or modes of thought of the society within which they obtain this education. This is attributable to the process of acculturation which occurs precisely because an educational system, like any societal enterprise, is itself a profoundly cultural phenomenon that is specific to a given nation.

It should, therefore, come as no surprise that an African leader such as former Senegalese President, Leopold Sedar Senghor, should seem more 'French' than the French themselves and remain so despite his championing of the seemingly anti-European doctrine of Negritude. Senghor declared that 'France remains our major partner, not only in cultural affairs, but in economic matters as well,' thereby echoing the position taken by Ivory Coast's President, Felix Houphouet-Boigny, in 1957, three years before his country's independence, when he asserted that, 'France's enlightened self-interest, but specially its keen sense of humanity, have led it to seek with us, actively and sincerely, the achievement of a new community' (Tunteng, 1976: 217–8). Negritude or no Negritude, Senghor has called for the establishment of a unity between Europe and Africa and, beyond that, a federation of the cultures of the various peoples of the world (Markovitz, 1969).

A slightly different hypothesis to explain the close relations between the new African states and their former colonial masters hinges on the dynamics of social class. The argument revolves around the variables of social structure, different class interests and class conflicts that characterize Africa's post-independence societies. More specifically, it is asserted that African states have emerged into independence under the leadership of a petit bourgeoisie whose interests were the same as those of the metropolitan bourgeoisie. This African elite was an essentially dependent, or 'comprador', bourgeoisie whose interests coincided with those of the imperialist bourgeoisie. Its interests were as a result at odds with those of the common people in the former colonies. In order to maintain its power and privileges this bourgeoisie resorted to a variety of tactics including the use of coercion and often a political ploy best defined as a form of 'defensive radicalism'. According to Professor Claude Ake, who has done much to popularize this concept, 'defensive radicalism' is essentially a mystification whereby African rulers seek to blunt the revolutionary pressures of the masses by the adoption of a radical rhetoric which masks the true intent and orientation of the bourgeoisie. As Ake puts it:

The assumption of a radical posture and the use of this posture [is] a cover for containing revolutionary pressures and for maintaining the status quo. There is no African country which is not involved in defensive radicalism which is manifested in the following tendencies:
a) the increasingly radical rhetoric against imperialism even among the most reactionary African leaderships such as those of the Ivory Coast, Senegal and Liberia;

   b) the radical rhetoric of the Organisation of African Unity against
      the continued colonization of Southern Africa;
   c) the verbal commitment of most African leaders to some form of
      socialism and the rejection of capitalism;
   d) the policy statements used to justify extensions of public
      ownership;
   e) the militant attack on inequality in some African countries;
   f) the policy statements explaining the curbs on the operations of
      foreign capital;
   g) the show of being friendly with socialist countries such as Cuba
      (Ake, 1978: 92).

Ake makes two further observations. Firstly, he concedes that there are a
few African states where the leadership takes its radical rhetoric seriously
and where steps have been taken to achieve socialism. However, he states
that even in these cases – e.g. Angola and Guinea-Bissau – the
radicalism of the official rhetoric tends to outstrip the radicalism of
official practice. Secondly, he argues that defensive radicalism is a
product of the objective situation in which post-colonial Africa finds
itself. Leaders must show that they are on the side of the masses if they
are to stay in power. To achieve a semblance of credibility leaders must,
however, translate some of their rhetoric into action. Hence, Ake
concludes, defensive radicalism can be a progressive phenomenon (Ake,
1978: 92–4.)
   However, the main contention advanced by Ake and other writers is
that African elites constitute local allies of imperialism and of the
international bourgeoisie that runs the global capitalist economy. The
implication of this perspective in respect of external relations is evident
enough. It is that the closeness of relations between African states on the
one hand and their former capitalist colonizers on the other is to be
explained at the level of the social dynamics that have their roots in the
global capitalist system. Chinweizu puts it more pungently:

   Since these leaders were concerned with acquiring for their class the
   privileges within colonial society, the freedom they sought had to be
   freedom within the imperial system, not outside it: not individual
   freedom within African societies liberated from the empires. They
   desired British or French liberties, not African liberty, and not
   African liberties . . .
   Encouraged in their march to freedom by the colonial authorities,
   they had use for neither national liberation nor a populist nationalism
   . . . While campaigning for civil liberties, they were granted local
   power as well and were persuaded that such local autonomy amounted
   to sovereignty. But in reality it was not sovereignty, since the states
   over which they were granted supervisory powers were still parts of the
   European imperial structure (Chinweizu, 1975: 98–9).

This interpretation, which hinges on a class analysis, clearly reflects a
considerable part of the reality of internal politics and international

relationships of African states. It puts in perspective and clearer relief much of internal and external social and political relationships which would otherwise be most difficult to comprehend. Yet it is by no means a definitive analysis.

In the first place, it tends to minimize the variations among African regimes, lumping them in the same basket and thereby producing an image of the African state that, for a number of countries, is in fact a caricature. The difficulties we encounter in understanding Africa's internal political processes and international relations arise from these very variations. Whilst generalization is necessary and important, as without it there can be no theory or meaningful analysis, its utility is reduced to the extent that numerous facts either do not fit or appear forced into the particular conceptual framework. Thus Algeria's degree of dependence on France can hardly be said to be the same as that of Gabon, even though both countries are former French colonies and both are oil-rich states. Similarly, Kenya and Tanzania, both members of the Commonwealth and former British colonies, have historically pursued significantly different policies towards the former colonial power. Several other examples could be cited. The point is that foreign policies or external relations are not to be considered as automatic, unilinear, or invariant by-products of the single variable of social class.

Second, if class if invoked as the sole explanatory category for state behaviour, it becomes difficult to explain why some states take their 'defensive radicalism' more seriously than others (as Ake himself admits they do) even though all African states are under the rule of the petit bourgeoisie. Variability in internal and external policies in Africa is not only an observable phenomenon but it is also one that requires modes of analysis that are more nuanced than is sometimes found in the literature.

Third, relations between African states and the former colonial powers reflect calculations of national interests on the part of both sets of parties to these relations. Having been colonized by one or the other of the European powers, it is hardly surprising that African states seek to exploit to their advantage any possibilities derived from the circumstances yielded to them as part of the legacy of history. It is the possibilities inherent in the previously imposed colonial relations which African states seek to translate into co-operative arrangements. It is naturally expected that these arrangements take full account of the new circumstances of independence and that they should be carried out on the basis of equality and mutual benefit. African governments reason that their success in achieving their objectives is more probable within the framework of these co-operative relations given the historical associations involved. Obviously, success will depend on other factors as well: one must also consider such factors as the nature of the independence bargain or the structure of relations between the given African state and its former colonizer; the degree of 'acculturation' of the particular African ruling elite; the nature of the issues that form the subject of such co-operation and the bargaining capabilities and advantages of the African states, individually or collectively, vis-a-vis their former colonizers. It is quite apparent, for example, that African states have, due to their unity of approach as part of the African–Caribbean–Pacific (ACP) grouping of states, been more successful in winning trade and aid concessions from the European Economic Community (EEC) than would have otherwise been possible. Under the Lome II Convention, which came into effect on 1 April, 1980 and which for a period of five years was to govern economic relations between the ACP and EEC states, forty-three African states, together with their twenty non-African partners in the ACP group, not only enjoy relatively free access to the EEC market, they also benefit from such arrangements as:

i) guarantees, under the so-called STABEX system, of compensation for losses of export earnings whenever the prices of certain of their commodities fall below an agreed 'floor' level.

ii) Provision of multilateral financial and technical assistance mainly under the auspices of the European Development Fund (EDF) and the European Investment Bank (EIB). An amount of 5.2 billion European Units of Account was to be set aside as the EDF resources to be used to finance development projects in ACP countries during the five year lifespan of the convention. The EIB also provides financial assistance for approved projects, particularly in the fields of industrial, agro-industrial, mining and infrastructural development.

Yet the ACP–EEC relationship is not without some serious problems and difficulties. In particular the expected gains for the ACP states have not been as large as expected so that dissatisfaction has been rampant within ACP ranks. This dissatisfaction relates to all the main issues of trade, aid, investment and technology transfers, and the pace of industrialization in the ACP states. This mood of disappointment and unhappiness is well reflected in a 1981 statement of Mr. T. Okelo-Odongo, Secretary-General of the ACP. Speaking before the German Institute of International Relations in Bonn, he observed:

In the trade area, for example, despite declaration by the European Communities to allow free access of ACP goods to European markets, no significant advance was made. In fact, the figures showed that during Lome I the balance of trade turned against the ACP states. In 1974, the ACP–EEC trade balance was about ECU* 4000 million in favour of the ACP states. In 1975 this figure moved down to ECU 593 million in favour of the ACP states. In 1976 the figure moved still further down and by 1978 the position was reversed, so that the trade figures showed a balance of ECU 800 million in favour of the EEC states.
The ACP share of the European Community market, excluding exports of petroleum products, was 4.6 per cent in 1975. In 1979, at the end of Lome I, the ACP share of the Community market had been reduced to 4.1 per cent.

* European Currency Unit.

Foodstuffs, raw materials and energy generating products accounted for 70 per cent of ACP exports. The share of manufactured goods increased from 3.3 per cent in 1975 to 4.6 per cent in 1978. This meant that the colonial pattern of trade, in which the ACP countries exported low-priced primary commodities and the European countries exported highly-priced manufactured goods seemed to have been kept intact during the lifetime of Lome I.

The effect of safeguard measures in Lome I was not encouraging. In 1980, Mauritius, an ACP state, was forced to reduce its exports of textiles to the Community by 50 per cent, despite the fact that ACP exports of textiles to the Community markets constituted only 1.8 per cent of Community imports while South-East Asia, for example, exported up to 25 per cent.

Industrial co-operation was no more encouraging. Despite the fact that some instruments for promoting industrial development in the ACP states were established, their impact was not felt. The resources allocated for industrial development in ACP states were most inadequate. This contributed to the lack of significant progress in this field.

At the expiry of Lome I one third of funds made available to ACP states had not been committed and only 43 per cent had been disbursed. (Okelo-Odongo, 1981).

Apart from the ACP–EEC framework African states have also sought assistance from their former colonial overlords within such institutions as the Commonwealth and the less formalized Francophone and Lusophone-African communities. Various mechanisms or understandings are incorporated in these institutions for purposes of promoting co-operation. The Commonwealth, for example, has established the Commonwealth Fund for Technical Co-operation to which all members are invited to make contributions and whose resources are used to facilitate the development process in the poorer member nations.

**TABLE 7.1 Africa's trade: former colonial powers as trading partners, 1976**

Note (1) Figures in parenthesis refer to former colonial power's comparative position in respect to trade with the African country concerned.
(2) N/A = Not available or not applicable.
(3) Figures not available or not applicable to Botswana, Cape Verde, Djibouti, Egypt, Equatorial Guinea, Ethiopia, Lesotho.

| Country | Former colonial power | % Exports to former colonial power | % Imports from former colonial power |
|---------|----------------------|-----------------------------------|-------------------------------------|
| Algeria | France | 13.8 (3) | 27.1 (1) |
| Angola | Portugal | 26.9 (2) | 22.0 (1) |
| Benin | France | 24.3 (1) | 28.6 (1) |
| Burundi | Belgium | 5.3 (4) | 18.1 (1) |

| Country | Former colonial power | % Exports to former colonial power | % Imports from former colonial power |
|---|---|---|---|
| Cameroun | France | 25.4 (1) | 44.3 (1) |
| Central Afr. Republic | France | 44.4 (1) | 46.2 (1) |
| Chad | France | 3.3 (4) | 36.6 (1) |
| Comoros | France | N/A | N/A |
| Congo | France | 15.9 (3) | 47.1 (1) |
| Gabon | France | 42.1 (1) | 68.8 (1) |
| Gambia | United K'dom | 29.8 (1) | 24.5 (1) |
| Ghana | United K'dom | 15.3 (1) | 14.7 (2) |
| Guinea | France | 13.0 (2) (1977) | 20.0 (1) (1977) |
| Guinea-Bissau | Portugal | 38.0 (1) (1977) | 27.0 (1) (1977) |
| Ivory Coast | France | 25.4 (1) | 38.2 (1) |
| Kenya | United K'dom | 29.1 (1) | 13.2 (2) |
| Liberia | USA* | 22.0 (1) | 31.4 (1) |
| Libya | Italy | 19.4 (3) | 25.5 (1) |
| Madagascar | France | 29.3 (1) | 40.9 (1) |
| Malawi | United K'dom | 47.3 (1) | 22.5 (2) |
| Mali | France | 30.8 (1) | 40.1 (1) |
| Mauritania | France | 11.8 (2) | 50.0 (1) |
| Mauritius | United K'dom | 69.3 (1) | 16.3 (1) |
| Morocco | France | 23.7 (1) | 29.4 (1) |
| Mozambique | Portugal | 23.8 (1) | 15.4 (2) |
| Niger | France | 63.7 (1) | 43.4 (1) |
| Nigeria | United K'dom | 10.9 (3) | 23.3 (1) |
| Rwanda | Belgium | 8.5 (1) | 19.8 (1) |
| Sao Tome and Principe | Portugal | 33.0 (2) | 61.0 (1) |
| Senegal | France | 31.5 (2) | 30.5 (1) |
| Seychelles | United K'dom | N/A | 21.0 (1) |
| Sierra Leone | United K'dom | 60.8 (1) | 21.5 (1) |
| Somalia | Italy | 6.5 (2) | 32.0 (1) |
| Sudan | United K'dom | N/A | 20.3 (1) |
| Swaziland | United K'dom | 33.0 (1) (1977) | N/A |
| Tanzania | United K'dom | 14.3 (2) | 13.4 (1) |
| Togo | France | 39.3 (1) | 33.1 (1) |
| Tunisia | France | 17.1 (2) | 32.2 (1) |
| Uganda | United K'dom | 20.5 (2) | 27.3 (1) |
| Upper Volta | France | 18.8 (2) | 44.5 (1) |
| Zaire | Belgium | 21.9 (1) | 15.4 (1) |
| Zambia | United K'dom | 13.6 (4) | N/A |
| Zimbabwe | United K'dom | 7.0 (4) (1981) | 11.0 (2) (1981) |

*Liberia, although dominated by the USA, was never formerly colonised.
Sources: *Africa Today,* London: Africa Journal Ltd., 1981, passim;
*Encyclopaedia Britannica 1982 Book of the Year,* London: Encyclopaedia Britannica, 1982 passim; Republic of Zimbabwe, *Monthly Digest of Statistics,* Harare: CSO, August 1982.

These multilateral arrangements notwithstanding, bilateral relations between individual African states and the former colonial powers still remain important features of the external relations of these states. This is best exemplified in the field of trade as Table 7.1 illustrates.

This table shows quite clearly the position of the former colonial powers as trading partners of the new African states. Of the countries listed, for twenty three, nearly half of the total, the former colonial power was the largest single market for their exports. A further nine countries looked to the former colonial power as their second largest market. As for imports, the table shows that the majority of the states — thirty five or 81 per cent of the total — drew the largest proportion of their imports from their former colonial rulers. When one considers that these figures, with a few exceptions, refer to trade in 1976 — some fifteen years after the achievement of independence by the majority of African states — the persistence of close relations between the African states and the former colonial powers is all the more remarkable. Whilst the level of export or import dependence on the former colonial power shown in the table is generally below 50 per cent the figures cited nonetheless reflect, in virtually all cases, a pattern of commercial links with a strong bias in favour of previous colonial linkages.

It should be noted that in maintaining or developing the relations discussed above African states have sought to shape or reshape relations with their former colonizers in such a way as to promote their interests. These relations have, in other words, been seen as an additional arena within which particular policy objectives can be pursued profitably. There is no doubt, for example, that African states which are members of the Commonwealth have used that arena repeatedly to urge Britain and other Commonwealth states to take more progressive positions on matters ranging from Southern Africa to other major conflict situations such as the Israeli–Arab dispute and to such major global issues as those relating to the so-called North–South Dialogue. (See, for example, the communique issued at the end of the Commonwealth Heads of Government meeting held in Melbourne, Australia in October 1981, particularly the 'Melbourne Declaration' issued by the meeting.)

Whilst it can be conceded that there are some positive aspects to the relations between African states and the former colonial powers, these have nonetheless to be seen in conjunction with the negative ones. Firstly, despite the progress made in the evolution of these relations, some fundamental problems remain unresolved. The most basic of these is structural. This refers to the fundamentally asymmetrical nature of these relations. The parties to these relations may, in terms of international law, be considered to be equal, but practice points to a real inequality. Elaborate argumentation is scarcely necessary to prove this point: African states, as suppliants, cannot, for example, dictate such matters as the volume, terms or conditions under which they receive international assistance; nor can they dictate the prices of their export commodities or of their manufactured imports from the developed countries. They are, as has been frequently stated, 'price-takers' rather than 'price-setters'. This is not to suggest that they are entirely powerless — some of the oil or mineral producers have in fact exerted considerable influence on the operation of the international economic system — but only that they are relatively or comparatively powerless. It can thus be argued that relations between African states and the former colonial powers reflect, at a sub-global level, the asymmetry that characterizes North–South relations at the global level. Yet it can also be said that the progress so far achieved in the evolution of such co-operative arrangements as those between the ACP and EEC states constitutes an important milestone towards the realization of a more equitable international socio-economic and political order.

A second major difficulty affecting relations between African states and the former colonial powers – or the 'North' generally – lies in the absence of a broad agreement on basic principles. There is no basic perspective to facilitate the resolution of problems. There is no, or at least only a tenuous, consensus so that all questions, including questions of principle, are matters for bargaining and compromise. In more specific terms, a consensus is yet to emerge in regard to, for example, how we explain the phenomenon of underdevelopment; whether the elimination of underdevelopment should constitute a priority question of contemporary international relations; how best to tackle North–South problems; and, finally, what should constitute the essential ingredients of a more civilized and just world order. These questions, not surprisingly, are at the centre of the debate concerning relations between both the African states and their former colonial overlords and, more generally, between the developing countries of the South and the privileged minority of states that constitute today's developed North.

# References

AKE, CLAUDE (1978) *Revolutionary pressures in Africa,* Zed Press, London.

CHINWEIZU (1975) *The West and the rest of us,* Vantage Books, New York.

MARKOVITZ, IRVING LOUIS (1969) *Leopold Sedar Senghor and the politics of Negritude,* Atheneum, New York.

NKRUMAH, KWAME (1965) *Neocolonialism, the last stage of imperialism,* Nelson, London.

OKELO-ODONGO, T (1981)The Lome Convention is a concrete demonstration of mutual cooperation between North and South, *The Courier* (Brussels).

SINGER, MARSHALL R (1972) *Weak states in a world of powers: the dynamics of international relationships,* The Free Press, New York.

TEVOEDJRE, ALBERT (1965) *Pan-Africanism in action: an account of the UAM,* Harvard Univ. Press, Cambridge, Mass.

TUNTENG, P KIVEN (1976) External influences and sub-imperialism in Francophone West Africa. In Peter C W Gutkind and Immannuel Wallerstein (eds) *The political economy of contemporary Africa,* Sage Publications, Beverly Hills, California.

# 8    Africa and the United Nations

Of the fifty-one founder members of the United Nations in 1945 only three – excluding the white minority-ruled Union (now Republic) of South Africa – were African. These were Egypt, Ethiopia and Liberia. Apart from the admission of Libya in 1955 the position regarding African representation remained essentially the same in the first decade of the UN's existence even though the total membership had in the meantime risen to seventy-six states. Five years later, however, African membership had risen dramatically to twenty-five in a General Assembly of one hundred. In 1980 fifty members, fully one-third of the UN's membership were African.

This rapid increase in the number of African states in the UN had a double significance. Firstly, it heralded Africa's ascendancy on to the stage of world politics from which it had been largely barred by nearly five hundred years of slavery and colonialism. In other words, it signalled the continent's new-found determination to participate fully in international relations as an actor rather than an object.

Secondly and more importantly, the increase in African representation in the General Assembly, coupled with the subsequent creation of two African (regional) non-permanent seats on the Security Council, meant that African issues and problems would henceforth receive greater international attention than hitherto had been the case. The issues of prime concern to African states were those of colonialism, in all its forms, apartheid, the cold war, great power intervention in African affairs and international economic relations and their effect on Africa's developmental prospects.

These concerns have, of course, not been exclusively African. Other Third World states have shared them. Indeed they constitute the prime focus of the Non-Aligned Movement. Yet the issues have been felt more keenly in Africa than elsewhere because Africa has suffered most from their persistence. It is in Africa that several of the most stubborn relics of colonialism remained in existence through the first three decades of the United Nations. It took protracted wars of national liberation, more or less politically backed by the UN, for independence to be gained in 1975 in Mozambique, Angola, Guinea-Bissau – all former Portuguese colonies – and in 1980 in Zimbabwe, the former British colony of Southern Rhodesia. The independence of these territories did not, however, complete the process of formal decolonization in Africa. In 1984 the UN Trust Territory of Namibia continued to be illegally occupied by South Africa despite numerous attempts, both at the UN and elsewhere, to remove this illegal control and promote the speedy independence of the territory. For seventeen years (1966–1983) African states invoked UN support and authority in an effort to terminate South African control of Namibia. Yet, despite favourable resolutions on the matter, especially Security Council Resolution No. 435 of 1978, South Africa continued its illegal occupation. It appeared in early 1984 that the South African regime would only relinquish its control under pressure from the freedom fighters of the South West African People's Organization (SWAPO), the Namibian liberation movement which the UN, at the prompting of African states, had recognized as the sole and legitimate representative of the Namibian people. SWAPO had little option but to intensify the war since South Africa was clearly committed to continuing the exploitation of the rich mineral resources of Namibia – copper, diamonds, uranium – and was, in any case, encouraged in its stubbornness by the attempt of the Reagan administration in the USA to make the independence of Namibia conditional upon the withdrawal of Cuban troops from Angola.

As for the issue of apartheid, or so-called 'separate development', it remains the official philosophy and practice of the white minority government of South Africa. Under this system the African people, who constitute over 70 per cent of the population, have no political or civil rights in 87 per cent of the country where the white minority, about 15 per cent of the population, exercises unfettered power. Under the system, the African majority can only enjoy 'political rights' and a social environment free of officially sanctioned racial discrimination in the 13 per cent of the country that consists of a patchwork of tribal reservations or tribal 'homelands'.

Although South Africa, a founder member of the UN, is independent, its apartheid system has attracted African and general international condemnation at the UN and in other fora. The struggle against apartheid has developed to the point where it virtually merges with the struggle against colonialism. Following the lead given by the OAU, the UN now recognizes the African National Congress and the Pan-Africanist Congress of South Africa as liberation movements whose struggle is not merely focused on the ending of racial discrimination in that country but also seeks to realize the full democratization of the country's political system. At the UN, the African states have been instrumental in crystallizing this perception of the struggle in South Africa as well as in seeking the isolation of that country at all levels – diplomatic, economic, military and cultural. Whilst this has not been notably successful, due to Western support of South Africa, it has nonetheless put that country on the defensive and has created an international climate supportive of, and favourable to, the struggles of the people of South Africa.

Finally, turning to Africa's position in international economic relations and to Africa's developmental performance, the outlook is bleak. In 1981 the World Bank made the following grim assessment:

The tragedy of . . . slow growth in the African setting is that incomes are so low and access to basic services is so limited. Per capita income was (US) $329 in 1979, excluding Nigeria, and $411 when Nigeria is included. Death rates are the highest in the world and life expectancy is the lowest (47 years). Fifteen to twenty per cent of the children die by their first birthday, and only 25 per cent of the population have access to safe water. Of the 30 countries classified by the United Nations Conference on Trade and Development (UNCTAD) as the poorest in the world, 20 are African (The World Bank, 1981: 3).

It is against this grim background that African governments have put economic issues to the forefront of their diplomatic activities both in the UN and in other fora. It can be said that for the bulk of African states international economic relations literally pertain to matters of life and death. Furthermore, the dismal performance of the African economies contributes in no small measure to political instability and the fragility of regimes on the continent. Having regard to these factors, the UN has been viewed by all African governments as a body which might significantly contribute to the socio-economic development of their countries.

African states' involvement in, and concern about, the issues outlined above can be understood from two further perspectives. In the first place, the objectives towards which African UN diplomacy was directed were consistent with the principles enunciated in the UN Charter itself. For example, Article I (2) proclaims as a major purpose of the UN the development of 'friendly relations among nations based on respect for the principle of equal rights and self-determination of peoples.' Chapter XI is devoted to a 'Declaration Regarding Non-Self-Governing Territories', while Chapters XII and XIII are directed to the adumbration of the principles and mechanisms to be applied towards the treatment of residents of trust territories in respect of whose governance the UN had specific legal responsibilities. Chapters IX 'International Economic and Social Co-operation' and X 'The Economic and Social Council' represent an elaboration of the broad organizational purpose stated under Article I (3), namely: 'To achieve international co-operation in solving international problems of an economic, social, cultural, or humanitarian character, and in promoting and encouraging respect for human rights and for fundamental freedoms for all without distinction as to race, sex, language, or religion.' The objectives pursued by the African states in the UN could thus be viewed as consistent with the organization's broad purposes.

A second factor to be noted with regard to the African states' involvement in the parliamentary diplomacy of the UN was the identification and formulation by these states of the tactical requirements for the effective conduct of this form of diplomacy. In order to facilitate speedy attainment of their objectives African states developed the tactic of coalition-building within the framework of the United Nations system. Initially they operated in the context of the Afro-Asian Group – an informal diplomatic forum comprising these countries' Ambassadors or Permanent Representatives at the UN. The group, essentially a forum for consultation with a view to achieving tactical and substantive consensus on issues before the UN had its origins in the Afro-Asian Conference held at Bandung, Indonesia, in April 1955. The conference drew attention to the unequal character of contemporary international relations as reflected in the persistence of colonialism and foreign economic, technological and military domination of Africa and Asia. The Afro-Asian Group merged with the broader Non-Aligned Movement which formally came into being at the Belgrade Conference of 1961. The Non-Aligned Movement embraced members of both the Afro-Asian Group and of certain European and, at a later date, South American and Caribbean countries. The movement initially focused on problems associated with the Cold War in the context of which it rejected any organic ties with either East or West, preferring, instead, to play a mediatory role between the two antagonistic camps. However, as the state of East/West relations became relaxed in accordance with the policy of detente in the 1960s and early 1970s to which the 1963 Moscow Nuclear Test Ban Treaty, the 1968 Nuclear Non-Proliferation Treaty, and the 1972 Strategic Arms Limitation Talks Agreement all bore witness, the Non-Aligned Movement began to pay more attention to problems in the economic relations between the developing and the developed countries (Mates, 1972).

The shift to problems of international economic relations was dramatized by the emergence in the UN in 1964 of the so-called Group of 77. The group, which has grown to encompass over ninety countries (although it retains its original appellation) played an important role in both the creation and the working of the UN Conference on Trade and Levelopment (UNCTAD). It has also played the leading role in the search for an international agreement on principles and mechanisms for governing a restructured New International Economic Order.

The role of African states in the UN cannot be viewed merely from the point of view of the objectives sought and the mechanisms utilized in pursuit of these goals. Account must also be taken of the underlying theoretical assumptions behind the establishment of the UN, as these assumptions more or less affect the extent to which particular objectives can be realized within the framework of the organization. Two such assumptions appear to have been uppermost in the minds of the founders of the UN. The first was that the organization, whose primary purpose was the maintenance of international peace and security, could not ignore the dimension of power and its role in international relations. The organization was not to operate as a democratic institution capable of making binding decisions on the basis of a majority vote. Instead, the decisions of the most important organ of the UN, the Security Council, would require 'the affirmative vote of nine members including the concurring votes of the permanent members'. The five permanent members of the Security Council are the USA, USSR, France, Britain and China. This 'veto' provision in the Charter gave recognition to the importance of power and military capability as the key factors in international politics. As Inis Claude has noted:

> The veto rule represents the proposition that the potential value of
> the United Nations with respect to the problems of war and peace at

the highest political level is defined and limited by the degree to which the major powers can discover a mutual interest in having it function as a stabilizing element within the context of the Cold War. Viewed in this way, the veto is not so much an obstacle to be circumvented, or a defect to be remedied, as a salutary reminder of facts that must be acknowledged and of realities that must be respected (Claude, 1964: 146).

In fact the veto provision merely symbolized the preponderant weight the great powers possessed by reason of their general level of socio-economic and technological development as well as their military capability or — as in the case of China — their readily recognized potential for achieving great power status. From this could be deduced what amounts to the unwritten operational code of the UN, namely, that whilst all member states participate in decision-making it is the great powers alone that in the end make the decisions.

Yet there is a dialectical character to the relation between the great powers and the small states. The evident predominance of the former should not be construed as implying that the latter, including the African states, wield no influence in the UN. They·do. Indeed, part of the reason why the great powers have at times sought to settle certain issues outside the UN has been that they did not wish to expose such issues to democratic discussion by the Third World states who form a majority of the UN member states. In other words, the increase in the number of non-aligned Third World states with a fairly strong sense of common purpose has rendered the UN less amenable to great power manipulation than has been the case hitherto. As Brucan has noted:

A sober evaluation of all pertinent factors will tell us that the United Nations is going through a stage marked by the adaptation of its structure and functioning to the new relationship of forces emerging in the world. The process of adaptation is pushed forward by the new historical actors, most of whom had no say in the drafting of the Charter. However, as any student of history knows, the beneficiaries of the old order will oppose change (Brucan, 1978: 116).

Apart from the power dimension, the UN system is structured and operates on the basis of functionalist or neo-functionalist assumptions. Functionalism presupposes that interstate co-operation in agreed fields of common interest not only yields results potentially beneficial to the co-operating parties, but is also likely to lead to a dimunition of state sovereignty through an almost imperceptible transference of decision-making authority in ever-widening spheres of activity to central institutions (Mitrany, 1933, 1943, and see Ch. 5 above). However, it is questionable whether the implied political impact of functional co-operation occurs with the inevitability that the above hypothesis suggests. It would seem that a more arguable hypothesis is the neo-functionalist concept advanced by Karl Deutsch which asserts that in any given region functional co-operation may lead to the emergence of 'a pluralistic security community', that is, a group of states which, precisely because they are linked together by a network of diverse transactions, have learned to conduct their relations in a manner that renders any recourse to war among them highly improbable (Deutsch, 1957; 1966).

Whilst the focus of this conception is regional there is no reason why it cannot be applied to the global level to the effect that the machinery and processes of functional co-operation in the UN system reflect the quest for a more peaceful world order. African states have a direct interest in such a world order and in the material benefits to be derived from practical co-operation within the UN system. Indeed, they and their partners in the Non-Aligned Movement have continued to expend energies in the effort to improve the structures and operational effectiveness of such UN agencies as UNCTAD, the International Monetary Fund (IMF) and the International Bank for Reconstruction and Development (IBRD). Whilst the results achieved to date have not been spectacular owing to the resistance and opposition of the developed countries for whom the achievement of the NIEO spells a diminution of their privileged status in the international economic system, there is little doubt that the pressure for fundamental change will continue to mount until justice is done to the Third World (Williams, 1981; Singham, 1977).

## Africa, the UN and the Congo crisis

Looked at politically, Africa's relations with the UN reached perhaps their most critical and intense phase during the so-called Congo Crisis of 1960–1964 which is discussed below as a case study of African attempts to use international machinery to solve an African problem.

The onset of the Congo Crisis coincided with a shift in the UN's, and especially the Secretary-General's, conception of the role of the organization in crisis situations. This new approach was encompassed under the concept of preventive diplomacy and was seen as a viable alternative to 'enforcement action' or collective military action under Security Council auspices. Preventive diplomacy was conceived as a strategy of crisis management which aimed at interposing UN military and/or political personnel between disputants with a view to preventing both the escalation of conflict and possible intervention by the superpowers. Such interposition would also allow for a 'cooling off' period and subsequent peaceful resolution of conflict. However, the central thrust of preventive diplomacy was to quarantine local conflict situations and to insulate them from superpower meddling. Such meddling, it was feared, would tend to internationalize or globalize such conflicts and this, in turn, would raise the spectre of world war (James, 1969). The intervention of a UN peace-keeping force in the Congo was intended to insulate the Congo from outside interference.

This operation, which followed the collapse of civil order and the onset of disintegration in the Congo (now Zaire) soon after the attainment of independence on 30 June, 1960, was both military and political in character. Militarily, it involved over 20 000 troops drawn from about a dozen small-to-medium powers in the UN while on the political front it entailed the introduction of UN personnel into the administrative machinery and decision-making processes of the new Congolese state.

The factors behind the collapse of civil order (manifested by the mutiny of the 25 000 strong colonially-trained and officered *Force Publique*) and the disintegration of the country (started by the secession of several regions of the country including the Katanga Province) were anchored in the country's history, strategic location and natural resources. In the first place, Belgian colonialism, imposed on the country in 1885, constituted one of the sorriest chapters in the history of colonialist plunder and exploitation in Africa. In the first twenty-three years of colonialism until 1908 the territory was ruled as the personal property of Belgian King Leopold II under the euphemistic name of the Congo Free State. During that period the country's population of over twenty million was progressively decimated to about eight million as a result of the slave-like exactions imposed by the Belgian king (Morel, 1920/1969: Ch. IX). The quest for labour required to gather rubber and ivory led to the emergence of a ferocious and genocidal regime in the 'Congo Free State'. The substitution of direct Belgian colonial rule in 1908 only changed the form but not the essential character of the system to which the Congolese people were subjected. At the same time large reserves of minerals including copper, diamonds and, later, uranium and cobalt were discovered and this resulted in the further exploitation of Congolese labour and resources in the service of foreign interests. Companies such as the Union Minière du Haut Katanga, Tanganyika Concessions and Société Générale de Belgique operated with scarcely any restrictions from a colonial regime whose raison d'etre was economic exploitation. It is thus hardly surprising that the Union Minière became the chief prop behind the Katangese secessionist movement headed by Moise Tshombe between 1960 and 1963 (O'Brien, 1963).

Furthermore, the colonial regime of the Congo thrived on an apparatus of rigid repression and the outlawing of all forms of political protest. Even in the face of the stirrings of African nationalism elsewhere on the continent after the Second World War, there was no expectation on the part of the Belgian colonialists of any such activity in their apparently quiescent colony. Furthermore, the colonialists assumed that Africans could be immunized against all rebellious temptations if their material circumstances were rendered tolerable. As Nkrumah puts it: The essence of the Belgian colonial system, as later developed, was to buy off any discontent by giving a certain amount of material comfort. The Congo became a model colony (Nkrumah, 1967: 11). The whole colonial political perspective amounted to a carrot-and-stick policy. In consequence, the development of nationalism was severely handicapped. Indeed, political parties and nationalist movements only emerged in the Congo a year or so before independence. And, not surprisingly, these parties were largely tribally-based, the nearest to an authentically national group being Patrice Lumumba's 'Congolese National Movement' (MNC). Of the major parties opposed to the MNC were the Bakongo-based ABAKO group of Joseph Kasavubu, the Katanga-based

Lunda CONAKAT group led by Moise Tshombe, and the 'Kasai Movement' of the self-styled 'King' Albert Kalonji of the then south Kasai province.

This severely fragmented political arena not only proved incapable of sustaining a stable government but also provided opportunities for external interference by various interested parties. The superpowers, and the erstwhile colonial power in particular, soon became involved in backing one or other of the contending groups, following the mutiny of the 'Force Publique' and the collapse of the national coalition government headed by Lumumba as prime minister and Kasavubu as president.

It is against this background that the Congolese government appealed to the UN for military assistance to enable it to restore peace and order in the country and to put an end to the secession of the Katanga and Kasai provinces. The matter was referred to the Security Council which passed its first operative resolution on 14 July, 1960. Other such resolutions were to be adopted on 9 August, 1960, 21 February, 1961 and 24 November, 1961. These resolutions essentially provided for the despatch of a UN peace-keeping force to the Congo; for all-round UN assistance to the Congolese government in the military, technical, economic and administrative spheres; and for the withdrawal from the territory of Belgian and other non-UN forces. More generally, they called upon all states to desist from interfering in the internal affairs of the Congo.

Almost from the start of its involvement the UN operation in the Congo (ONUC) was bedevilled by controversy. There was, firstly, disagreement as to the scope of its mission and even the nature of its mandate. For example, the Congolese government, with the support of 'radical' African and socialist states, demanded that ONUC should not only expel the Belgian troops from Katanga but also that the secession of the latter province be terminated by force if necessary. UN Secretary-General Dag Hammarskjoeld, on the other hand, insisted that the role of ONUC was non-political and was to be confined to purely police actions. In this he was supported by the major Western powers headed by the United States. Until his death in a plane crash over Zambia (then Northern Rhodesia) in 1961, Hammarskjoeld steadfastly maintained this narrow interpretation of ONUC's mandate. It was only under U Thant as Secretary-General that Katanga's secession was forcibly ended in December 1962. By then Lumumba had been deposed in a military coup d'etat led by General Joseph Mobutu and had been handed over to the Katangese secessionists who executed him and two of his ministerial colleagues early in 1961.

Behind all the clashes concerning the mandate of ONUC were basic differences of principle and interest that adversely affected the unity of key actors including the African Group in the UN. Some African states, mostly those that came to form the Casablanca Group in January 1961, preferred to see a Congolese state that would be freed from any form of external control. They had placed their hopes in the UN and were sorely disappointed when that organization seemed powerless to restore legality and normality to the Congo (Nkrumah, 1967). Other African states, mostly those that in May 1961 formed the Monrovia Group, took a more moderate stance on the Congo issue. The group fully supported the UN effort and refrained from any criticism of the organization, policy and operation of ONUC. Unlike the Casablanca Group which tended to view major Western powers as having subverted ONUC for their own economic and strategic reasons, the Monrovia Group harboured no such fears or suspicions.

Polarization or divisions in African ranks over the Congo issue obviously weakened Africa's capacity to influence the course of events. This, unfortunately, was not to be the last time that such divisions revealed themselves in respect of a crucial African question. History was to repeat itself in regard to Africa's posture over, for example, the illegal declaration of independence by the white minority regime of Ian Smith in Rhodesia in 1965 and the factional struggle for power in Angola on the eve of that country's independence ten years later. Such instances of African disunity were themselves related to the lack of African political and diplomatic influence over the course and outcome of events. This inability has had serious implications for the destiny of millions of Africans.

# Conclusion

As an international forum for the examination and possible resolution of major issues facing the international community as a whole the UN has been of considerable value to Africa. It has provided a platform for the expression of the continent's grievances. Its specialized agencies have played and continue to play an important role in assisting in the socio-economic development of Africa and other developing countries. While its capacity for problem-solving in the political and security fields has been limited due largely to superpower rivalries, it has nonetheless provided a forum which African states can use to achieve broader international legitimization of their policy objectives, especially in regard to the issues of decolonization and development.

Nonetheless, there is a long list of UN failures on African questions. Indeed, even in clear-cut cases requiring decisive UN intervention the performance of the organization has, at best, been modest and at worst, dismal. An example of this was the inability of the UN to terminate the illegal regime in Southern Rhodesia (now Zimbabwe) through a programme of economic sanctions. Other examples include the failure to bring about a speedy end to South Africa's illegal occupation of Namibia or to hasten the elimination of the racialist apartheid policies of the South African regime. Progress towards the restructuring of the international economic system has, for the African states and their partners in the Non-Aligned Movement, been disappointingly slow.

Thus we are left to conclude that in a world characterized by great inequalities of resources and power, the UN's capacity to translate its ideals and principles into concrete accomplishments must inevitably be limited by the reality of the inequalities that exist between its member states.

# References

CLAUDE, INIS L (1962) *Power and international relations,* Random House, New York.

CLAUDE, INIS L (1964) *Swords into plowshares: the problems and progress of international organisation,* Random House, New York.

BRUCAN, SILVIU (1978) *The dialectic of world politics,* The Free Press, New York.

JAMES, ALAN (1969) *The politics of peacekeeping,* F A Praeger, New York.

DEUTSCH, KARL W (1957) *Political community in the north Atlantic area,* Princeton Univ. Press, Princeton.

DEUTSCH, KARL W (1966) *International political communities,* Doubleday, New York.

MATES, LEO (1972) *Non-Alignment: theory and current practice,* Oceana Publications, Dobbs-Ferry.

MITRANY, DAVID (1933) *The progress of international government,* Yale Univ. Press, New Haven.

MITRANY, DAVID (1943) *A working peace system,* Chicago Univ. Press, Chicago.

MOREL, E D (1920) *The black man's burden,* Monthly Review Press, New York 1969 (first published London, 1920).

NKRUMAH, KWAME (1967) *Challenge of the Congo,* Nelson, London.

O'BRIEN, CONOR CRUISE (1963) *To Katanga and back: a UN case history,* Simon and Schuster, New York.

SINGHAM A W and VAN DIHN, TRAN (1976) *From Bandung to Colombo: conferences of the Non-Aligned countries, 1955–1975,* Third Press Review, New York.

SINGHAM, A W (ed) (1977) *The Non-Aligned Movement in world politics,* Lawrence Hill & Co., Westport, Conn.

WILLIAMS, GWYNETH (1981) *Third World political organisations: a review of developments,* MacMillan, London.

WORLD BANK (1981) *Accelerated development in Sub-Saharan Africa,* The World Bank, Washington, D.C.

# 9 Causes of conflict in the relations of African states

## Conflict as a characteristic of international relations

A study of conflict can be viewed at two levels: intra-state and extra-state. Intra-state conflict may take the form of a struggle between two or more groups of power contenders within a state, each seeking to acceed to political power in order to advance its interests and goals. At worst intra-state political conflicts can cause costly civil wars, especially when the state apparatus fails to mediate successfully between the conflicting parties. Extra-state conflict occurs because of competition between two or more states. Because no state is self-sufficient states are interdependent. Interdependence produces a degree of integration (by which we mean increased interactions or close contacts) among independent and sovereign African states. However, because states pursue different interests, increased contact is as likely to cause conflicts as it is to promote co-operation.

Intra-state conflicts may even occur within a well organized state system with a legally constituted state apparatus for the mediation and arbitration of conflicts. Within the state system there is a government endowed with the monopoly of the legitimate means of violence — the police and the military — together with a judiciary which permits the system to regulate competition within it. Furthermore, the state is endowed with resources for allocation among conflicting interest groups. Through the manipulation of power and allocation of resources among interest groups the state system produces consensus which is necessary for the maintenance of the system.

The international system, unlike the state system, does not possess either any consensus or any institution which holds the monopoly of the means of violence in the world at large. Consequently war, the expectation of war, and the diplomatic and the strategic behaviour consequent upon it become the very stuff of international relations (Modelski, 1970). Robert J. Lieber has remarked that 'The causes of conflicts constitute the primordial question in the study of international politics' (Lieber, 1972: 89).

African states have been brought closer by independence and sovereignty. They interact with one another and with non-African states. Interactions within Africa take place in a sub-international system, or what William Zartman has called 'the subordinate state system', a term which suggests the incomplete and dependent nature of the system (Zartman, 1967). The African subordinate state system, like the international system lacks a consensus and an organization capable of mediating effectively in inter-African conflicts. As a result, conflict is a characteristic of the subordinate state system as well as of the international system.

## Causes of conflict

A list of the causes of conflict in the relations between African states must include the following factors: ideology, personality, internal power struggles, the treatment of ethnic minorities, decolonization, territorial disputes, refugee problems and, finally, external interference. Within this list it is useful to distinguish between those causes which relate to the internal affairs of a state and those causes which relate to external factors. Ideology, personality, internal power struggles and the treatment of ethnic minorities belong to the first group. Decolonization, territorial disputes, external interference and refugee problems belong to the second. However, it should be stressed that in practise both sets of causes are closely related: the problem of refugees, for example, is often created by internal power struggles.

### Domestic sources of inter-state conflict

The origins of inter-state conflict are often to be found in domestic developments. A change of government in a state may have a dramatic effect on international relations. For example, if a traditionally conservative state, allied to other conservative states, changes from a conservative to a radical government its allies are likely to be alarmed by the new government and to view it with suspicion and disfavour. Another domestic source of inter-state conflict is civil war. In a civil war each faction normally has international allies and as a result civil wars can easily develop into an international conflict. In these examples of domestic sources of inter-state conflict ideology, personality and internal power struggles are all major factors.

### Ideology

Conflict over ideology and points of principle is common in African international relations. Even the principle shared by all African governments, namely opposition to the racist policy of apartheid has, at times, been the source of conflict between African states. Since the conference of independent African states in April 1958 in Accra a general consensus has prevailed among African states that apartheid and racism must be brought to an end. The OAU has taken the position that no African state should have diplomatic and commercial relationships with the Republic of South Africa. But some African states have disagreed. Some southern African states – Malawi, Lesotho, Swaziland and Botswana – whose national economies are dependent on South Africa have maintained diplomatic and commercial relationships with the apartheid regime. The moderate state of Kenya permits commercial airlines flying to and from South Africa to refuel in Nairobi and even radical Mozambique has allowed the practice which started in the colonial era of exporting African workers to South Africa to continue. It does so because it cannot afford to lose this valuable source of the foreign exchange. Kenya's deeply rooted western orientation and dependency makes it unwilling to refuse refuelling facilities to Western European airlines flying to and from South Africa.

The issue of dialogue with South Africa which was raised by President Felix Houphouet-Boigny of the Ivory Coast in 1969 has divided African states. The call for dialogue came in spite of the Lusaka manifesto in April 1969 which had registered strong opposition to apartheid and racism and to any dialogue with South Africa or with the white minority regime in Rhodesia. But by the early 1970s the Ivory Coast, Chad, Benin, Gabon, Ghana and the Malagasy Republic had all endorsed the idea of dialogue in the belief that dialogue with South Africa would encourage moderate whites and influential business opinions in South Africa to exert pressure on the apartheid government to modify racist policy and seek accord with blacks. Houphouet-Boigny and, more recently Kenneth Kaunda of Zambia have both engaged in dialogue with South Africa.

However, the majority of African states opposed the idea of dialogue with South Africa. The former Nigerian Head of State, General Gowon, and President Julius Nyerere of Tanzania led the opposition. General Gowon declared on 8 May, 1971 that a dialogue with South Africa would be a great betrayal of the African people and that Nigeria would not be a party to such an action. By a majority resolution the OAU summit meeting in Accra in June 1971 rejected dialogue with South Africa. However, there was little public opposition to President Kaunda's decision in 1982 to renew attempts at dialogue with South Africa. While the dialogue had long been fruitless, in early 1984 President Kaunda initiated a dialogue which led to the signing of a Non-Agression Pact between South Africa and both Mozambique and Angola.

Non-alignment is another area in which African states have agreed to disagree. African states have not only disagreed on the application of non-alignment (Olympio, 1961; Nkrumah, 1958), but they have also disagreed on what the concept means. The anti-communist President Houphouet-Boigny and the former Senegalese President Leopold Sedar Senghor both equate non-alignment with alliance with communists. In their view non-alignment is a device used by radical states to undermine African governments allied to Western Europe and North America (Aluko, 1977: 15; Adelman, 1980: 12). Sékou Touré and Nyerere, on the other hand, have denied that non-alignment inevitably leads to a closer identification with socialist countries. Many other African leaders share this view and support non-alignment in order to achieve equitable relationships with both the East and the West.

Conflicts that arise out of ideological differences follow a similar pattern to disagreements over the issue of non-alignment. African states which think of themselves as socialists view non-socialist states as agents of neo-colonialist and imperialist interests. At the same time the non-socialist countries regard their socialist counterparts as puppets of Soviet imperialism. Both groups suspect each other of colluding with non-African powers in order to undermine their respective political and economic systems. Each camp accuses the other of an unholy alliance with imperialists.

Ideological differences have created an atmosphere of hostility between many African states. In East Africa, where Kenya and Tanzania pursue different modes of production and social organization, it is not uncommon to find Kenya claiming that the reason for Tanzania's apparently unfriendly attitude lies in the failure of its socialist experiment. Kenyans say that Tanzanian leaders envy Kenya's capitalist achievements. Tanzania, for its part, retaliates by referring to Kenya as a 'man-eat-man society'.

The power struggle between Ghana and Nigeria, which started in the years preceding the founding of the Organization of African Unity and which continued until Nkrumah was overthrown in 1966, was partly a result of ideological differences. Nkrumah's strong commitment to socialism and his call for immediate unification of African states alienated both the conservative and the moderate states. Nigeria led a strong and successful campaign against Nkrumah's efforts to mould a continental system based on his own ideology of African unity (Aluko, 1976). Similarly, Guinea's alienation from the conservative Francophone states throughout the whole of the 1960s was due to Sékou Touré's radicalism which many Francophone states interpreted as a form of communism.

The conflict between Angola and Zaire between 1975 and 1979 can in part also be explained by ideology, although it is true that President Mobutu was also interested in the oil resources of the exclave of Cabinda. The existence of a socialist government in Angola at a time when internal opposition to Mobutu's rule was strong, alarmed the government in Zaire. Mobutu feared that a hostile Angola would provide operational bases for his opponents. This concern was shared by the United States, who encouraged Mobutu to pursue an anti-Angolan policy. The United States had made a concerted effort to prevent the 1975 OAU summit meeting in Addis Ababa from recognizing the Angolan government (Nzongola-Ntalaja, 1978: 144–70; Bender, 1978: 63–143; El-Khawas and Cohen, 1976; Stockwell, 1977). A final example of ideological conflict can be seen in the failure to hold the 1982 OAU summit meeting scheduled to take place in August in Tripoli. Many African states objected less to the admission of the Sahrawi Arab Democratic Republic (SADR) as the 51st member of the OAU than to Colonel Gaddafi's radical Islamic ideology.

## Military coups and inter-African relations

Since the independence of the former Belgian Congo on 30 June, 1960 and the subsequent military intervention in the political process of the country, African armed forces have increasingly become power contenders in the domestic politics of many countries. The military has done this by overthrowing civilian governments. This intervention has been made possible by the decline in the established machinery for the transfer of power, which has made political change within a state very problematic. Often the military have been the only force capable of challenging the government. Furthermore, disrespect for political institutions has in many cases led to rampant corruption at the top of the political and civil administration. Together with the steady weakening of political leadership and the intense and uncompromising rivalry among the political elites these factors have combined to give the military a rationale for overthrowing civilian governments (Foltz, 1966; Greene, 1972). The importance of military intervention in African politics is underlined by the fact that by 1981 more than half of the OAU member states either had military governments or had experienced attempted military takeovers.

Military coups are internal matters which fall outside the jurisdiction of the OAU. Nonetheless they can affect the inter-state relations of the OAU member states. For example, following the overthrow of Kwame Nkrumah by the military in 1966, Guinea refused to recognize the military regime in Ghana. Instead, Nkrumah was made a 'co-President' of Guinea with Sékou Touré and was allowed to live in Guinea. Relations between Ghana and Guinea deteriorated further as a result and the quarrel spilled over to the OAU itself. In February 1966 seven African delegations walked out of the OAU conference of the Council of Ministers in Addis Ababa 'in protest against the seating of the Ghanaian delegation sent by the National Liberation Council of Ghana'. In October the OAU again had to face a crisis when the Ghanaian military government detained in Accra the Guinean delegation travelling to the OAU conference in Addis Ababa (Cervenka, 1969: 8). A similar incident occurred in 1971 when the OAU was divided over the seating of a Uganda delegation as one group supported the delegation sent from Dar-es-Salaam by Milton Obote whilst another group wished to see Amin's delegation represent Uganda.

Military coups may have an even more fundamental effect on the bilateral relations of African states than the frequent wrangling over delegations which have been characteristic of many OAU conferences. Military takeovers tend to increase internal instability and contribute to a breakdown in law and order. The institutional framework always becomes dysfunctional. Such conditions lead to the dislocation of the society and this in turn leads to the displacement of nationals who, through fear of persecution, are forced to become refugees in neighbouring countries.

The influx of political refugees, which has become a major feature in Africa, produces political consequences of its own. One such consequence is political tension between the countries concerned, especially when the refugees attempt to use the host's territory as an operational base against their home government. The problem between Tanzania and Uganda from February 1971, when Amin took over government, to April 1979, when he was finally driven out by Tanzanian troops, had much to do with the behaviour of Ugandan refugees residing in Tanzania.

In spite of the problems created by military intervention in politics, there exists no formula for dealing with the issue of military coups. Since military coups had become a reality in African politics at the time the OAU was founded, one might have expected member states to include in the charter a provision for collective action against the military usurpation of political power. But this did not happen. There exists no mechanism in the OAU Charter for either repudiating or denying recognition to a military government. The framers of the OAU Charter felt this problem was an internal matter, and that individual states themselves ought to decide whether or not to recognize a military government. The result of this oversight has been conflict among African states and, as Nicholas Nyangira has observed, the situation is likely to remain the same unless the OAU Charter is amended to take the problem into account (Nyangira, 1980).

## Civil war

Civil war is one of the most explosive of intra-state conflicts and it often transcends national boundaries. The 1967 Nigerian civil war started strictly as an internal conflict. It stemmed from a number of factors – power struggle among the military leaders, religious and ethnic differences and regional grievances all being among the main causes. The military coup, which preceded the civil war, had destroyed the constitutional framework for change of leadership. It had, therefore, weakened the political system and, when the political system failed to mediate between all the conflicting interests civil war broke out when the Ibos declared themselves independent and proclaimed the state of Biafra.

The civil war between the Biafrans and the Federal Government did not remain internal for long. When both parties sought external assistance it developed into an international issue. The international aspect was, however, partially contained by the OAU which invoked the principle of an African solution for an African problem. This principle was partially respected by the superpowers. However, the Soviet Union did support the Federal Government and some groups in France rallied behind Biafra.

Among African states the problem was whether or not the OAU should uphold Biafran independence and sovereignty. The recognition of Biafra would have run counter to the OAU's principle of protecting the territorial integrity of member states (Chimes, 1969: 75–6). The crisis arose when despite the fact that a majority of African states upheld the OAU Charter and supported the Federal Government, four African countries (Gabon, Ivory Coast, Tanzania and Zambia) recognized Biafra, and a few more supported Biafra's claim to independence without according it full political recognition. The decision by some states to recognize Biafra made it very difficult for the OAU to solve the conflict. More importantly, it strained relations between the Nigerian government and those countries which had extended recognition to Biafra. The OAU was also divided by the Angolan civil war in 1976 when twenty-two member states supported the MPLA government and twenty-one opposed it (Bender, 1978; Nzongola-Ntalaja, 1978).

The endless Chadian civil war has had an even greater impact. Libya's intervention in Chad in 1981 was greeted by one of the strongest and most universal continental protests ever witnessed in Africa. It is this intervention which led to the July 1981 Nairobi OAU resolution to send a peacekeeping force to Chad. Unfortunately, the subsequent failure of the OAU peacekeeping operation has damaged the image of the OAU as a potential continental peacekeeper.

## External sources of inter-state conflict

### Territorial disputes

Territorial or boundary disputes are the most explosive conflicts in the African subordinate state system. Since 1961 more than half of the OAU member states have been involved in at least one territorial dispute (Waters, 1969; Matthew, 1977). Territorial dispute in its restricted sense refers to conflict over a whole territorial entity. It means the denial by one of the disputants that the territory claimed has any right to self-determination, independent existence or sovereignty. Morocco's claim on Mauritania at the time of the latter's independence constituted a territorial dispute. Since the late 1970s Morocco has laid claim to the Western Sahara (Sahrawi Arab Democratic Republic) and this claim too falls within the category of territorial dispute. But the term territorial dispute can be used broadly to apply to claims involving large areas of another state's territory. The 1963 Moroccan claim to a part of Algeria which was larger than the Kingdom of Morocco itself, and Somalia's 1961 claim on the whole of Kenya's North-Eastern Province, and on three-quarters of Eastern and Coast Provinces, the Ethiopian Ogaden and the state of Djibouti all fall within this broader usage. The Moroccan and Somali claims may also be described as boundary disputes because they call for the redrawing of the existing boundaries in order to effect a territorial adjustment. Boundaries are 'imaginary lines which define the [limit of] an area' or territorial entity (Allott, 1974: 117). Boundary lines mark where one territorial area ends and where another territorial area begins. Both territorial and boundary disputes involve an attempt to induce one state to surrender either all, or a portion, of its territory to another state. We therefore do not draw a sharp distinction between territorial and boundary disputes.

Modern territorial or boundary disputes in Africa have their origins in colonialism. European colonialists drew up African boundaries without any thought to their future impacts. Boundaries were drawn in order to suit European interests and did not accurately reflect ethnic divisions. This was the case with regard to the Ewe of Ghana and Togo, and to the Somali-speaking peoples of Djibouti, Ethiopia, Kenya and

Somalia. Historical relationships were also ignored. Morocco, for example, has evoked pre-colonial historical experiences and religious affinity in order to justify its claim on Mauritania and the Western Sahara (Gretton, 1980: 343–4).

Territorial conflicts in Africa arise when the legality of the colonial boundaries are challenged. Countries which reject the legality of colonial boundaries declare them illegitimate because they were drawn and agreed upon by Europeans. These countries argue that the treaties legalizing colonial boundaries were signed by Europeans alone and that as a result the treaties lack legality in independent Africa, and should, therefore, be adjusted in order to take historical and ethnic realities into consideration. The countries on which territorial claims have been made reject this argument and insist that colonial treaties inherited by independent African states constitute international obligations on the new governments. It is worth noting here that the OAU has bestowed legality and legitimacy on the existing inter-state boundaries. Article III, paragraph three of the charter calls upon all member states 'to respect . . . the sovereignty and territorial integrity of each State . . .' while the 1964 OAU resolution in Cairo regarding the status of the colonial boundaries held that the existing boundaries must be respected, thus conferring legitimacy upon them.

Since territorial claims affect national territorial integrity and therefore challenge a state's independence and sovereignty, African states have fought and will probably continue to fight over them until permanent solutions are found, either by all states accepting the legitimacy of the present boundaries or by the creation of a continental government.

## Natural resources

Territorial disputes can also be explained by the presence of natural resources. Morocco's claim on Algerian territory in 1963 appears to have had an economic motive – the presence of oil deposits in the desert area. Likewise, its war with the POLISARIO involves more than territorial interest. If Morocco controlled the Western Sahara it would be able to monopolize the production and marketing of phosphate and to exploit the area's iron ore deposits. Libya's claim to the northern Aouzou strip of Chad stems from the presence of uranium in the region. The Nile water is a potential source of inter-state conflict among the Nile Valley states (Mazrui, 1974). Since the coming of a socialist government in Ethopia, Egypt has on several occasions declared it would go to war with Ethiopia if it interfered with the flow of the Blue Nile which originates from the Ethiopian Highlands. The Blue Nile is important for the annual flooding of the River Nile on which both Egypt and Sudan depend heavily for agricultural activities.

## Decolonization

If territorial disputes lead to military engagement in Africa, decolonization is another cause of violent conflict. The support of independent African states for liberation movements expose these states to colonialist military aggression. During the 1960s Tanzania had to endure armed attacks from Mozambique because Tanzania supported FRELIMO's war against Portuguese colonialists. In the 1970s Guinea's support for the liberation struggle in neighbouring Guinea-Bissau brought it into conflict with the Portuguese authorities. The white minority regime in former Rhodesia made repeated raids into Mozambique and Zambia because both countries allowed Zimbabwean nationalists to operate from their territory. Angola, which gives support and shelter to SWAPO's fight for the liberation of Namibia, has suffered considerable hardship from South African aggression and interference. In its attempt to prevent the liberation of Namibia, South Africa has resorted to full-scale military invasions of Angola and it is doubtful whether the early 1984 agreement between the two countries would lead to peaceful co-existence as long as Namibia remains under South African occupation.

*The military factor*

In East Africa and the Horn of Africa inter-state armed conflicts appear to correspond to the level of growth in military strength. Immediately after independence armies were very small and their weapons unsophisticated. Therefore the military skirmishes in the Horn of Africa between 1963 and 1967 had involved small and poorly equipped armies and had never grown out of proportion. The picture changed significantly during the second half of the 1960s.

The change followed from a combination of internal and external factors. In Uganda Milton Obote's government had faced formidable opposition from the Baganda. The government became increasingly dependent on the military to maintain itself. Internal opposition also created fear of external intervention. These three factors combined to convince the Obote regime of the need to expand and modernize the Ugandan army. An air force was also established. Under Obote the Ugandan army increased from an estimated 5–7 000 men in 1967 to over 10 000 by 1970. Following the overthrow of the Obote regime by Idi Amin the army was increased to about 23 000 men. Amin also followed the trend already set by Obote by acquiring more advanced Soviet-made military equipment – MiG 19s and MiG 21s combat aircraft, battle tanks and armoured cars. Tanzania, too, had embarked on the process of building its army. It had a territorial dispute with Malawi just as Kenya and Ethiopia had had with Somalia. Amin threatened the security of the country because Tanzania had given refuge to the deposed Milton Obote and supported groups opposed to Amin. Earlier Tanzania had been subjected to Portuguese armed attack for sheltering and supporting FRELIMO fighters. As a result by the early 1970s the Tanzanian professional army had increased from about 7 000 men in 1967 to over 20 000 men. In addition Tanzania developed a people's militia which provided a reservoir of trained military personnel. But the most rapid military growth occurred in Somalia. With the assistance of the Soviet Union the Somali army increased from about 2–3 000 men in 1969 to about 22 000 men in the early 1970s out of a population of 4 million people. Kenya had, until after 1976, maintained an army of less than 20 000 men and Ethiopia had an army of about 43 000 men, but these were in keeping with their relatively large populations (Orwa, 1981).

It is clear then that East Africa experienced an arms race during the second half of the 1970s. Kenya joined the race immediately after Amin's claim on its territory in 1976. By the time of the Ethiopian–Somali war of 1977 and Tanzanian–Ugandan war of 1978–9, the regional balance of power appeared altered. Each of the countries in the region had an army of not less than 20 000 men. Each had an air force, the smallest of which, the Kenyan air force, was equipped with 12 United States F5E and F5F fighter aircraft and employed some 700 men. All the ground forces in the region were armed with advanced battle tanks, armoured cars, heavy artillery and long-range field guns, among other military material. Somali forces were the most heavily armed. Its ground forces could field 250 T-34, T-54 and T-55 Soviet-made battle tanks and more than 300 BTR-152 armoured cars. Its air force of 2 700 men boasted 66 combat aircraft including MiG-15s, MiG-17s and MiG-21s. At the time of its war with Ethiopia the Somali army had reached an estimated 53 000 men (US Arms Control and Disarmament Agency, 1979; SIPRI, 1979, 1980; Orwa, 1981; *Military Balance,* 1978, 1979, 1980; *Africa Contemporary Record, Record,* 1973/74: B176, B269-270, B309; *Strategic Survey,* 1977: 19, 25).

In North Africa an arms race occurred between Egypt and Libya. Following the 1969 military coup Libya began to devote much of its resources to military expenditure. In 1979, Libya, given its small population of slightly over 4 million, accounted for 12 per cent of total African military expenditure, while Egypt with a population of more than 30 million accounted for 22 per cent and South Africa 17 per cent *(Africa Guide,* 1981: 28). The ongoing conflict between Egypt and Libya, which went as far as a limited military engagement in 1977, can be explained in part by this arms race. Ideological and religious differences apart, there appears to exist a power struggle between the two countries. Gaddafi, with oil wealth, wishes to increase Libya's influence not only in the Middle East and North Africa but also in black Africa. This move by Libya challenges the traditional Egyptian perception of itself as the regional power. Egypt has responded to the Libyan challenge by forming a military alliance with Sudan to counter the possible spread of Libya's influence. Egypt's close military ties with the United States can also be explained in part by Libya's heavy dependence on the Soviet Union for military supplies.

Thus, throughout Africa arms build-ups have increased inter-state tension and have transformed disagreements into violent conflicts. In leaders like Amin and Gaddafi the acquisition of arms has bred adventuristic sentiments whilst in expansionists like Siad Barre of Somalia and King Hassan of Morocco it has created the temptation to play the power game by deploying military force in order to achieve territorial ambitions.

## Prospects for the future

Conflicts in Africa are in a state of flux. They fall under two main categories – those conflicts involving violent confrontations and conflicts over matters of principle. The latter type are the most common as they represent the expression of attitudes and a national way of life. In the experience of Africa since independence conflicts over principles alone have not been a cause of violent conflict between African states. However, conflict of principles when accompanied by a threat to vital national interest, may produce a war. This can be seen in the Tanzanian–Ugandan war of 1978–9. It can therefore be observed that differences on matters involving principles will continue to be a characteristic of inter-state relations in Africa. However, few, if any, wars are likely to be fought over issues such as ideology and non-alignment.

So far it seems that inter-state violence is a product of concern for vital national interests – territorial integrity, national honour and access to resources – and the personality of leaders. As long as territorial claims remain a major objective of some African states the possibility of future wars between two or more African states cannot be discounted. It is also worth noting that leaders such as Amin and Gaddafi tend to increase regional tension.

Equally important is the growing strength of African armies – strength, that is, in relation to each other. Military armament may for a time act to maintain an equilibrium through the operation of a balance of power. But, as we have shown in the case of the Horn of Africa and in East Africa, the current arms race on the continent has the potential of increasing inter-African tension, with a possible increase in inter-state violence. Military build-up is going to be more of a threat to the territorial integrity of some African states than had been the case in the early 1960s. Strong armies are also likely to induce unilateral interventions in the internal affairs of other states. Unfortunately, the OAU in its present form cannot be expected to deal effectively with any upsurge in inter-state violence.

## References

ADELMAN, KENNETH L (1980) *African realities,* Crane, Russak and Co. Inc., New York.

ALUKO, O (ed) (1977) *Foreign policies of African states,* Hodder and Stoughton, London.

ALUKO, O (1976) *Ghana and Nigeria, 1957-1970: a study in inter-African discord,* Rex Collings, London.

ALLOTT, ANTHONY (1969) Boundaries and the law in Africa. In Carl Gosta Widstrand (ed) *African boundary problems,* The Scandinavian Institute of African Studies, Uppsala.

BENDER, GERALD (1978) Kissinger in Angola: anatomy of failure. In René Lemarchand (ed) *American policy in Southern Africa: the stakes and stance,* Univ. of America Press, Washington, D.C.

CERVENKA, ZDENEK (1969) *The Organisation of African Unity and its Charter,* Frederick A Praeger, New York.

CHIMES, SAMUEL (1969) The Organisation of African Unity and African boundaries. In Carl Gosta Widstrand (ed) *African Boundary Problems,* The Scandinavian Institute of African Studies, Uppsala.

EL-KHAWAS, MOHAMED AND COHEN, BARRY (eds) (1976) *The Kissinger study of Southern Africa,* Lawrence Hill and Company, Westport, Conn.

ENAHORO, PETER (1971) Dialogue, *Africa,* London.

FOLTZ, WILLIAM J (1966) Military influence. In Vernon McKay (ed) *African diplomacy: studies in the determinants of foreign policy,* Frederick A Praeger, New York.

GREENE, FRED (1972) Toward understanding military coups. In Irvin Leonard Markovitz (ed) *African politics and society: problems of government and development,* The Free Press, New York.

HAAS, MICHAEL (1974) *International system: a behavioural approach,* Chandler Publishing Company, New York.

HOLSTI, J K (1967) *International politics,* Prentice-Hall, New Jersey.

HVEEM, H and WILLETS, P (1974) The practice of nonalignment: on the present and future of a continental movement. In Yashpal Tandon and Dilshad Chandarana (eds) *Horizons of African Diplomacy,* East African Literature Bureau, Nairobi.

IISS (1978, 1979, 1980) *Military Balance* International Institute of Strategic Studies, London.

IISS (1979) *Strategic survey,* International Institute of Strategic Studies, London.

LEGUM, COLIN (ed) (1973-4) *Africa Contemporary Records,* Africana Publications, New York.

LEGUM, COLIN and LEE, BILL (1977) *Conflict in the Horn of Africa.* Africana Publications, New York.

LEGUM, COLIN (1979) Communal conflict and international intervention in Africa. In Colin Legum et al *Africa in the 1980s: a continent in crisis,* McGraw-Hill Book Co.

LIEBER, ROBERT (1972) *Theory and world politics,* George Allen and Unwin, London.

McKAY, VERNON (1966) Introduction. In Vernon McKay (ed) *African diplomacy,* New York, 1966.

MATTHEW, K (1977) The Organisation of African Unity, *India Quarterly,* XXXIII.

MAZRUI, ALI A (1974) The Indian Ocean and the Nile Valley: the view from East Africa. In Yashpal Tandon and Dilshad Chandarana (eds) *Horizons of African diplomacy,* East African Literature Bureau, Nairobi.

MBOYA, TOM (1970) *Challenge of nationhood,* Andre Deutsch, London.

MODELSKI, GEORGE (1970) The promise of geocentric politics, *World Politics,* XX.

NKRUMAH, KWAME (1958) African prospects. *Foreign Affairs* **XXVIII.**

NORTH, ROBERT C, KOCH Jr, HOWARD E and ZINNES, DIANA A The integrative functions of conflict. In Julian R Friedman, Christopher Bladen and Steven Rosen (eds) *Alliance in international politics,* Allyn and Bacon Inc., Boston, Mass.

NYANGIRA, NICHOLAS (1980) Regional organisation and integration: the case of the OAU. Seminar Paper given in the History Department, University of Nairobi.

NZONGOLA-NTALAJA (1978) The US, Zaire and Angola. In René Lemarchand (ed) *American foreign policy in Southern Africa,* Univ. Press of America, New York.

OLYMPIO, SYLVANUS (1961) African problems and the Cold War, *Foreign Affairs* **XXXI.**

ORWA, D KATETE (1981) Balance of power theory and Kenya's foreign policy in East Africa. Unpublished paper read at the Historical Association of Kenya Annual Conference in Nairobi.

SIPRI (1979, 1980) *Year Book,* Stockholm International Peace Research Institute.

STOCKWELL, JOHN (1978) *In search of enemies: a CIA story,* Andre Deutsch, London.

THORNE, C T (1966) External political pressures. In Vernon McKay (ed) *African diplomacy,* Frederick Praeger, New York.

US ARMS CONTROL AND DISARMAMENT AGENCY (1979) *Arms Control,* 1978, Government Printer, Washington D.C.

WALTZ, KENNETH N (1959) *Man, State and War,* Columbia University Press, New York.

WATERS, ROBERT (1969) Inter-African boundary disputes. In Carl Gosta Widstrand (ed) *African boundary problems,* The Scandinavian Institute of African Studies, Uppsala.

ZARTMAN, WILLIAM I (1966) National interest and idealogy. In Vernon McKay (ed) *African diplomacy,* Frederick Praeger, New York.

ZARTMAN, WILLIAM I (1967) Africa as a subordinate state system in international relations, *International Organisation,* **XXI.**

ZARTMAN, WILLIAM I (1979) Social and political trends in Africa in the 1980s. In Colin Legum et al *Africa in the 1980s,* McGraw-Hill, New York.

# 10 Regional co-operation and integration

Regional co-operation can be defined as 'any inter-state activity with less than universal participation designed to meet some commonly experienced need' (Haas, 1971: 77). The need can be military, political, economic, or it may be of social, technical or residual public interest.

So defined, regional co-operation is not entirely new to Africa. In the colonial era co-operative arrangements abounded among territories ruled by each colonial master. For example the 'Royal West African Frontier Force' met a regional military need, and the Union Douanière de l'Afrique de l'Ouest' (the West African Customs Union) met a regional economic need. The motive for co-operation was imperial interest, the co-operative arrangements serving the colonial master's administrative convenience and fiscal needs or ensuring their trading companies' monopoly and profits.

From the terminal years of colonialism when Africans began to occupy responsible political positions, and particularly since 1960, African states have been struggling to develop new patterns of continental and regional co-operative arrangements. Their efforts have often involved what Green and Krishna (1967: 3) call a 'creative destruction' of the colonial arrangements or their modification to meet African needs and aspirations. Thus for example the West African Currency Board and the West African Airways Corporation were dissolved and replaced with national institutions while the Federations of French West Africa and French Equatorial Africa were linked and transformed via various stages into what is now the 'Organization Commune Africaine et Mauricienne' (OCAM). The motive in the post-colonial struggle for co-operative arrangements has been primarily economic. As Professor Jalloh rightly observes:

A motivating factor was consciousness of the small size of most of the countries involved and the realization of many of them that without joining others in larger groups, they faced serious obstacles in promoting their economic development. In this, they were particularly influenced by the creation and success of the EEC. The reasoning was that if even major countries like France and Germany felt the need for regional integration, such a need was even greater for far smaller and underdeveloped countries (Jalloh, 1980: 72).

Secondary politico-security motives reinforce the economic rationale behind the post-colonial efforts at co-operation. Small, economically and militarily weak, and politically insecure, the new states needed to present a collective front against the rest of the world, particularly the most developed part of it, in order to break down dependencies, political control and inferior status and to arrest the balkanization of Africa. There was also a defensive motive, arising from fear of larger and more powerful neighbours. Thus the Union Douaniere et Economique de l'Afrique Centrale (UDEAC) was formed in part out of fear of the economic threat from Nigeria and Zaire and OCAM was partly inspired by fear of Ghana and the Casablanca bloc (Jalloh, 1980: 72). The Communauté Economique de l'Afrique de l'Ouest, (CEAO), was formed 'to counterbalance Nigeria's political and economic weight, in particular, check her attempts to organize a larger economic community' (Ojo, 1980: 518).

Co-operation and unity for collective betterment has been at the centre of African international relations since 1960. Indeed, Pan-Africanism, as an idea and as a movement on the African continent, was predicated on co-operation and unity. The struggle to develop new patterns of post-colonial, continental and regional co-operative arrangements was, in a real sense, an aspect of the struggle to institutionalize Pan-Africanism.

## Post-colonial efforts at co-operation

Efforts to institutionalize the concept of Pan-Africanism in the 1960s structured and shaped the debate on the proper form and scope of African unity. Attention became focused on the geographical scope as well as the intensity or degree of co-operation deemed necessary. One proposal for institutionalizing Pan-Africanism was Nkrumah's 'Continental Union Government' or, at the very least, a political union of West African States. A Ghana–Guinea union, Ghana–Guinea–Mali union and a Ghana–Congo (Zaire) union were each envisaged by Nkrumah as a nucleus of a continental union. This proposal failed largely because Nigeria opposed it. Nigeria's position was that economic integration must precede political union and that economic integration itself must begin at the sub-regional level and proceed in stages beginning with functional co-operation and co-ordination and leading towards, perhaps, a common market. Nigeria thus favoured functionalism, the theory that co-operation in non-controversial areas leads to the acquisition of knowledge and skills which spill over to make co-operation in politically sensitive areas possible (Haas, 1964: 1958; Mitrany, 1943; Claude 1964). Clearly, too, Nigeria was imbued with the notion of the struggle for power of the realist school (see Ch. 1). In West Africa Nigeria was the dominant power, but continentally it clearly had competitors in Egypt and Congo (Zaire). The very possibility of Nigerian domination, however, was one reason for Nkrumah's insistence on immediate continental union.

This disagreement over the proper form and scope of African unity started a power struggle between Nigeria and Ghana which became a struggle for leadership in West Africa (Ojo, 1974; Aluko, 1976). The struggle was broadened to include the rest of Africa as Nkrumah embarked upon his 'nucleus' unions and engaged in subversive activities against weaker recalcitrant African states. He succeeded only in creating the Casablanca bloc. Nigeria, for its part, sought support for its position in diplomatic fora such as the conferences of Independent African States in Monrovia (1961) and Lagos (1962). Most Francophone states were wary of Nigeria's position but their opposition to Nkrumah's position and personal ambition was strong enough for them to endorse the Nigerian position as the lesser of two evils (Thompson, 1969: 196–269, 305–89). Thus emerged the Monrovia bloc. But Francophone wariness of Nigeria's position in particular and of co-operation with the Anglophones in general led to their forming of the Brazzaville group within the Monrovia bloc. To the extent that the divisions among these blocs formed the stuff of inter-African relations in the early 1960s (see Chapter 5) we can say that disagreement over the proper form and scope of co-operation was the essence of African states' relations between themselves.

The question of political unity on a continental, or even regional, basis was laid to rest with the formation and subsequent development of the OAU. The OAU, it should be noted, was not formed to bring about unity; hence the strong objections by most of the founding fathers to it being called the Organization *for* African Unity. Rather the organization represents itself the extent and scope of political unity, the embodiment and expression of that unity, so it is rightly called the Organization *of* African Unity (Wolfers, 1976:1–45). After the formation of the OAU the various political groups fizzled out. Meanwhile under the impetus of those states which favoured functional co-operation and co-ordination, and with the backing of the UN General Assembly resolutions as well as the relentless independent efforts of the Economic Commission for Africa (Ojo, 1980; Gardiner, 1965), it became generally accepted that for the purpose of economic co-operation and development Africa should be divided into five economically viable sub-regions. These were North Africa to comprise the Arab states; West Africa (from Mauritania to Nigeria); Central Africa (from Chad and Cameroon to Sudan and Zaire); East Africa (from Ethiopia to Tanzania) and Southern Africa (from Angola to Mozambique).

Co-operative efforts and organizations centred on these regions. However, a number of mini-schemes inherited from the colonial era persisted and others emerged in response to divergent political and ideological philosophies and needs. At the same time, the search continued for viable region-wide complements or successors. To date only in West Africa do we have a region-wide organization–ECOWAS. But West Africa also has the largest number of mini-schemes. By one count in 1979 there were thirty inter-governmental or semi-governmental organizations with an exclusive or predominant West African membership (Renninger, 1979). For Africa as a whole there were nearly fifty such organizations in 1980 and this excluded affiliated institutions, those that cover the continent (e.g. the OAU or the African Development Bank), those that are primarily external in membership (e.g. the Commonwealth) and those which are basically UN agencies and institutions (e.g. the Economic Commission for Africa and its affiliates). Few of these organizations are purely political. The vast majority are concerned with economic development thus underlining the fact that the motivation for regional co-operation has been economic. A list, which is far from exhaustive but which, nonetheless, reflects the wide range of forms, memberships and functional scopes of African regional organizations is shown in Table 10.1

As can be seen from the table, a large number of the economic organizations deal with specific issue areas such as specific crop development and/or marketing; joint development and exploitation of water basins; or development banks and clearing houses. In their own ways they contribute to development and are therefore important. The others tend to be multifunctional in the sense that they deal with economic development on a broad range of issues such as trade and commerce, foreign investment and industrial development, education and research and transport and infrastructures. Among such multifunctional organizations are: OCAM, CEAO, UDEAC, ECOWAS, Conseil de l'Entente, the East African Community and the Southern African Customs Union. These organizations are involved in activities designed to eliminate progressively discrimination across national borders, creating in the process new institutions to make, and sometimes implement, the requisite decisions. The removal of discriminations and the creation of new institutions is referred to as economic integration. We are particularly interested in the variety of regional organizations engaged in economic integration for it is that variety which, when successful, brings greater unity and more comprehensive development.

# Forms of regional economic integration

Economic integration itself can take many forms, depending on the level or degree of discrimination which is eliminated. Bela Balassa (1961) identifies five levels at which discrimination may be removed and, by implication, five ideal-types of regional integration. At the lowest level is the free trade area in which tariffs and quotas are eliminated among the members of the integrating region. A customs union goes further. In addition to the elimination of tariffs and quotas, a customs union also eliminates discriminatory tariffs by non-member countries. This it does by setting up common external tariffs against such non-member countries. A third ideal-type (or level) of integration is the common market. This combines the features of the free trade area and the customs union with the elimination of obstacles to the free flow of the factors of production, namely labour and capital. Economic union or community goes one step further. It harmonizes economic policies among its members, sometimes including a common currency. Finally, at the highest level of integration we have political union. Here the very

**WEST AFRICA**

| | BENIN | CAPE VERDE | GAMBIA | GHANA | GUINEA | GUINEA-BISSAU | IVORY COAST | LIBERIA | MALI | MAURITANIA | NIGER | NIGERIA | SENEGAL | SIERRA LEONE | TOGO | UPPER VOLTA |
|---|---|---|---|---|---|---|---|---|---|---|---|---|---|---|---|---|
| Association des Chirurgiens Francophones de l'Afrique de l'Ouest | | | | | | | O | | ● | | ● | | ● | | ● | |
| Conference des Administrations des Postes et Télécommunications des Etats de l'Afrique de l'Ouest | ● | | | | | | ● | | ● | ● | ● | | ● | | | ● |
| Comité conjoint du Programme de Lutte contre l'Onchocercose | ● | | | ● | | | ● | | ● | | ● | | | | ● | O |
| Communauté Economique de l'Afrique de l'Ouest (CEAO) | | | | | | | ● | | ● | ● | ● | | ● | | | O |
| Comité Permanent Inter-Etats de Lutte contre la Sécheresse dans le Sahel | | ● | ● | | | | | | ● | ● | ● | | ● | | ● | O |
| Comité Sous-Régional de l'Afrique de l'Ouest de l'Association des Banques Centrales Africaines | ● | | ● | ● | ● | ● | ● | ● | ● | | ● | ● | ● | ● | ● | ● |
| Economic Community of West African States (ECOWAS) | ● | ● | ● | ● | ● | ● | ● | ● | ● | ● | ● | O | ● | ● | ● | ● |
| Conseil de l'Entente (ENTENTE) | ● | | | | | | O | | | | ● | | | | ● | ● |
| Multinational Programming and Operational Centre for West Africa | ● | ● | ● | ● | ● | ● | ● | ● | ● | ● | ● | O | ● | ● | ● | ● |
| Mano River Union | | | | | ● | | | ● | | | | | | O | | |
| Organisation Commune Benin-Niger des Chemins de Fer et Transports | O | | | | | | | | | | ● | | | | | |
| Organisation de Coordination et de Cooperation pour la Lutte Contre les Grandes Endemies | ● | | | | | | ● | | ● | ● | ● | | ● | | ● | O |
| Organisation pour la Mise en Valeur du Fleuve Gambie | | | ● | | ● | | | | | | | | O | | | |
| Organisation pour la Mise en Valeur du Fleuve Senegal | | | | | | | | | ● | ● | | | O | | | |
| Régie du Chemin de Fer Abidjan-Niger | | | | | | | O | | | | | | | | | ● |
| Regional Training Centre for Training in Aerial Surveys | ● | | | ● | | | | | | | | | O | ● | | |
| Secrétariat Permanent Sene-Gambien | | | O | | | | | | | | | | ● | | | |
| Union Monétaire Ouest Africaine | ● | | | | | | ● | | | | ● | | ● | | ● | ● |
| West African Bankers Association | ● | | ● | ● | | | ● | ● | ● | | ● | ● | ● | O | ● | ● |
| West African Clearing House | ● | | ● | ● | | ● | ● | ● | ● | | ● | ● | ● | O | ● | ● |
| West African Examinations Council | | | ● | O | | | | ● | | | | ● | | ● | | |
| West African Rice Development Association | ● | | ● | ● | ● | ● | ● | O | ● | ● | ● | ● | ● | ● | ● | ● |
| West African Sub-Regional Pool of the Pan-African News Agency | ● | ● | ● | ● | ● | ● | ● | ● | ● | ● | ● | O | ● | ● | ● | ● |

**Key for all tables.**

O outline circle indicates
location of headquarters

## Table 10.1 Membership of regional organizations in Africa

(a) West African organizations only

| | BENIN | CAPE VERDE | GAMBIA | GHANA | GUINEA | GUINEA-BISSAU | IVORY COAST | LIBERIA | MALI | MAURITANIA | NIGER | NIGERIA | SENEGAL | SIERRA LEONE | TOGO | UPPER VOLTA |
|---|---|---|---|---|---|---|---|---|---|---|---|---|---|---|---|---|
| African Agricultural Credit Commission | | | | | | | ● | | | | | | ● | | | |
| African Development Bank | ● | ● | ● | ● | ● | ● | ● | ● | ● | ● | ● | ● | ● | ● | ● | ● |
| African Groundnut Council | | | ● | | | | | | ● | | ● | ○ | ● | | | |
| African Timber Organisation | | | | ● | | | ● | ● | | | | | ● | | | |
| Agence pour la Securite de la Navigation Aerienne en Afrique et Madagascar | ● | | | | | | ● | | ● | ● | ● | | ○ | | ● | ● |
| Air Afrique | ● | | | | | | ○ | | ● | ● | ● | | ● | | ● | ● |
| Arab Bank for Economic Development | | | | | | | | | ● | | | | | | | |
| Autorite de Developpement Integre de la Region Liptako-Gourma | | | | | | | | | ● | | ● | | | | | ○ |
| Cocoa Producers Alliance | | | | ● | | | ● | | | | | ○ | | | ● | |
| Comite Inter-Africain d'Etudes Hydrauliques | ● | | | | | | ● | | ● | ● | ● | | ● | | ● | ○ |
| Conference of East and Central African States | ● | | | | | | | | | | | | | | | |
| Conference Internationale des Controles d'Assurances des Etats Africains | ● | | | | | | | | | | | | | | | |
| Conference des Ministres des Etats de l'Afrique de l'Ouest et du Centre sur les Transports Maritimes | ● | ● | ● | ● | ● | ● | ○ | ● | ● | ● | ● | ● | ● | ● | ● | ● |
| Conseil Africain et Malgache pour l'Enseignement Superieur | ● | | | | | | ● | | ● | ● | ● | | | | ● | ○ |
| East African Community (EAC) | | | | | | | | | | | | | | | | |
| Economic Community of the Great Lakes Countries | | | | | | | | | | | | | | | | |
| Lake Chad Basin Commission | | | | | | | | | | | ● | ● | | | | |
| Lakes Tanganyika and Kivu Basin Commission | | | | | | | | | | | | | | | | |
| Organisation of African Unity (OAU) | ● | ● | ● | ● | ● | ● | ● | ● | ● | ● | ● | ● | ● | ● | ● | ● |
| Organisation Commune Africaine et Mauricienne (OCAM) | ● | | | | | | ● | | | | ● | | ● | | ● | ● |
| Organisation Commune de Lutte Antiacridienne et Antiaviare | ● | | | | | | ● | | ● | ● | ● | | ○ | | | ● |
| Organisation Interafricain de Cafe | ● | | | ● | ● | | ○ | ● | | | | ● | | | ● | ● |
| Organisation Internationale contre le Criquet Migrateur Africain | | | ● | ● | | | ● | | ● | ○ | ● | ● | ● | ● | ● | ● |
| River Niger Commission (Niger Basin Authority since 1980) | ● | | | | ● | | ● | | ● | | ○ | | | | | ● |
| Section Regionale de l'Association des Aeroports Civils en Afrique de l'Ouest et du Centre | ● | ● | ● | ● | ● | ● | ● | | ● | ○ | ● | ● | ● | ● | | |
| Societe Africaine de Developpement des Industries Alimentaires a Base de Mil et de Sorgho | | | | | | | | | ● | ● | ○ | | | | | ● |
| Societe de Developpement Hoteliere et Touristique de l'Afrique de l'Ouest | ● | | | | | | | | | | | | | | | |
| South African Customs Unions (SACU) | | | | | | | | | | | | | | | | |
| Southern African Development Coordination Conference | | | | | | | | | | | | | | | | |
| UDEAC | | | | | | | | | | | | | | | | |
| Union Africaine des Postes et Telecommunications | ● | | | | | | ● | | ● | ● | ● | | ● | | ● | ● |

(b) West African membership of pan-African organizations

| | ALGERIA | EGYPT | LIBYA | MOROCCO | TUNISIA | CAMEROON | C.A.R. | CHAD | CONGO | GABON | EQUIT. GUINEA | SAO TOME & PRINCIPE | ZAIRE |
|---|---|---|---|---|---|---|---|---|---|---|---|---|---|
| African Agricultural Credit Commission | ● | | ● | ○ | ● | | | | | | | | |
| African Development Bank | ● | ● | ● | ● | ● | ● | ● | ● | ● | ● | ● | ● | ● |
| African Groundnut Council | | | | | | | | | | | | | |
| African Timber Organisation | | | | | | ● | ● | | ● | ○ | ● | | ● |
| Agence pour la Securite de la Navigation Aerienne en Afrique et Madagascar | | | | | | ● | | ● | ● | ● | | ● | |
| Air Afrique | | | | | | ● | ● | ● | | | | | |
| Arab Bank for Economic Development | ● | ● | ● | ● | ● | ● | ● | ● | ● | ● | | ● | ● |
| Autorite de Developpement Integre de la Region Liptako-Gourma | | | | | | | | | | | | | |
| Cocoa Producers Alliance | | | | | | ● | | | | ● | | ● | |
| Comite Inter-Africain d'Etudes Hydrauliques | | | | | | ● | | ● | ● | ● | | | |
| Conference of East and Central African States | | | | | | | ● | ● | ● | ● | ● | | ● |
| Conference Internationale des Controles d'Assurances des Etats Africains | | | | | | ● | ● | ● | ● | ○ | | | |
| Conference des Ministres des Etats de l'Afrique de l'Ouest et du Centre sur les Transports Maritimes | | | | | | ● | ● | ● | ● | ● | | | ● |
| Conseil Africain et Malgache pour l'Enseignement Superieur | | | | | | ● | ● | ● | ● | ● | | | ● |
| East African Community (EAC) | | | | | | | | | | | | | |
| Economic Community of the Great Lakes Countries | | | | | | | | | | | | | ● |
| Lake Chad Basin Commission | | | | | | ● | | ○ | | | | | |
| Lakes Tanganyika and Kiru Basin Commission | | | | | | | | | | | | | ● |
| Organisation of African Unity (OAU) | ● | ● | ● | ● | ● | ● | ● | ● | ● | ● | ● | ● | ● |
| Organisation Commune Africaine et Mauricienne (OCAM) | | | | | | | ○ | | | | | | |
| Organisation Commune de Lutte Antiacridienne et Antiaviare | | | | | | ● | | ● | | | | | |
| Organisation Interafricain de Cafe | | | | | | ● | ● | | ● | ● | | | ● |
| Organisation Internationale contre le Criquet Migrateur Africain | | | | | | ● | ● | ● | ● | | | | ● |
| River Niger Commission (Niger Basin Authority since 1980) | ● | | | | | ● | | ● | | | | | |
| Section Regionale de l'Association des Aeroports Civils en Afrique de l'Ouest du Centre | | | | | | ● | ● | ● | ● | ● | | | ● |
| Societe Africaine de Developpement des Industries Alimentaires a Base de Mil et de Sorgho | | | | | | | | | | | | | |
| Societe de Developpement Hoteliere et Touristique de l'Afrique de l'Ouest | | | | | | | ● | ● | ● | ● | | | |
| South African Customs Union (SACU) | | | | | | | | | | | | | |
| Southern African Development Coordination Conference | | | | | | | | | | | | | |
| UDEAC | | | | | | ● | ○ | | ● | ● | | | |
| Union Africaine des Postes et Telecommunications | | | | | | | ● | ● | ○ | | | | |

(c) North African and (d) Central African membership of pan-African organizations

| ANGOLA | BOTSWANA | BURUNDI | ETHIOPIA | KENYA | LESOTHO | MALAGASY REP | MALAWI | MAURITIUS | MOZAMBIQUE | RWANDA | SEYCHELLES | SOMALIA | SOUTH AFRICA | SUDAN | SWAZILAND | TANZANIA | UGANDA | ZAMBIA | ZIMBABWE |
|---|---|---|---|---|---|---|---|---|---|---|---|---|---|---|---|---|---|---|---|
| ● | ● | ● | ● | ● | ● | ● | ● | ● | ● | ● | ● | ● |  | ● | ● | ● | ● | ● | ● |
|  |  |  |  |  |  |  |  |  |  |  |  |  |  | ● |  |  |  |  |  |
|  |  |  |  |  |  | ● |  |  |  |  |  |  |  |  |  | ● |  |  |  |
|  |  |  |  |  |  | ● |  |  |  |  |  |  |  |  |  |  |  |  |  |
|  |  |  |  |  |  |  |  |  |  |  |  |  |  | ● |  |  |  |  |  |
|  |  | ● | ● | ● |  |  |  |  |  | ● |  | ● |  | ● |  | ● | ● | ● |  |
|  |  |  | ● |  |  | ● |  | ● |  | ● |  |  |  |  |  |  |  |  |  |
|  |  |  |  | ● |  |  |  |  |  |  |  |  |  |  |  | ● | ● |  |  |
|  |  |  | ● |  |  |  |  |  |  | ○ |  |  |  |  |  |  |  |  |  |
|  |  |  | ● |  |  |  |  |  |  | ● |  |  |  |  |  | ● |  | ● |  |
| ● | ● | ● | ○ | ● | ● | ● | ● | ● | ● | ● | ● | ● |  | ● | ● | ● | ● | ● | ● |
|  |  |  |  |  |  |  |  | ● |  | ● |  |  |  |  |  |  |  |  |  |
| ● |  | ● | ● | ● | ● |  |  |  |  | ● |  |  |  |  |  | ● | ● |  | ● |
|  |  |  |  |  | ● |  |  |  |  |  |  |  |  |  |  | ● | ● |  |  |
|  |  |  |  |  |  |  |  |  |  |  |  |  | ● |  |  |  |  |  |  |
|  | ● |  |  | ● |  |  |  |  |  |  |  |  | ● |  | ● |  |  |  |  |
| ● | ● |  |  |  |  | ● |  | ● |  | ● |  |  |  |  |  | ● | ● | ● | ● |
|  |  |  |  |  |  |  |  |  |  | ● |  |  |  |  |  |  |  |  |  |

(e) East and Southern African membership of pan-African organizations structures and political institutions which harmonize policies are themselves harmonized and become unified. The various ideal-types and the nature of discriminations removed are set forth in Table 10:2.

**TABLE 10.2 Ideal-types of economic integrative action to eliminate discrimination**

| Ideal-types | Elimination of tariffs and quotas | Common external tariff | Free flow of labour and capital | Harmonization of economic policies | Unification of political institutions |
|---|---|---|---|---|---|
| 1. Free trade area | ● | | | | |
| 2. Customs union | ● | ● | | | |
| 3. Common market | ● | ● | ● | | |
| 4. Economic union or community | ● | ● | ● | ● | |
| 5. Political union | ● | ● | ● | ● | ● |

Adapted from Joseph S. Nye (1968: 860) and Renninger (1979: 39)

Given these various forms of economic integration we would say that the African regional organizations which deal with economic integration are, by and large, economic communities or, intended to be so even when they call themselves by different names. Jalloh (1980) reviewing the respective treaties which created the various economic communities observed that:

They all aim at creating free trade among their members and joint co-ordination of commercial policies with respect to third parties. Besides the free movement of goods, there are also provisions for the movement of persons among the members. Co-ordination of other policies, notably policies on foreign investments, transportation, and industrial and economic development, is also provided for. Finally, there is the agreement to create and operate joint services in the area of education, infrastructure and research. Two of these regional organizations, OCAM and the Conseil de l'Entente, also include co-ordination of foreign policies among the tasks of the regional organizations.

Jalloh concluded that 'African regional organizations tend to have very broad functions which if realized will result in the emergence of at least an economic union'.

Seven of these African regional integration efforts are of particular interest because of their historical and continuing impact on African international relations. In their successes and failures they also provide lessons for other integration efforts. We outline the course of five of them (UDEAC, Conseil de l'Entente, OCAM, CEAO, and SACU) and examine the sixth (the East African Community) in greater detail. On the basis of insights gained from these studies we will discuss the development and assess the prospects of the seventh and newest of them – ECOWAS.

## UDEAC

UDEAC's origins lie in the Federation of French Equatorial Africa. After the Federation broke up in 1956 Congo (Brazzaville), Gabon, Central African Republic and Chad chose to maintain their former economic links in the form of a customs union and by co-ordinating fiscal policies. A treaty to that effect established the Equatorial Customs Union in 1959. In 1961 the Federal Republic of Cameroon joined the customs union. In 1964 a new treaty sought to strengthen the union in the direction of a common market. The treaty formally established UDEAC on 1 January, 1966 and was re-negotiated in 1974 (Robson, 1967).

Since 1966, however, not much has been achieved beyond the unification of tariffs and import dues, a steady growth in inter-union trade and attracting more foreign aid than would otherwise have been the case. The union has remained stagnant. A full customs union has not yet been achieved and little progress has been made in other areas of co-operation. Thus the free movement of labour and capital provided for in the treaty has virtually remained a dead letter. And despite unified tariffs and import dues members still impose a 'complementary import duty' to supplement their budgets. Similarly, although the treaty states that industrial goods and processed agricultural products from member states should be progressively subject to a single, uniform tax this has not occurred. On the contrary, members use discriminatory tax to protect their industries against those in partner countries producing similar products.

The main reason for stagnation concerns the inability to distribute the costs and benefits of union fairly between the member states. The two poorest members, Chad and the Central African Republic, have persistently complained that most of the gains go to Cameroon while they receive little or nothing. They therefore asked for a system of industry allocation which would guarantee that despite their unattractiveness for investment in comparison with the richer and better endowed coastal states of Gabon and Cameroon, some industries would be located exclusively on their territories. Although some concessions were made, these amounted to little in practical terms owing to the reluctance of the more developed Gabon and Cameroon to 'subsidize' their poorer partners. For instance the Industrial Development Bank, which was proposed in 1964, has yet to take off effectively, and Chad and the Central African Republic have not attracted industries from the union. The recent allocation of petrochemical industries to Gabon, aluminium to Cameroon and pharmaceutical and watch-making to the Central African Republic is little more than a recognition and legitimization of accepted facts.

Given this kind of situation, little institution-building has been possible. The principal decision-maker is the Committee of Direction comprising two representatives of each member state. The Council (of heads of state) merely gives its approval or decides in case of differences. The Secretariat is charged with mere administrative tasks and has no autonomous decision-making authority. One assessment was that the Secretariat was 'more or less equivalent to a statistical office combined with a multilateral mail forwarding agency' (Green and Krishna, 1967: 109).

The problem of equitable distribution of gains and the failure of integration to move forward have led Chad and the Central African Republic to see their more powerful Nigerian and Zairean neighbours as alternatives to UDEAC. A substantial part of Chad's trade passes through Nigeria with which it also has cultural links and with which it participates in the Chad Basin Commission. Frustrated by UDEAC, Chad and the Central African Republic withdrew membership and joined Zaire to form the Union of Central African States (UEAC) though the Central African Republic soon reconsidered her stand and returned to UDEAC, and Chad may yet do the same.

## Conseil de l'Entente

The dismemberment of the Federation of French West Africa also led to attempts by some of its members to maintain previous economic ties on a new basis and to co-ordinate foreign economic and political policies. In 1959 Benin (then Dahomey), the Ivory Coast, Niger and Upper Volta agreed to set up a Conseil de l'Entente. (The Ivory Coast had put forward a plan to merge with Niger and Upper Volta.) Togo joined the Conseil in 1966. The main objectives were to promote economic development and integration of members via a customs union, co-ordination of policies in the fields of communication, administration and fiscal measures, and assistance in preparing economic and industrial projects and finding foreign aid to implement them.

The Conseil succeeded in establishing a mutual aid and loan guarantee fund to guarantee foreign public and private investments in member states. The fund, with substantial capital ($19 million in 1976), has expanded its activities to embrace virtually the entire field of economic development. It has sponsored co-operative actions in telecommunications, regional industrial developments, health care programmes for animals, stabilization of prices and supplies of cereals, and feasibility studies of commercial production of fruits and vegetables. By 1977 it had also succeeded in attracting USAID loans totalling about $13.5 million and various European and Canadian loans amounting to over $5.5 million (Yansane, 1977: 45).

Despite these successes the Conseil has had to weather many storms. It has survived primarily because the problem of equitable distribution of costs and benefits has not been acute. Three reasons account for this. First its members are approximately equal in population (except Benin and Togo which are much smaller) and of approximately equal wealth (except the Ivory Coast which is twice as rich in GNP as any of its partners. Secondly, the fund's assets have been very substantial and its benefits have been fairly distributed with each state receiving in inverse ratio to its contribution thus putting the poorest at an advantage. Finally the Ivory Coast, the core state in the organization is, for political reasons, willing and able to make special pay-offs to its partners and bends over backwards to satisfy their needs within the limited resources of the organization.

These advantages notwithstanding, the Conseil has not made much progress towards a common market and has not succeeded in establishing supra-national institutions to move integration forward. Even trade among its members remains a small fraction of their trade with non-member countries. With the formation of CEAO and ECOWAS it is likely that the organization will either continue to stagnate or even disintegrate as members come to cast their eyes on the benefits of these larger integration schemes.

## OCAM

OCAM is an outgrowth of the efforts of former French African colonies (other than Mali and Guinea) to co-ordinate matters of currency, transport and technical assistance as well as foreign policy among themselves, and between them and France. On a larger plane it aimed to foster peace, mutual aid and non-interference in the internal affairs of members. In 1961 these former colonies established the Organisation Africaine et Malgache de Coopération Economique (OAMCE) to take care of the economic aspects. It immediately established Air Afrique to be followed soon by the Association of Development Banks and the Afro-Malagasy Organization for Industrial Property. A political wing, the Union Africaine et Malgache (UAM), was also established to co-ordinate political, diplomatic and security matters. This wing immediately set up a defence organization (the Afro-Malagasy Union for Defence) as well as a Posts and Telecommunication Union. But with the establishment of the OAU which eclipsed political unions, these organizations were consolidated into the Union Africaine et Malgache de Coopération Economique (UAMCE) in 1964 to deal solely with economic, socio-cultural and technical matters. But because the OAU was still finding its feet, it was felt that UAMCE should meanwhile acquire a strong organization and political significance. Accordingly, in 1965 after admitting Rwanda and the Congo (Zaire) UAMCE was reorganized into OCAM (Julienne, 1967: 349–51).

The objectives of OCAM include: harmonization of economic, social, technical and cultural policies and activities, co-ordination of development programmes; and consultation and co-ordination in foreign policy matters though with due respect for the sovereignty and freedom of action of member states. Guy de Lusignam (1969: 293) notes that there were also more immediate political objectives as OCAM attempted to restore peace in the war-torn Congo (Zaire); to exert a moderating influence on the more extreme African revolutionary outlooks; and to restrict Nkrumah whom they accused of subversive activities in Africa.

OCAM had the blessing of the French government and became a major instrument by which France maintained cohesion among Francophone states. The political aspects of the organization, however, brought severe strains. Matters worsened because of divergencies in attitude towards such issues as the Arab–Israeli conflict and the way to deal with South Africa's apartheid policy. A number of leaders such as Ould Daddah of Mauritania also became conscious of their dependency on 'Mother France' and publicly began to demand reforms in the co-operation agreements governing their relations with that country, especially after the demise of de Gaulle in 1969. There was, too, the conflict between Senegal and the Ivory Coast over leadership in OCAM, a conflict exacerbated by Senegal's denunciation of Houphouet-Boigny's suggestion that a dialogue be maintained with apartheid South Africa. Cameroon, Chad, Madagascar, Mauritania and Zaire soon withdrew their membership, though Mauritius later joined (the name OCAM could thus be retained the 'M' now standing for Mauritius instead of Madagascar). By 1974 OCAM had to resolve to make itself completely non-political and become a true instrument of economic, cultural and social development. Accordingly in 1975 its charter eliminated any reference to political consultations among member states (Yansane, 1977: 46–7).

On the economic front, agreements were reached to guarantee markets for certain products from member states, notably sugar. These agreements have been ineffective, in part because of financial difficulties among the sugar importing countries and in part because of the defection of the sugar exporting countries, Zaire and Madagascar. OCAM's major achievement to date has been its aggressive and successful lobbying for higher prices for its exports in keeping with the higher prices of its imports from the EEC and its agreement to create three new joint enterprises: the African and Mauritian Institute of Bilingualism, in Mauritius; the Inter-State School of Architecture and Town Planning, in Lomé, and the Institute for the Training of Statisticians, in Kigali, Rwanda. Its budget remains small (around $2 million a year) and members often fail to honour their debts. Accordingly its projects, including its show-case achievement, Air Afrique, have run into hard times. In sum OCAM has not been able to move forward: it has been in a state of encapsulation, or stagnation.

*CEAO*

CEAO can be said to represent a metamorphosis of the Union Douanière de l'Afrique de l'Ouest (UDAO) first created in Paris in 1959 to cushion the economic effect of the pending break-up of the Federation of French West Africa. As each member state attained independence in 1960 and began to manage its own budget and plan its own trade and development policies, the customs union ran into difficulties. Disputes arose over the distribution of customs duties collected by the coastal states on goods travelling to and from the landlocked and poorer states. In 1962 UDAO collapsed. It was revived in 1966 as UDEAO with a less ambitious objective than a full custom union.

UDEAO allowed common external tariffs and fiscal charges only on certain imports from non-member states and reduced taxes on imports from members to 50 per cent and in exceptional cases, to 70 per cent of the most favourable rate applied to similar products from outside the union. It also introduced a system of distributing the proceeds of the common external tariffs and fiscal charges in a way that would favourably compensate the landlocked countries. But these provisions remained largely a dead letter as members often applied duties on goods from partner states that were substantially higher than what was provided for. This was both a cause and an effect of the meagre volume of trade among the members (about 1 per cent of total imports and 2 per cent of total exports). One country, Mali, complained of being cheated of what little trade increase there was on account of the Ivory Coast's special trading relationship with Upper Volta and Niger, two of its partners in the Conseil. By 1969 UDEAO had been pronounced a failure by its Council of Ministers and a proposal was made to replace it with CEAO.

These developments were occurring at a time when OCAM, as we have noted, was running into difficulties, when de Gaulle, symbol of French mystique and the engineer of Francophone Africa's neo-dependence on France, was no longer on the scene and when 'anti-Nkrumahism' another rallying cry for unity among Francophone states, no longer applied as Nkrumah was, himself, in exile. In short all the instruments and avenues through which France and its former colonies maintained cohesion with each other were in decline. Gaullism appeared to be at an end in Africa, and some feared that chaos would result. France, therefore, needed an issue to help rekindle sentiments of Francophone solidarity and unity with France. Anti-Nigerianism was one such issue. Nigeria's potential influence in West Africa had long worried France. It had also worried some Francophone states, notably the Ivory Coast, which is why the Ivory Coast recognized Biafra during Nigeria's Civil War and put pressure on France to do the same. Nigeria's emergence from the war as a united and a stronger country politically and, thanks to the emergent oil boom, economically, created concern in Paris, given the fears of disarray in Francophone West Africa. The French President, Georges Pompidou, embarked on a series of African tours beginning in February 1971, during which he urged the Francophone states to 'harmonize their efforts so as to counterbalance the heavy weight of Nigeria' in the West African region. Senghor and Houphouet-Boigny took the suggestion seriously enough to compose their differences and for Senghor to pay an unprecedented official visit to Abidjan in December 1971. There the two leaders affirmed their commitment to the formation of CEAO the proposal for which had been written at a meeting held in Bamako in May 1970.

CEAO was deemed to be a customs union of seven states – Benin, Niger, Senegal, the Ivory Coast, Mali, Upper Volta and Mauritania (Togo was an observer and Guinea was excluded). Its final treaty, signed in Abidjan in April 1973, provided for free trade in certain commodities, free movement of persons, a common external tariff to be established over a two-year period and a community fund for compensation to those who benefit less from the union.

CEAO has made some advances since its formation. Trade among its members a mere 5.8 per cent of total trade in 1969–70 increased to 9.4 per cent in 1974–75 and it is estimated to be about 10 per cent in 1980. Steps have been taken to establish free trade in non-industrial goods and to give preferential tariffs to certain manufactured goods. But this is as far as developments have gone. Tensions remain among members over the relative share of regional trade and no significant progress has been made in the area of co-ordinating and harmonizing industrial and economic development plans. Its institutions remain inter-governmental rather than supra-national. Jalloh (1980: 75) pessimistically observes 'CEAO gives the impression of stagnating with little prospects for the expansion of regional tasks'. It seems likely that CEAO functions might soon be eclipsed by the larger grouping, ECOWAS.

## SACU

This is a customs and currency union instituted by South Africa with its independent African enclaves, Lesotho and Swaziland and the landlocked neighbour, Botswana. It is of interest primarily because it represents an instrument of South Africa's control over the economy of the 'partners'. Tied, via this union, to South Africa's economic apron-string these 'partners' will be unable to contribute to political, diplomatic and military efforts to liberate the oppressed black in the Republic. SACU will also offer South Africa a propaganda weapon internationally to demonstrate how 'beneficial' the association is to the satellites and will thus strengthen its case for its Bantustan policy, the so-called 'home-rule for the Africans'. It is unlikely that a system based on the separation of races, itself based on a belief in the inferiority of one race, could successfully foster a genuine economic union at any level among allegedly incompatible races.

The sum of our discussion thus far is that while African regional organizations have had laudable objectives of bringing about economic integration and development, their achievements have been minimal. One obvious reason has been disagreement among members over relative shares of actual or potential gains of integration. Another reason has been differences in political outlook and political orientations towards extra-regional (non-African) powers while another problem has been the failure to build supra-national institutions which have a regional rather than a parochial national outlook in matters of benefit sharing and development planning. The result has been stagnation rather than a spur to a higher level of integration. We shall look at these and other problems in greater detail and deduce from them some general theories regarding Third World integration. To do this we turn to the most spectacular failure, the East African Community, which was once regarded as the most successful and the most promising in Africa.

## The East African experience

The East African Community, a regional grouping of Kenya, Uganda and Tanzania, was formed by a treaty which came into force in 1967. The treaty was the final stage in the efforts to foster regional co-operation in British East Africa. The efforts began with the British colonial measures to promote more unified administrative control over their East African territories by establishing the Court of Appeal for East Africa (1902), a postal union (1911) a customs union (1917) and the East African currency board (1920). Tanganyika, a British mandate later to become Tanzania after unification with Zanzibar in 1963, was gradually absorbed into these institutions. In 1948 a quasi-federation was established with a common market and a number of common services such as the East African Railways and Harbours Administration, the East African Posts and Telecommunication Administration, and the Agricultural and Medical Research Services. A High Commission (comprising the three territorial governors) with a secretariat, manned by technocrats with region-wide outlook and expertise co-ordinated the common services. There was also a central legislature although its authority over regional institutions was limited not only because it could be over-ruled by the High Commission but also because it had no legislative competence over significant areas of regional activity such as regional planning or fixing of tariffs and customs rates. In any case the Africans distrusted the legislature because its elective and voting systems gave disproportionate influence to the white settlers (Springer, 1980).

The quasi-federal system was revamped in 1961 – partly because of Tanganyika's independence (1961) and partly because of Ugandan and Tanganyikan resentment of the disproportionate benefits accruing to Kenya in terms of growth in the GNP, foreign investment, international trade and location of common services headquarters in Nairobi. An East African Common Services Organization (EACSO) was introduced. Under this new system, the High Commission was replaced with a Common Services Authority composed of the three elected leaders of the three territories. The authority was assisted by four ministerial committees and a revamped central legislature with wider legislative competence. The question of inequitable distribution of benefits was partially settled by setting up a distributable pool account into which a fixed percentage of customs and excise duties as well as corporate income taxes collected by each territory was paid. One half of the proceeds was retained by the Authority to operate the common services while the balance was shared equally among the member states. Since Kenya obviously would contribute the lions share of the proceeds, the distributive formula clearly put the other two territories at an advantage and thus partially redressed the inequity about which they previously complained. But the problem of locating the Common Services Organization headquarters in Nairobi remained a sore point. However, because the EASCO was deemed a transitional organization to be superceded by a federation whenever Uganda and Kenya achieved independence (Tanganyika even offered to delay its own independence for that purpose!), this and other outstanding problems were put on ice for the time being.

The anticipated federation failed to materialize. Serious negotiations to establish it in 1963 broke down largely because Uganda opposed the high degree of centralization which its partners wanted to build into the federation. Subsequently EACSO came on the verge of disintegration. In June 1965 the dissolution of the East African Currency Board was announced, to be replaced with national central banks and currencies. The East African Navy had earlier broken up in 1961 followed by Ugandan withdrawal from the East African Tourist Travel Association in 1963. The common market faced the throes of death as Tanzania threatened to withdraw. Although the Tanzanian and Ugandan economies expanded at a faster rate than Kenya's they accused Kenya of getting a disproportionate share of the benefits on account of its inter-territorial trade surpluses and its industrial expansion. An ad hoc arrangement drawn up after meetings in Kampala and Mbale failed to save the situation. The Kampala–Mbale agreements provided that certain industries such as tyre, bicycle parts and fertilizer manufacture be exclusively located in Tanzania or Uganda. The agreements also permitted these two countries, through the agency of a regional quota committee's authorization, to institute quotas on certain Kenyan products like beer and galvanized iron. Kenya, however, not only failed to ratify these agreements but also proceeded to establish a tyre factory on its territory thus opening the way for Tanzania to impose unilateral import quotas and other restrictions on Kenyan products. A commission comprising three ministers from each state and headed by Kjeld Philip, a UN expert, had to be appointed to negotiate what was envisaged as a permanent solution, namely the Treaty for East African Co-operation (Springer, 1980).

The Treaty, which was signed in June 1967 and came to force on 1 December, placed the common market and the common services within one framework and gave the former a solid legal foundation. But more important it made provisions aimed at achieving equitable distribution of cost and benefits and it created a number of community organs to co-ordinate activities and provide executive direction. An innovation in this regard was the Community Minister, an individual appointed by each state to promote the Community's interests and project its viewpoints in his or her own cabinet.

This new effort by independent African states to create an economic community by treaty lasted ten years. By 1977 the common services had collapsed: the Kenya–Tanzania border had closed halting all economic intercourse, and Tanzania had engaged in border clashes with Uganda, culminating in full-scale war in 1978–79 which ended with the overthrow of Idi Amin's regime.

Several factors account for the disintegration of the East African Community. While some are idiosyncratic, others are fundamental in that they afflict all integration schemes in the Third World. We group these factors into five and examine their relative importance.

*Polarization and perception of unequal gains*

Although its prime objective was to promote 'the accelerated, harmonious and balanced development and sustained economic expansion of economic activities the benefits whereof shall be equitably shared' the EAC could not fully realize that objective. Kenya, the most developed of the countries as a result of a deliberate colonial policy in favour of the white settlers, continued to develop more and gain more. The Common External Tariffs (CET) had the effect of protecting its industries against competition from outside the community and guaranteed it a ready market in Uganda and Tanzania. The latter two countries, with fewer and less efficient industries, could not compete with Kenya. They had no option but to buy Kenyan products at relatively higher prices than they would have to pay, had the CET not effectively shut out similar products from outside the community. In addition, they had to forgo the revenue from import duties they would have collected had they imported from outside the community. Furthermore, foreign companies wishing to beat the CET by establishing industries within the Community naturally preferred to invest in Kenya which already had a large manufacturing base and a better infrastructure. Thus net foreign private capital inflow into Kenya between 1969 and 1976 (estimated from incomplete returns) was $184.9 million compared with $95.9 for Tanzania and $31.0 for Uganda (Mazzeo, 1980: 103).

The effect of all these was that, although the GNP of Kenya was growing at about the same rate at least as that of Tanzania (100 per cent between 1967 and 1976), Kenya dominated the Community trade, accumulated trade balances against its partners and widened the industrialization gap among them. Thus Kenya's share of the Community trade which was 63 per cent in 1968 climbed to 77 per cent in 1974 whereas Tanzania's rose from 11 per cent to 17 per cent, while that of Uganda, partly because of its domestic troubles, actually declined from 26 per cent to 6 per cent. Its trade balance against Tanzania and Uganda steadily rose from 280 million shillings in 1968 to 749 million shillings in 1976 (1 shilling = $0.14). By contrast Tanzania ran a trade deficit against the two partners, amounting to 187 million shillings in 1969 and worsening to 221 million in 1976. The Ugandan case was worse: its deficit of 59 million shillings in 1967 had increased to 528 million in 1976. Significant, from the point of view of the industrial gap, was the fact that whereas the share of manufactured goods in Kenya's intra-Community exports increased from 87 per cent in 1971 to 89.6 per cent in 1975, the share of manufactured goods in Tanzania's exports declined from 68.6 per cent to 61.1 per cent and Uganda's plummetted from 84.9 per cent to 41.0 per cent over the same period (Ravenhill, 1980; Mazzeo, 1980). This situation became intolerable for Tanzania and Uganda. Matters would have been worse had the EAC permitted the free flow of labour and capital. Had that been the case labour and capital would have moved from Tanzania and Uganda to the relatively more prosperous Kenya accentuating its advantages and leaving Tanzania and Uganda worse off. Nevertheless there was an uneven distribution of gains among the members of the community and this fact needed to be dealt with. The normal way to tackle the issue is to apply compensatory and corrective measures. But, as we shall see in a moment, such measures proved grossly inadequate, resulting in frustration, suspicion and mutual acrimony.

The kind of increasing gap between Kenya and its partners illustrates one popular theory among students of regional integration and it challenges another. The first theory is that when states at different levels of development engage in integration schemes involving a customs union or common market, there is a tendency for growth to occur in those states that have an initial advantage. They become the poles of growth. Resources move from the states that were initially at a disadvantage to the more advantaged, leaving the former even poorer. As a result they become the poles of stagnation. The phenomenon is called the 'backwash effect' in contrast to the 'spread effect' where resources move from the richer area to accelerate growth in the poorer areas. Backwash effects lead to polarization, the rich getting richer and poor getting poorer.

The second theory, one challenged by the pattern of trade and economic growth in the EAC, is the traditional, neo-classical theory of integration of a customs union or common market type. According to the theory popularized by Balassa (1961), Viner (1950), Meade (1955) and Lipsey (1960) among others, customs unions are beneficial only when they lead to trade creation, that is when high-cost products in one state are replaced by low-cost imports from other members of the union. In removing trade barriers to form the union, competition will ensue among similar industries in the member states as they produce for the large union market. This competition will:

> Lead to a pattern of specialization in which each country produces and supplies to the other members of the union the products in which it has a comparative advantage. The high-cost industries in each country will tend to be displaced by their low-cost competitors in other members of the union. Through the creation of intra-union trade, each member will be supplied from the lowest cost source within the union (Hazelwood, 1967: 6).

For trade creation to occur, however, the potential union members must already be relatively industrialized, conduct substantial trade with each other despite existing high tariff barriers, have complementary rather than competitive economies and have a relatively low ratio of foreign trade to the GNP. Where these conditions are absent, trade diversion is likely to be the result of union, in other words the substitution of high-cost imports from union partners for lower cost, perhaps better quality goods previously imported from non-member countries. For the EAC countries (perhaps less so than most developing countries) these background conditions were for the most part absent and there can be little doubt that trade diversion occurred in the community. But higher growth and development also took place than would have otherwise been the case and it more than offset the disadvantages of trade diversion.

Import substitution industries on a regional scale were facilitated (e.g. in cement, cigarettes and beer), regional corporations developed, employment increased, inter-territorial trade which amounted to 1 631 million shillings representing less than that 15 per cent of total international trade in 1964 had climbed to 2 499 million shillings by 1976 representing about 26 per cent of total external trade (Ravenhill, 1980: 58–61) while net foreign capital flow which was around $35 million in 1969 had risen to about $140 million in 1976.

It is these kinds of gains that have shifted the attention of scholars away from the neo-classical theories of trade creation/diversion (with their focus on efficient utilization of resources) to the more dynamic developmental theory of integration. The emphasis of the development theory is not on efficient use of productive capacity, for Third World countries have little productive capacity to start with, but on how to stimulate the creation of that productive capacity in the first place. For the adherents of the developmental theory, trade diversion is the very essence (or ought to be the essence) of integration. Kahnert and his associates (1969), Linder (1966), Mikesell (1963: 205–29) and Axline (1977) argue that trade diversion is the regional equivalent of import-substitution at the domestic level and, like the latter, it is a tool of development. For the region it is the main means of expanding production, as firms attempt to supply other member countries' markets, triggering off economies of scale. The attendant smaller unit cost of production in turn stimulates consumption and demand and, hence, expansion and growth in investment. The larger regional market also enhances the capacity and ability to sustain heavy industries that would otherwise be unprofitable. Import-substitution at the regional level is also a main source of savings of scarce foreign exchange which can then be used for input (rather than consumer) imports, thus enhancing capacity use and growth. These benefits are reaped without sacrificing alternative uses of resources which remain in the region and thus permit a more efficient combination of production factors, external economies and inter-industry linkages which ultimately lead to greater trade not only within the region but also with the outside world.

The EAC had obviously only partially reaped these benefits when it disintegrated. And its demise hinged on the question of the perceived and objective inequitable distribution of what little benefits accrued. This brings us to the problem of inadequate compensatory and corrective measures both to offset inequitable gains and to ensure balanced regional development.

*Inadequate compensatory and corrective measures*

Two types of mechanisms are normally employed to offset perceived or objective unequal gains from integration and polarization. The first is the compensatory or equalization mechanism in which certain measures are taken to transfer some of the gains of integration from those who benefit more to those who benefit less or even suffer net losses. One such measure is the collection and sharing of customs revenue in accordance with a pre-negotiated formula which favours the disadvantaged. Another is the transfer tax which provides revenue as well as protecting infant industries in the disadvantaged members.

The second type of mechanism for redressing unequal gains and polarization is the corrective mechanism, so called because it entails measures which aim to create conditions of industrialization and development at the poles of stagnation and thus correct the underlying cause of polarization and unequal gains. Such measures include the setting up of funds for industrialization and/or development banks from which members derive benefits in inverse ratio to their contribution under a pre-agreed formula. Harmonization of fiscal incentives to private investors and a system of industrial licensing which discourages duplication of industries and encourages dispersal in locations are also common corrective measures. Deliberate regional economic planning whereby decisions are taken to locate certain regional industries in certain places can also be said to be a corrective measure.

In the EAC several of these mechanisms were adopted. First, there was the East African Development Bank whose initial capital was to be provided with equal contributions from the member states. The bank's main purpose was to promote balanced industrial development in the area through investment loans and guarantees, the priority (38.75 per cent of the loans and guarantees) going to Tanzania and Uganda. Second, the member-states were to develop a common scheme of fiscal incentives for industrial development, that is to say to adopt a common policy on foreign investment and thus avoid unhealthy competition in granting concessions. This third equalizing measure was a temporary one: during the first fifteen years a state which suffered deficit in its total trade in manufactured goods with the other two member states was allowed to impose 'a transfer tax', equivalent to no more than the amount of the deficit, on imports of manufactures from the partner states. This was intended to protect domestic industries in the state imposing the tax. Finally, the treaty effected a geographical distribution of headquarters of common services to encourage a more equitable distribution of their benefits: the harbour corporation was separated from the railway corporation and transferred to Dar es Salaam, the posts and telecommunications corporation moved to Kampala where the Development Bank had its headquarters, the Community headquarters was sited in Arusha and Nairobi retained the railways and airways corporations.

The various compensatory and corrective measures, however, proved grossly inadequate. Tanzania and Uganda each imposed a transfer tax against their partners and benefited as a result. For instance Tanzania realized from it some 221 million shillings in revenue between 1968 and 1974 while Uganda accummulated 231.5 million shillings (Fredland, 1980: 73–4). But in the process, the principle of free movement of goods within the region was defeated and the aim of discouraging duplication of inefficient industries so as to realize economies of scale was also partially lost, largely because the transfer tax was subjected to all manner of abuse. The industrial licensing system also failed to promote the growth of efficient regional industries and it lapsed in 1973. As for the harmonization of fiscal incentives, no final agreements were ever reached on the subject and the widening gap in income tax policy among the partners negatively affected inter-state co-operation, leading to the break-up of the East African income tax department in 1973.

The Development Bank failed to meet expectations. Its initial capital of 120 million shillings (contributed equally by the three partner states) had reached only 238 million by early 1973, raised by selling equity shares to foreign banks and by raising loans from the World Bank and the Swedish International Development Authority. The modest assets meant that the bank's activities had to be on a limited scale. Thus while the partners' shares of approved loans approximated to the pre-agreed formula (22 per cent Kenya, 38 per cent Tanzania and 40 per cent Uganda in actual disbursement in 1973) the amount involved represented no more than 4 per cent of the annual industrial investment in each partner state. Apart from this, the bank also failed to act as a catalyst for complementary industrial investment. Its investments in textiles, sugar, tyres, cement and paper, for example, were said to be not particularly relevant to the aim of making the economies of the partners complementary. But, then unless there was regional planning so that there would be a 'clear and agreed pattern of industrial specialization in which the bank's investment could fit', the bank alone could not effect complementarity (Mazzeo, 1980: 86; Hazelwood 1980; 129). Unfortunately, the Economic Planning Council was purely advisory, and this was another inadequacy of the EAC.

The expectations of the impact of relocating the headquarters of common services, decentralizing some of its operations and subsidizing different parts of the services and different regions, were clearly too high. The reality was that the bulk of activities (60 per cent) and, therefore, of investment (57 per cent) and employment (54 per cent) continued in Kenya (Mazzeo 1980: 86). Some services became almost a Kenyan preserve: 80 per cent of the activities of the airways corporation, for example, were estimated in 1977 to originate and terminate in Kenya. Conflicts developed between national and community policies. The most acute was over land transport where Kenya developed excellent road networks that competed with the community's railway corporation and helped to make it impossible for the railways to show a profit. Different attitudes towards transport issues and other policy matters exacerbated the situation. Tanzania, for instance, favoured railways while Kenya opted for road transport. Tanzania also wanted the airways to concentrate on developing and expanding domestic routes whereas Kenya favoured the more profitable international flights. The international routes brought in tourists and foreign exchange. 'The typical tourist' Richard Fredland (1980: 67–8) 'flew into Nairobi's international airport via East African Airways, lodged at a Nairobi hotel . . . and drove or was chauffeured to Tanzania for two or three days of game viewing in a Tanzanian national park . . . Consequently, of perhaps US $2 200 paid by the tourist, as little as $200 was earned by

Tanzania while the remainder, excluding air fare, was earned by – or at least in – Kenya'.

Kenya's preference for road transport caused additional difficulties for its partners. For while rail capacity lay idle (because of deliberate Kenyan preferential regulations and treatment in favour of highway transport) foreign exchange was being consumed to import, sometimes at uncompetitive prices, capital goods and highway transport equipment, thus raising commodity costs and lowering productivity. It is not surprising therefore that as the balance of payments of the partner states worsened after the 1973 oil crisis, unilateral actions began to be taken. Tanzania and Uganda started withholding funds which should have been transferred in foreign exchange to the railway corporation headquarters. Dismissal and deportation of community workers from partner countries followed. In 1977 Tanzania closed its borders with Kenya after its attempts to undercut Kenya's monopolistic exploitation of the tourist trade had failed – the building of the Kilimanjaro International Airport 'within sight of the fabled peak and a short drive from Arusha, the usual jumping-off point for tours to Tanzania's game areas' had not stemmed the tide of tourism via Nairobi (Fredland, 1980: 66).

The EAC experience emphasizes the relevance of two current theories in regard to integration among Third World countries. First compensatory measures are never, in themselves, adequate to move integration forward to a higher level. Indeed, in so far as they involve mere fiscal transfers, these measures tend to be seen by the less developed of the partners as little more than the equivalent of the customs revenue they would have collected had the integration scheme not excluded or restricted extra-regional imports. In any case such fiscal transfers are not, and can in no way be a 'substitute for the employment opportunities and such spin-offs as improved local skills, technology and infrastructure – not to forget prestige – which are brought by industrial development' (Ravenhill, 1980: 47). In other words compensatory measures are seen as far less important than corrective ones since it is the latter which, when successfully implemented, lead to real redistribution of productive capacity and assure the less developed partners of a share in the structural transformation of the community. Because of the importance attached to them, corrective measures play the central role in determining the cost of participation in Third World integration schemes.

The second theoretical point is that precisely because of their central role in determining the opportunity cost of participation, corrective measures represent the most significant and most divisive issue in the integrative process and are likely to be the central political issue in negotiating the integration treaty and in the actual implementation of its terms. Agreement on corrective measures is always difficult because the more developed partners, on the one hand, and the less developed partners, on the other, have different perceptions of the cost -benefit as well as having different negotiating strategies and style. The more developed partners are being called upon to forgo in favour of their less developed partners the scarce resources for development that would, in the absence of a corrective mechanism, ordinarily accrue to them. This they are reluctant to do for obvious economic reasons. Moreover it is politically unwise for leaders to be seen to sacrifice domestic economic advantages for the sake of regional partnership. The less developed partners insist on positive or 'dirigiste' mechanisms such as direct transfer of funds from their richer partners, guaranteed investment and direct allocation of industries. Failure to implement corrective measures makes the integration scheme less attractive than going it alone or maintaining close relationships with extra-regional powers.

One way of bridging the differences between the more and less developed partners is to have package deals. Here there is a linkage of issues such as treating tariff reduction with allocation of industries, harmonization of incentives, Development Bank loans, and fiscal transfers. Such linkages would not only 'result in updating the common interest and [would] thus enhance both the scope and level of regional integration', but they would also offer members 'the opportunity to trade concessions in different areas, compensating a member that fails to gain in one area with advantages in another' (Jalloh, 1980: 79).

In Africa, unfortunately, issues tend to be treated in narrow isolation, and there is a reluctance to accept the linkage of issues. One main reason for this is that integration is seen as coming in stages, each stage having its unique problems that must be solved at the appropriate time. The piecemeal approach is grounded in historical experience and fear of the unknown. The attitude of 'crossing the bridge when we get to it', which is a product of underdevelopment itself, makes it much more difficult to predict or anticipate with reasonable certainty the scope and extent of problems. We know we have to cross a bridge, but how long a bridge, where it is located and the maximum tonnage it can handle —these facts we do not know. Linking present issues with future ones appears unrealistic as it would put some members in the unenviable position of accepting some real immediate costs in the hope of some possible but uncertain gains in the future. This limitation, when coupled with the importance attached to industrial development, explains why many members of Third World integration schemes give the impression that 'They want to see the smoke coming from the factories before signing the agreement for the common market' (Axline, 1978: 953–73).

It should now be clear that integration treaties represent the maximum concessions that could be extracted from the partner states at the time of negotiation. Deviations from them can be made only on the terms of the least co-operative partner. The implementation of the treaty terms also creates its own problems as the specific problems are worked out. One major problem is the changing perception of equity and the yardstick for measuring it. For example, can one say that the allocation of a tyre factory to Tanzania is equitable to the allocation of, say, a metal window factory to Uganda or a textiles factory to Kenya?

These problems are not totally insurmountable. For example, there is nothing sacrosanct about the various phases or stages of integration, nor indeed about the sequence of these stages. Later stages may be put before earlier ones. In the EAC, for example, considerable harmonization of fiscal and monetary policies preceded the free flow of capital and labour. It has been suggested that indeed two stages be combined, not simply to ensure acceptable package deals, but because it is a pre-requisite of success in Third World integration. As Axline (1977: 102–3) puts it:

Rather than a logic which moves from rather modest beginnings of economic integration to incrementally higher levels of political co-operation, the logic of integration among underdeveloped countries foresees little likelihood of success if integration is undertaken at relatively low levels, and a greater possibility of success only if a relatively high level of political integration is undertaken at the outset. Efforts based on less comprehensive political integration are more likely to be subject to a disintegrative dynamic.

The need for 'a relatively high level of political integration at the outset' is quite obvious: given the extreme nationalisms in Africa and other Third World countries, more complex supra-national institutions, with a wider scope of decision-making will be needed to evolve a comprehensive, dirigiste integration scheme.

### Inadequate supra-national institutions: the problems of personalization of the decision-making process

The EAC established many regional institutions to help with the progress of co-operative tasks. The basic community organs, however, remained inter-governmental with the heads of state constituting the East African Authority, the supreme decision-making body. Five ministerial councils advised the Authority and provided executive direction to the secretariat. An innovation was the Community Minister, an individual appointed by each state to promote the community's interests and project its view-points in the cabinet of that state. There was also provision for a Legislative Assembly whose members were appointed by the governments of each member state but which had limited constitutional powers. Judicial organs were also established, among them the Common Market Tribunal.

None of these organs, however, had the power of, say, the colonial civil service which was a surrogate regional authority which established a veritable hegemony over the area, performing the 'task of conflict resolution and initiating new areas of regional co-operation'. With independence, and particularly under the EAC treaty, co-operation as Ravenhill puts it, moved away from 'hegemony to bargaining'. Furthermore, the bargaining was among equals in the settlement of conflict and in the initiation of new areas of co-operation. There was, moreover, no intention or willingness to cede to a regional secretariat the powers necessary to enable planning to be based on regional market requirements rather than on national needs (Ravenhill,1980: 40).

Notwithstanding that co-operation has moved from hegemony to bargaining it is wholly incorrect to assert that the EAC organs were inadequate for moving integration forward by providing the long-term solution to the distributive problem, namely regional industrial planning. Although the institutional machinery looked impressive in its diversity it lacked the autonomous decision-making power such as characterizes the Commission of the European Economic Community. The retention of this power by the three Presidents circumscribed the bureucracy and dampened its initial enthusiasm and at the same time it 'discouraged too bold initiatives by ministers for fear of being disavowed by their Presidents' (Mazzeo, 1980: 92–3). But these are essentially defects of ability and skills on the part of the operators of the institutional machinery. For, as Mazzeo has argued, the institutional machinery of the EAC in many respects compared favourably with those of other regional schemes including the EEC. If it lacked a relatively autonomous decision-making body, it nonetheless enjoyed remarkable financial autonomy and its legislature had nothing to envy in the European Parliament. The Authority initially provided the necessary direction for Community institutions. When, later, the Authority broke down, the secretariat and other institutions devised new procedures to avoid any consequent problems of budget approval and policy-guidance. 'The fact that the EAC survived [this way] for seven years . . . is an indication of . . . the suitability of most of the components of the institutional machinery, and the commitment and ability of Community officals, notably those in high positions, like the Secretary-General and the East African Ministers' (Mazzeo,1980: 93–4).

The EAC did not fail because of the inadequacy of its institutions. Rather, it was what Mazzeo calls the 'personalization of power in the Authority' which increased the danger of instability and of transforming personal rivalries into national and intra-regional conflicts. Personalization of power and the decision-making process enabled each head of state, by an act of his own individual whim and caprice to determine the fate of the Community. Nyerere's refusal to convene a meeting of the Authority because of his dislike for Idi Amin can only be explained in these terms and would be almost unthinkable in conditions of institutionalized power.

Personalization of power is rooted in the colonial inheritance and the structural conditions prevailing in Africa. Colonial rule was essentially an authoritarian administrative/traditional grid which gave potential African leaders no experience or tradition in institutionalized and shared power-wielding. Nor did it suggest any clear conception of what politicians do other than wield power. At independence this colonial authoritarian inheritance was strengthened by the problems of nation-building, the low level of industrialization and the lack of organizational pluralism:

The stress and urgency of nation-building demand the creation of a strong central government facilitating the identification of governmental with presidential power. The low level of industrialization, by making it difficult for pluralistic interest groups to emerge, equally strengthens the tendency towards concentration and personalization of power, breeding instability (Mazzeo, 1980: 111).

In this kind of situation it is not easy to relinguish domestic power, hence the high incidence of coups d'etat as the means of changing governments. It is much more difficult to relinguish power to external institutions over which one would have even less control. The economic and political cost may simply be too high. Ceding power to regional institutions may mean sacrificing domestic economic growth and foregoing certain industries for the sake of regional partnership and overall betterment. But domestic business interests and civil servants may be hostile to an extension of regional authority which might encroach on their own. No rational political leadership is likely to want to alienate such powerful interest groups.

These observations support the view that governments of countries preoccupied with nation-building are usually poor partners for economic integration as they cannot be relied upon to make vital decisions for fear these might undermine their control at home (Haas, 1971: 15). It is also clear that unwillingness to give regional institutions autonomy is more than a matter of disinclination to cede newly won independence. It relates also in part to the structural conditions which still churn out king-type presidents. In conditions such as these the optimum decision-making organ that is generally feasible is the Authority of Heads of State which, it is hoped, will increasingly institutionalize rather than personalize power as the structural conditions improve.

### Ideological differences and economic nationalism

There is little question that there was a growing ideological division between the EAC partners. What is not so certain is whether this increasing ideological divergence was a cause or an effect of the growing polarization resulting from the unequal gains in the integrative process. Kenya clearly became increasingly capitalist while Tanzania became increasingly socialist as did Uganda until Idi Amin's regime. The pursuance of these divergent ideological paths appeared to have consequences which magnified stresses among the partners: socialism caused significant socio-economic disruption in Tanzania, especially in regard to the Ujamaa villages, and in Uganda, whereas capitalism, albeit dependent capitalism, ostensibly accounted for Kenya's socio-political and economic stability.

But while Kenya's stronger economic base and stable capitalist system enabled it to attract external investment and to exploit the opportunities which the Community offered, Tanzania's weaker economic base and socialist system had the opposite effect: external investors were reticent and the country's ability to exploit Community opportunities to the full was not as strong. Kenya, for example, was able to exploit and develop her tourist trade whereas Tanzania's tourist activities stagnated and even declined.

The widening economic gap and domestic stresses were soon

couched and explained in ideological terms. Tanzania was to ridicule Kenya's stable growth as based on a 'man-eat-man' philosophy to which Kenya replied by describing Tanzanian socialism as founded upon the principle of 'man-eat-nothing'. Tanzania then sought to prevent the intrusion via Kenya of 'bourgeois capitalist values and decadence', to terminate Kenyan exploitation of the Tanzanian market, and to insulate its people from the affluence of Kenya which was already causing large-scale smuggling of currency, coffee and other consumer items and thus jeopardizing its socialist programmes. It became impossible to reach an agreement on regional industrial planning and monetary harmonization. The increasing degree of mutual hostility led to the closing of the borders which precipitated a chain of reactions ending in the collapse of the EAC.

It is obvious from this analysis, however, that it was not ideological differences in themselves which brought disagreements, resulting in the collapse. Rather, it was the widening economic gap, resulting in the economic nationalism of the partners, which structured, gave content to, and reinforced ideological differences. It is economic nationalism and competition among partner states which intensify and harden attitudes towards ideological differences and not the other way round. Ideology, in this context, is merely a substitute for economic nationalism. We agree with Hazlewood (1980: 137), therefore, that it 'would be a conclusion of despair that mutually beneficial economic co-operation requires a close similarity of social and political outlook'. Our analysis is instead, that matters would have been different had Kenya, the linchpin and core state of the community, been willing and able to close the economic gap between itself and its partners by making greater sacrifices of national gains. Indeed, there is a theory of increasing popularity that the existence of a core state, with economic and political interests in the furthering of regional integration, and capable of making the necessary side payments to weaker partners is essential to the success of the integration effort (Ojo, 1981).

*External actors and influences*
Numerous multinational corporations and their subsidiaries capitalized on Kenya's initial advantage, extracted generous concessions on further foreign investment, and then tried to service the regional market from plants located in Kenya (Mutharika, 1975: 26–7). The emergent close relationship with these foreign partners – notably the UK, the USA and West Germany – tended to be viewed by the Kenyans as an attractive alternative to the EAC, especially as prospects increased for export, rather than mere import-substitution, industries. Naturally this precipitated the development of a similar relationship by Tanzania not only with the Western bloc but also with the Socialist bloc, principally China. The competition among the regional partners extended to external markets for their raw materials and agricultural products as well as to efforts to attract foreign skills and technology.

Competition for foreign partners and markets have had three main consequences. First, disparate conditions are created in terms of tax incentives, patent laws, labour conditions and foreign exchange privileges, all of which 'impede the co-ordination and harmonization of national development plans with respect to external resource procurement so essential for Pan-African economic integration' (Nnoli, 1978: 69–70). Such divisive competition partly accounted for the neutralization of the intent of the transfer tax and the investment policies of the East African Development Bank. Similarly, competition for foreign aid helps to reinforce dependence on the donor countries as these aids are tied to the purchase of the donor's goods and equipment, which often set off local demands for certain complements such as spare parts and technical skills. The task of integration schemes to generate transactions is as a result made much more difficult (Nnoli, 1978: 65). Tanzania's aid and trade agreements with China, for example, affected its economic relations with its EAC partners. The tied aid and its own need for technologically advanced equipment and skills resulted in the re-direction of Tanzania's imports from intra-Community to extra-Community sources.

A second consequence of intra-Community competition for foreign partners is the duplication of inefficient plants within the Community. The multinationals are the primary beneficiaries of these since it is they who are normally able to establish uneconomic plants that are protected from within the Community by the tax system and from extra-regional rivals by the external tariff. These inefficient mini-plants, however, undermine the realization of economies of scale which is one of the principal justifications for the creation of customs unions. In the EAC the influence of multinationals and other external interests led to such decisions as the building of a tyre factory in Kenya that was supposed to be sited in Tanzania; the construction of the Tan-Zam railway without due reference to the East African Railway Corporation; the establishment of an international laboratory for research on animal diseases in competition with the widely acclaimed East African Veterinary Research Organization; and the building of plywood manufacturing facilities in each member state in competition with the single existing large facility (Mazzeo, 1980: 104; Fredland, 1980: 74).

A result of inefficient mini-plants is the problem of higher prices. Inefficient production means high cost and higher prices. When this is added to the natural proclivity of multinationals to inflate prices one appreciates why goods manufactured in African countries are notoriously more expensive than imported brands. As we noted the multinationals are able to do this because the pattern of demand and consumption are induced by them and are related to the maximization of their own profits rather than to the needs of the host countries. In the EAC inflated prices of imported machinery worsened the balance of trade of Kenya and Tanzania who, in order to conserve their foreign exchange, were compelled to curtail intra-Community imports of largely consumer goods and to stop transferring funds to the headquarters of Community corporations.

A third consequence of a competitive relationship between integrating states as a result of the interference of external actors is 'inter-imperialist rivalry'. This leads to the creation of de facto zones of influence which in turn alters the 'strategic image' of the partners, changes their perceptions of the balance of power amongst themselves and creates mutual distrust and suspicion. Kenya's Western connection, for instance, when added to its increasing economic superiority, elevated it to the status of an African middle power, 'a sub-imperial state' capable of undermining the interests of Tanzania and Uganda. Tanzania and Uganda in turn perceived themselves as relegated to a subordinate position and sought to compensate their loss of regional influence by making political connections with other extra-regional actors. Tanzania, established bilateral co-operative and trade agreements with China. Uganda, for its part, chose Arab financial aid and Soviet arms. As these divergent external affiliations strengthened over time, intra-regional ties correspondingly weakened (Nnoli, 1978; Mugomba, 1978).

# ECOWAS: The bright star in the sky?

The inauguration of ECOWAS in Lagos on 28 May, 1975 was a breakthrough in the long series of efforts to institute some form of economic co-operation and integration embracing the entire West African region. The treaty provisions and the progress in their implementation so far seem to tackle in a realistic fashion the five major types of problems that afflicted the EAC and other African integration schemes, hence the optimism that ECOWAS might be the bright star in the sky (Ojo, 1981; Jalloh, 1980: 77). How justifiable is this optimism?

The ECOWAS treaty, which defines its objectives and the way in which they are to be achieved, aims to achieve an economic community over a fifteen year period in three stages. The first stage, lasting two years, is to be devoted to fact-finding and organization of the community institutions. During this period no new import duties may be imposed nor existing ones increased against member states. In the second stage, lasting the next eight years, there will be gradual elimination of customs duties and quantitative restrictions in accordance with a schedule to be agreed upon in a protocol. There will also be the abolition of obstacles to the free movement of persons, services and capital. The third stage, the next five years, will be devoted to the abolition of the existing differences in the member states' external tariffs. Beyond this, the treaty calls for the harmonization of agricultural, industrial, economic and monetary policies, including measures on foreign investment, the setting up of joint ventures, reduction of dependence on the outside world and, implicitly, the establishment of collective bargaining with the industrialized world. To achieve its aims and objectives ECOWAS has adopted a number of protocols which define the modus operandi of the new body. Five such protocols were annexed to the treaty within eighteen months. We now turn to how the treaty provisions, the protocols and the actual implementation process have so far dealt with the problems faced by previous attempts at economic integration and assess the overall future prospects for ECOWAS.

*Problems of unequal gains and polarization*

The founding fathers anticipated the problems of unequal gains and polarization and agreed in principle to have compensatory and corrective measures, notably through the instrumentality of a Fund for Compensation, Co-operation and Development. The details of the mode of operation of the Fund were to be embodied in a separate protocol.

But even before the protocol could be worked out and implemented, sensitivities to potential polarization borne of disproportionate costs and benefits had begun to find expression. Negotiations were affected by those sensitivities and the adoption of the protocol was delayed. The more developed of the West African countries (Ghana, the Ivory Coast, Liberia and Senegal) appeared pitched against the less developed countries and both groups were antagonistic towards the core state, Nigeria. Nigeria is designated the core state because of its economic and political preponderance: in 1977–8 it accounted for 57 per cent of the population, 70 per cent of the GDP, 60 per cent of the agricultural production, 94 per cent of the mining, 60 per cent of the manufacturing, 69 per cent of the commerce and transport, 70 per cent of the total exports and 64 per cent of the total imports of the West African region (Ojo, 1981: 31).

In the negotiations of the protocols on the Fund and on member contributions to the ECOWAS budget all countries except Nigeria insisted on using the GDP as the basis for determining member contribution. Nigeria, however, argued in favour of using the per capita income, by which the more developed group of countries would each have paid much more than Nigeria. Although Nigeria finally backed down, agreeing to a formula which placed equal weight on both GDP and per capita income, thus making Nigeria contribute the single largest proportion of 32 per cent to the Fund and to the budget (its closest competitors, Ghana and the Ivory Coast each contribute 13 per cent) the Ivory Coast and Senegal caused a seventeen month delay in adopting the protocols. They made adoption dependent upon a broadening of the community to include the Francophone states of Central Africa, Zaire in particular. They backed down only after extensive and intensive diplomatic activities which elicited the commitment of every one, particularly the core state and the more developed countries to provide equitable benefits to all.

Of particular significance was the decision in accordance with the treaty to distribute the principal administrative and financial organs and offices equally among all the states as a symbol of the commitment to equitable distribution of benefits. Thus the Secretariat of ECOWAS was sited in Lagos and a Nigerian was appointed as the Financial Comptroller. The Fund was located in Togo, the Secretary-General came from the Ivory Coast and the Managing Director of the Fund from Liberia, and his Deputy from Benin. How sensitive a symbol this arrangement was, was dramatized in a dispute over the removal of the first Managing Director of the Fund, Dr Horton. For some time Dr Horton had been criticized for insubordination to the Executive Secretary-General, Dr Quattara, and for favouring certain countries in the recruitment of staff for the Fund. He was also accused of mismanagement. At the stormy second session of the fourth summit in Dakar, Liberia insisted that if Dr Horton was removed, the Secretary-General should also be relieved of his post. The less developed countries largely held that for the sake of good management and maintenance of confidence in the staff all the senior officers of ECOWAS should be removed, including the Nigerian Financial Comptroller whose audit report had revealed Dr Horton's irregularities. This solution, it was felt, symbolized the concept of sink or swim together. But Nigeria's head of state, General Obasanjo, who felt that any little idiosyncracy of an individual official must not be allowed to hamper the development or growth of ECOWAS, strove hard to reconcile all divergent interests. His solution, which restored the original symbol of unity without a general massacre, was to have Liberia provide a replacement for Dr Horton. Mr Robert Taubman subsequently filled the post. Meanwhile the Authority of heads of state affirmed that the letter and the spirit of Article 8 (a) of the Treaty was that the Executive Secretary had authority over the Managing Director of the Fund and anything in the Treaty or the protocol to the contrary must be amended (Doc A/DEC 13/5/79).

Sensitivity to unequal distribution of gains and costs has slowed the development of the organization somewhat. The task of study and institution-building, for which a period of two years was earmarked, has taken four years. The first phase of establishing free trade is off to a slow start. According to the ECOWAS Treaty, member states are required during the first two years of the definitive enforcement of the Treaty, to impose no new duties and taxes nor to increase existing ones. But this provision came into force on 28 May, 1979, after the fourth summit of the ECOWAS Authority. It is only after the 28 May, 1981 that reductions in tariff rates and non-tariff barriers could be applied and their effects analyzed for the purpose of compensating those who, relative to the consolidation period, evidently suffer hardships.

By the time of the fifth summit in May 1980 only modest though significant progress had been made on this issue. It was agreed that non-tariff barriers, the elimination of which had to be started by 28 May, 1981 in accordance with certain schedules should be completely eliminated in respect of Nigeria and the more developed group of countries by 28 May, 1985 for industrial products and by 28 May, 1987 for all other products. For the less developed group, customs duties and other barriers on industrial products were scheduled to be eliminated completely by 28 May, 1987 and those on other products by 28 May, 1989. Details of the compensation procedures for loss of revenue arising from the trade liberalization were also agreed upon (Documents A/DEC 18/5/80 and A/DEC 19/5/80).

Meanwhile, only an interim agreement has been possible on the implementation of free movement of persons which the Treaty had accepted in principle. Because most states have been concerned about the impact of influx of immigrants and some of the less developed countries worry that free movement might result in nationals of the core state and the more developed countries dominating their economies it was agreed to experiment with a phased programme of implementation, beginning with the abolition of visa requirements for community citizens intending to stay for a maximum of ninety days in any member state. Account of the visa abolition could then be taken during the next phase of effecting the right of residence and establishment.

This interim agreement on free movement of persons has already run into trouble as Nigeria, in early 1983, had cause to expel an estimated two million 'illegal' aliens – nearly all of them citizens of member states of ECOWAS. Admittedly the vast majority of these aliens did not come under the ninety-day legal residence provisions of ECOWAS, and several thousands who came under those provisions had abused the privilege by over-staying their welcome in Nigeria and taking up employment. Nevertheless the mass expulsion cast doubt on the feasibility of effective free movement of persons within the Community. Nigeria's official argument was that the expulsion was legal, that it affected only illegal aliens and that it was aimed at curtailing violence 'often traced' to these aliens. The point, however, is that had the provisions been for permanent residence, as they are in a full Community, rather than for just ninety days, the aliens would not have been 'illegal'. The question is then whether even with permanent residence provisions the aliens might still have been subject to mass expulsion because of accusations of 'violence' (the official line) or because of the 'unhealthy economy' (the popular belief and justification)? Clearly the expulsion was not illegal but it did, and still does, have serious implications on the possibility of moving ECOWAS into a fully-fledged common market.

It is also doubtful that the compensatory and corrective mechanisms are adequate to overcome the problems of unequal gains and polarization. There are essentially three of these mechanisms:

(i) The safeguard clause (Article 26 of the Treaty) empowering any member state to take necessary measures for a period of one year to redress serious disturbances to its economy resulting from trade liberalization and movement to customs union;

(ii) The Council of Ministers' power to review and correct any deflection of trade (Article 16 (2) and (3));

(iii) The Fund for Co-operation, Compensation and Development. As the name implies, the Fund is not only directed at compensating member states who have suffered revenue loss as a result of the freeing of trade, the application of CET, and the location of Community enterprises, it is also a corrective mechanism aimed at redressing the more fundamental causes of unequal development. Thus the Council of Ministers is empowered not only to determine the revenue loss of member states and the appropriate compensation to be paid from the Fund, but also to use the Fund to create conditions of industrialization and increasing productive capacity by structural transformation of the subregion. Specifically the Fund can be used to finance feasibility studies and developmental projects of national and community interest; to guarantee foreign investments in member states for enterprises established in pursuance of harmonization of industrial policies; to furnish the means to facilitate sustained mobilization of internal and external financial resources for member states and the community; and to aid and promote development projects in the less developed countries (Article 52 of the Treaty and Article 2 of the Protocol on the Fund).

In view of the tremendous burden placed on the Fund as the main compensatory and corrective mechanism, its initial capitalization of $500 million of which $100 million was expected to come from the member states is grossly inadequate. Firstly, infrastructure is abysmally deficient everywhere, especially in the poorer countries. A co-ordinated infrastructural development in the area of transportation and communication network over a vast expanse of territory is a prerequisite to a rapid and comprehensive expansion of trade and industry (Ogundana, 1974; Hazlewood, 1967: 11). Extremely large investment is required for this. Secondly, the mere development of infrastructure will not be sufficient to mollify the less developed countries over polarization of resources and wealth, whether this is perceived or real: they want to see the smoke coming from factories on their soil as well. This means that even greater capital investment is required to be effective. But it also in practice requires regional industrial planning and a common regime on foreign investment, and these are two necessities which in turn require supra-national institutions if they are to be successfully achieved. However, there are no provisions for a supra-national planning agency. It is to be hoped that the logic of the provisions on comprehensive plans for transportation networks, on the co-ordination and harmonization of common policies on agriculture, energy, natural resources and Africanization and on industrial integration and development should in time lead to 'incrementalism' and 'spill over in the scope of collective action' and that this logic will necessitate some form of regional planning agency. Meanwhile the Secretariat is filling the gap.

Nor has the Treaty anything to say on a common regime on foreign investment. But as Ojo (1980: 600–1) argues the silence is deliberate for tactical and political reasons and it conforms with the gentleman's agreement to adopt a 'pragmatic and flexible approach' and to deal with only 'specific issues calling for immediate attention'. When the appropriate time comes in the near future 'to have a common stand on many issues and to bargain together with other countries' the omission will be rectified, as Adebayo Adedeji and some political leaders acknowledge (Adedeji, 1976).

Meanwhile Nigeria, as a core state willing and able to make side-payments, has been filling some of the gaps in order to blunt the sensitivity to potential inequality in the gains of integration. Its intensive and extensive diplomatic activities, its large share of financial contributions and voluntary expenditures, its investments in joint venture projects, and its granting of many concessions towards the implementation of the terms of the treaty agreements all demonstrate Nigeria's commitment to the success of ECOWAS. Apart from its $32 million contribution to the Fund and the Budget and its estimated $1 billion voluntary expenditure up to May 1978, within the ECOWAS framework Nigeria has also been supplying 400 000 tons of crude oil annually to Togo's Lomé refinery since 1976, while the Ivory Coast's refinery at Vridi has relied heavily on Nigerian crude since 1975 as has the Senegalese refinery at Cayor since 1978. Under various agreements Nigeria supplies oil and oil products to Ghana, Benin and Sierra Leone (which it also supplies with coal). It has also established joint industrial projects with various West African countries, among them cement and sugar factories in Benin, and a five per cent share in iron ore companies in Guinea.

Nigeria's rather extensive participation in joint ventures with other ECOWAS member states has had a domino effect and has resulted in a plethora of similar investments among other member states. Thus Benin and Togo have agreed on joint phosphate extraction and its delivery to other member countries of ECOWAS. Ghana, Togo and the Ivory Coast have agreed on joint cement production and delivery as well as on oil extraction. Such joint ventures have great potential for forging stronger intra-West African links and, by enhancing the degree of interdependence, they create backward and forward linkages among their industries. Significantly in formulating policy and identifying projects to be funded by ECOWAS the Council of Ministers has decided to put emphasis on multinational regional projects with good production, transportation and communications as the area of top priority. Indeed by mid-1980 a special fund for the development of telecommunications had been set up, a financing loan of about $50 million had been approved in principle by the EEC and a feasibility and reinvestment study had been carried out on a plan to connect the telephone networks of all ECOWAS capital cities by March 1981. The Executive Secretariat had also drawn up a programme for the co-ordination of transport development, including harmonization of future roads and harbour projects and modernization of existing ones (*West Africa*, 9 June, 1980).

It is clear, then, that sensitivity to problems of unequal gains and polarization and the attendant pre-occupation with proper institution building all caused the Treaty to move slowly towards implementation during its first four years. However, as Renninger (1979: 35) correctly observes, 'progress has been more rapid [since the] Secretariats [were constituted] to guide the implementation process'. The role of Nigeria has also been significant in this progress. It has continued to bear the major cost and to demonstrate its willingness to forego immediate economic gains and advantages in order to ensure the proper growth of the organization and a stronger commitment on the part of the weaker neighbours. It has often served as the bridge between conflicting positions within ECOWAS, sometimes by setting examples of forebearance and at times by supporting the position of the less developed countries. Its role to date can best be described as one of a catalyst. It has provided the essential 'dynamic centre of gravity within the prospective integrative area . . . willing to act as leaders in the process of integration' (Abangwu, 1975: 131).

## Institutions and organs of administrations

The major institutions and organs established to perform the integrative tasks are the Authority of Heads of State and Government, the Council of Ministers, the Executive Secretariat and a number of technical and specialized institutions. The supreme decision-making organ is the Authority of Heads of State and Government which meets annually. Its decisions and directions are binding on all institutions of the community and on member states. It is assisted in its duties by the Council of Ministers consisting of two representatives of each member state. Ordinarily the Council of Ministers meets twice a year, one meeting immediately preceding the annual meeting of the Authority. Its principal responsibility is to direct and keep under review the operations and development of the community and make policy recommendations to the Authority. Its decisions are taken by unanimous vote. But where an objection is recorded on behalf of a member state to a proposal, unless the objection is withdrawn, the matter is referred to the Authority for final resolution.

The principal administrative organ of ECOWAS is the Executive Secretariat whose personnel are appointed with due regard 'to the desirability of maintaining an equitable distribution of appointments . . . among citizens of the Member States' (Article 8 of the ECOWAS Treaty). The appointees, however, are expected to owe their loyalty entirely to the Community. Together they are responsible for the day to day administration of the Community and its institutions, servicing and assisting these institutions in the performance of their duties, implementing decisions of the Authority and the Council of Ministers and initiating and carrying out studies and making proposals for the efficient and harmonious functioning and development of the Community.

There are other technical and specialized institutions, among them: the Tribunal of the Community; the Fund for Co-operation, Compensation and Development; the Trade, Customs, Immigration, Monetary and Payments Commission; the Transport Tele-communications and Energy Commission; the Industry, Agriculture and Natural Resources Commission; and the Social and Cultural Affairs Commission.

This institutional decision-making structure is similar to that of the EAC especially in the fact that in both cases the Authority of Heads of State and Government was the ultimate decision-making body and that both structures lacked the large dose of 'dirigisme' which in theory is important in successful integration schemes. Yet there are sufficiently wide differences to enable ECOWAS to avoid or attenuate the kind of problems that bedevilled the EAC. For instance, the Council of Ministers can take decisions as well as make recommendations to the Authority. The latter, in effect, merely ratifies the Council's decisions. Its most important function is to serve as an appeal court, the court of last resort when there is disagreement within the Council. While it is thus arguable that the unanimity rule in the Council of Ministers could weaken the Community, permitting the intrusion of particularistic, nationalistic claims to thwart its decisions and progress it would appear that the essence of the rule appears to be to permit some flexibility and allow second thoughts. A veto by a member state gives the Council an opportunity to reassess its stand and be convinced that its majority position is in the overall interest of the Community. Once so convinced, the Council can inform the Authority of this fact. It is nonetheless true that as a veto in the Council must be presumed to have the sanction of the head of state of the member state concerned, that it will still be a contentious issue for the Authority. It is also true that heads of state and government in general rarely look behind their immediate national interests even in matters of community-wide concern. But objections in the Council of Ministers are more easily dealt with in the atmosphere of camaraderie, of purposeful interaction among supreme authorities, and under the pressure not to be the odd-man-out that has become characteristic of summits of African heads of state in recent years. This is the reason why there is the provision for referral to the Authority of proposals vetoed in the Council. In any case, as Okon Udokang (1976) has rightly pointed out, because they are the wielders of supreme power in their respective states (and who themselves have formulated the goals of the Community and who are determined to see them realized), the heads of state and government acting as the Authority, are better equipped than a supra-national authority to get the organization moving forward. Decisions by the Authority are bound to take into account the peculiar national interests of every member state. The decisions, once made, have the aura of finality and are more certain to be implemented. It is still true that the unanimity rule can cause delays or slow down the tempo of integration. It can even mean the taking of decisions (or non-decisions) that are irrational from the point of view of the Community. But it avoids the crippling false starts that often arise when authority is vested in supra-national institutions which tend to go too fast too soon, driven only by the technically rational requirements of their task, but which are insensitive to the political realities. In other words the control of Community institutions by political leaders may not necessarily be the quickest avenue of success for the integration scheme, but it promises to be the optimum solution for the West African situation.

A second difference between ECOWAS and the EAC has been the limited incidence of personalization of decision-making in West Africa. Two factors account for this. In the first place, a majority of social and economic interest groups and classes in a number of key countries (e.g. Nigeria, Ghana and Sierra Leone) support ECOWAS and this makes personalization of power at the domestic level increasingly difficult. This has a spill-over into decision-making at the regional level. Secondly, at the regional level the sheer number of states involved and the various powerful interest groups concerned is a guarantee against the sort of behaviour, witnessed in EAC, where two presidents form a coalition against a third. In East Africa this reinforced the personalization of regional decision-making by the three presidents. As we have pointed out the pressure not to be the odd man out and the threat of exclusion (i.e. of going ahead without the recalcitrant state) tend to result in yielding to the majority wish or striking compromises.

Finally, unlike the EAC, the Secretariat of ECOWAS can take independent initiatives to make studies as well as receive instructions from the Council of Ministers and can thus propose policies and actions in the interest of the Community as a whole. It has in certain respects been a surrogate supra-national planning agency. Given this trend and given the logic of incrementalism and spill-over in the scope of collective action inherent in the ECOWAS objectives, either the Secretariat will evolve into a veritable regional planning agency or some supra-national structures will emerge to perform that role.

## Ideology and economic nationalism

We noted that in the failure of the EAC it was not ideology that was the culprit, but rather economic nationalism parading in the guise of ideology. The question of ideology is even less important in West Africa. There are few ideologies in West Africa. Guinea, one of the few ideological states, has had so many co-operative ventures with so unrepentant a capitalist state as Nigeria as to suggest the theory that ideology is no bar to economic co-operation. As for economic nationalism, it was suggested that in the absence of regional planning agencies, the existence of a core state able and willing to make side-payments may attenuate its dangers. Nigeria, it has been noted above, appears to be playing this role, albeit on a low key. Whether it can play it on the grand scale as does Venezuela with respect to the Andean Group is yet to be seen. Venezuela was able to make a £60 million unilateral voluntary contribution to the Andean Development Corporation and alone provided $500 million to a special fund for energy and agro-industrial projects to promote Andean integration. Whether Nigeria can match this kind of financial generosity will depend on the outlook for petroleum as well as on domestic politics and public attitudes towards ECOWAS.

## External actors

Imperial rivalries have both hindered and spurred integration in West Africa. There is little doubt for instance, that the initial hesitation of most Francophone states in rallying round ECOWAS was based upon their fear of possible French economic and political sanctions. All of these states virtually rely on France for internal defence and a few even for their recurrent expenditures. The other West African countries also considered their political and economic relationships with Western

Europe and North America and worried whether ECOWAS was worth the possible disorientation in those relationships and the sacrifice which that would entail. It might be said, then, that perception of interdependence with a non-regional actor has tended to hamper West African regional integration and it might be of continuing significance in the future.

On the other hand the perception of dependence on the imperial powers and increasing awareness of its dangers (in terms of security and economic development) were a crucial driving force behind Nigeria's commitment to the formation of ECOWAS and behind the agreement by the other West African states to institute the organization. The reality of increasing economic, and indirect political, dependence on foreign powers and their multinational corporations and the implications for overcoming underdevelopment was a major factor in the North–South confrontation at the sixth special session of the UN General Assembly in 1974 as well as in the ACP–EEC negotiations. The mutual suspicion between France and Nigeria noted in our discussion of CEAO, the continuing French support for that organization and the general French anti-Nigerian and anti-Anglophone proclivity hardened Nigeria's resolve to make ECOWAS a reality. It was hoped thereby to thwart France, reduce its influence and curtail Francophone dependence on France. Because relationships between France and Francophone states are much more formally and elaborately structured than relationships between Britain and Anglophone Africa, the French presence constitutes the bulwark of Western imperialism in West Africa. On balance, then, the integrating impact of non-regional actors may be said to be significantly stronger than their disruptive role, thus supporting the theory that the existence of strong non-regional actors tends to persuade the regional actors to co-ordinate and harmonize policy more intensively.

The other major external factors, the multinational corporations, have also, on balance, spurred integration. Generally, they have supported ECOWAS. This is in part because given the economic conditions of West Africa where industrialization is just about to begin on a large scale, integration is in the interest of these multinationals: they can reduce overheads by having one or two larger plants to serve the entire region instead of several mini plants in several states. There are few of these multinationals already in manufacturing who have vested interests in opposition to integration, the vast majority is only now beginning to enter manufacturing in a big way. They are now attempting to transform themselves from general trading companies handling the full range of merchandise imports into specialized marketing units and import-substitution manufacturers. In doing so they capitalize on their accumulated experience, operating methods, local contacts and knowledge of the market to engage in market-protecting investments. Indeed, it appears that ECOWAS is one of the few instances where multinationals, because of their acknowledged advantages over national firms and because they would obtain the larger benefits of integration, have not actively opposed the process of integration and might actually promote it (Vaitsos, 1977–8: 251–6).

There is no guarantee that ECOWAS will be able to deal effectively with the problems of unequal gains and polarization to everyone's satisfaction. But given the number of states involved; that it has a core state willing and able to make side payments; that it has the threat of exclusion to force the recalcitrant into line; given also the increasing functional scope and salience of the secretariat and the external actors who, on balance, constitute an integrative force, ECOWAS may indeed be the bright star on the horizon of African international relations.

# References

ABANGWU, G C (1975) Systems approach to regional integration in West Africa, *Journal of Common Market Studies* **13** (1 & 2).

ADEDEJI, ADEBAYO (1976) Collective self-reliance in developing Africa: scope, prospects and problems. Keynote Address at the International Conference on ECOWAS, Lagos, Nigeria Institute of International Affairs, 23-27 August, Mimeo.

ALUKO, OLAJIDE (1976) *Ghana and Nigeria 1957-70: a study in inter-African discord,* Rex Collins, London.

AXLINE, W ANDREW (1978a) Underdevelopment, dependence, and integration: the politics of regionalism in the Third World, *International Organization* **31** (1).

AXLINE, W ANDREW (1978b) Integration and development in the commonwealth Caribbean: the politics of regional negotiations, *International Organization* **32** (4).

BALASSA, BELA (1961) *Theory of economic integration,* Richard Irwin, Homewood, Illinois.

De LUSIGNAN, GUY (1969) French-speaking Africa since independence, Praeger, New York.

FREDLAND, RICHARD (1980) Who killed the East African Community? In Christian P Potholm and Richard A Fredland (eds) *Integration and disintegration in East Africa,* Univ. Press of America, Lanham, Maryland.

GARDINER, ROBERT K (1965) Integrated economic development in Africa: the role of the economic commission, *International Development Review,* June.

GREEN R H and KRISHNA K G V (1967) *Economic cooperation in Africa: retrospect and prospect,* Oxford Univ. Press, London.

HAAS, ERNST B (1958) *The uniting of Europe,* Stanford Univ. Press, Stanford.

HAAS, ERNST B (1971) The study of regional integration: reflections on the joy and anguish of pre-theorizing. In Leon N Lindberg and Stuart A Scheingold (eds) *Regional integration: theory and research,* Harvard Univ. Press, Cambridge, Mass.

HAZELWOOD, ARTHUR (ed) (1967) *African integration and disintegration* Oxford Univ. Press, London.

HAZLEWOOD, ARTHUR (1980) Economic instrumentalities of statecraft and the end of the EAC. In Christian Potholm and Richard Fredland (eds) *Integration and disintegration in East Africa,* Univ. Press of America, Lanham, Maryland.

INIS, CLAUDE L Jr (1964) *Swords into plowshares: the problems and progress of international organization,* Random House, New York.

JALLOH, ABDUL AZIZ (1980) Recent trends in regional integration in Africa, *Nigerian Journal of Internal Affairs* **6** (1 & 2).

JULIENNE, ROLAND (1967) The experience of integration in French-speaking Africa. In Hazelwood, Arthur D (ed) *African integration and disintegration,* Oxford Univ. Press, London.

KAHNERT, P, RICHARDS O, STOUTESDYK E, and THOMOPOULOS, P (1969) *Economic integration among developing countries,* Development Centre of OECD, Paris.

LINDER, S B (1966) Customs unions and economic development. In Wionczek, Miguel S (ed) *Latin American economic integration,* Praeger, New York.

LIPSEY, R G (1960) The theory of customs unions: a general survey, *Economical Journal* **70** (279).

MAZZEO, DOMENICO (1980) Problems of regional co-operation in East Africa. In Christian Potholm and Richard Fredland (eds) *Integration and disintegration in East Africa,* Univ. Press of America.

MEADE, J E (1955) *The theory of customs unions,* North Holland Publishing Co, Amsterdam.

MIKESELL, RAYMOND F (1963) The theory of common markets as applied to regional arrangements among developing countries. In Roy Harrod and Douglas Hague (eds), *International trade theory in a developing world,* St Martin's Press, New York.

MITRANY, DAVID (1943) *A working peace system,* Royal Institute of International Affairs, London.

MUGOMBA, AGRIPPAH T (1978) Regional organizations and African Underdevelopment: the collapse of the East African Community, *Journal of Modern African Studies* **16** (2).

MUTHARIKA, B W T (1975) Multinationals in regional integration: the African experience, *The African Review* **5** (4).

NNOLI, OKWUDIBA (1978) External constraints on Pan-African economic integration, *Nigerian Journal of Internal Affairs* **4** (1 & 2).

NYE, JOSEPH S (1968) Comparative regional integration: concept and measurement, *International Organization* **22**.

OGUNDANA, BABFEMI (1974) Seaport development and multination co-operation in West Africa, *The Journal of Modern African Studies* **12** (3).

OJO, OLATUNDE J B (1974) 'Nigeria's foreign policy, 1960-1966: politics, economics and the struggle for African leadership' Doctoral Dissertation, University of Connecticut.

OJO, OLATUNDE J B (1980) Nigeria and the formation of ECOWAS, *International Organization* **34**.

OJO, OLATUNDE J B (1981) *The core state in Third World economic integration: Nigeria and ECOWAS* Unpublished manuscript, University of Port Harcourt Library.

RAVENHILL, JOHN (1980) The theory and practice of regional integration in East Africa. In Christian P Potholm and Richard Fredland (eds) *Integration and disintegration in East Africa,* Univ. Press of America, Lanham, Maryland.

RENNIGER, JOHN P (1979) *Multinational co-operation for development in West Africa,* Pergamon Press, New York.

ROBSON, PETER (1967) Economic integration in Equatorial Africa. In Arthur Hazlewood (ed) *African integration and disintegration,* Oxford Univ Press, London.

SPRINGER, ALLEN L (1980) Community chronology. In Christian P Potholm and Richard A Fredland (eds) *Integration and disintegration in East Africa,* Univ. Press of America, Lanham, Maryland.

THOMPSON, WILLARD SCOTT (1969) *Ghana's foreign policy, 1957-66,* Princeton Univ. Press, Princeton.

UDOKANG, OKON (1976) ECOWAS and the problem of regional integration, *Nigeria: Bulletin of Foreign Affairs* 6 (3).

VAITSOS, CONSTANTINE V (1977/78) The attitudes and role of transnational enterprises in economic integration processes among the LDCs, *Millenium: Journal of International Studies* 6 (3).

VINER, JACOB (1950) *The customs union issue,* Carnegie Endowment for International Peace, New York.

WOLFERS, MICHAEL (1976) *Politics in the Organization of African Unity,* Methuen, London.

YANSANE, A Y (1977) West African economic integration: is ECOWAS the answer? *Africa Today* 24 (3).

# Index